The Purposed Woman
365 Day
Devotional

A Collaboration with Over 300 Inspiring Women

Purposeful Woman All Over the World,

I introduce to you and present to others a Devotional written by Women from all throughout the countries of the world. This book is sure to be what you need Any time of Day to Inspire you to know that you are not alone, and that you can make it through anything with God!

January 1
Shannon L. Turner

Psalm 23:1

The Lord is my Shepherd, I lack nothing. This faith journey can be a bit of a roller coaster at times, with its ups and downs, twists and turns. Lord when my mind races or heart grows anxious please calm with your peace that surpasses all understanding. Lord please help me to always see that You are with me and providing for me especially in the times I am in survival mode, in my own strength, trying to handle what life seems to have thrown at me. You are my Savior, my Friend, the Lover of my soul, my Constant.

Shannon L. Turner

Email: embracinglife@shannonlturner.com

Romans 12: (NIV) Do not conform to the pattern of this world, but be transformed by the renewing of your mind. Then you will be able to test and approve what God's will is—his good, pleasing and perfect will.

Stop Apologizing. Don't strive to be people pleasers, but pleasers of God. If your habits are disruptive then by all means change them out of love and obedience to God's word. When we open ourselves up to His transformative power, we are at the same time opening the door to God's plan for our lives. If you change (or pretend to change) ONLY to be someone's friend or part of a group, you will eventually expose yourself. Starting from a perspective of love and relationship with God, you can forge a lasting change that you will never make you sorry.

Celestine is a writer, visual artist, emerging filmmaker, speaker, and community arts promoter. She is the Director of the annual Down East Flick Fest held in Greenville, NC and the creator of the visual journaling workshop, "ReCreations: Rewriting Your Life Script ™" and facilitates writing-to-heal workshops.

Email: forthecre8or@gmail.com
https://www.linkedin.com/in/celestine-davis-75147422/
https://www.instagram.com/faithdame/
http://celestinedavis.com/
https://www.facebook.com/4thecreator/
downeastflickfest.org

January 3
Charlette Fairchild

The Purposed Woman
Isaiah 41:10
"Fear not, for I am with you; be not dismayed, for I am your God; I will strengthen you, I will help you, I will uphold you with my righteous right hand."

God's word is a beautiful thing!! Sometimes life gets hard. There are probably days you feel as if you can't go on or want to just lay in bed and sleep life away! TODAY IS A NEW DAY!! Be encouraged! You have a God that loves you so much that he will provide the strength you don't have! No matter what you do or where you go, he is with you! To think at this very moment he is uplifting you, encouraging you and bringing you peace! Get up and rejoice in God's blessings!! YOU are loved, valued and cherished!

Dr. Charlette Fairchild (Charlie) is a graduate of ODU and went on to receive her Masters and Doctorate from The College of William and Mary. She is a sales expert and works for GE Appliances, A Haier Company. Charlie is a motivational speaker, a mother, an author and a God-fearing woman.

January 4
Marnie Pouget

"On the last and greatest day of the festival, Jesus stood and said in a loud voice, 'Let anyone who is thirsty come to me and drink. Whoever believes in me, as Scripture has said, rivers of living water will flow from within them.'"
John 7:37-38

Water is crucial to a beautiful, healthy physical life. Living water is crucial to a beautiful, healthy spiritual life. As our physical bodies thirst, so our spirits thirst. In comparison to the desert the oasis is a lush and vibrant place of refuge. The word oasis is defined as "a fertile spot in a desert where water is found."

When we dwell at the source of the living water, in communion with God, that refreshing living water will overflow from us. We will be an oasis. A fertile spot, in a desert, where water is found.

I am the very blessed wife of my best friend and mother of five precious children. Walking a life-road that is more amazing than I could ever imagine.

I enjoy sharing my love of fabulous hair I can be found blogging at http://thelittlehilllife.blogspot.com/

Social media tags: https://www.facebook.com/naturallybased/

Instagram: blbc.mamarazzi

Email: the7pougets@gmail.com

January 5

Marnie Pouget

"For you created my inmost being; you knit me together in my mother's womb." Psalm 139:13

When you were created, God had his hands all over you. You were created with intention and purpose.

As a work is completed the artist adds his mark, identifying it as his own. The painter adds his signature, the potter adds her stamp, the photographer adds his watermark.

An artist's work is their creation. A reflection of themselves. A precious piece of who they are. They created this work and it is theirs.

You are the creation of the Master Artist. Made in His image. A reflection of who He is. He created you and you are His.

I am the very blessed wife of my best friend and mother of five precious children. Walking a life-road that is more amazing than I could ever imagine. I enjoy sharing my love of fabulous hair I can be found blogging at http://thelittlehilllife.blogspot.com/

Social media tags: https://www.facebook.com/naturallybased/

Instagram: blbc.mamarazzi

Email: the7pougets@gmail.com

January 6
Mary Davis

Rest in God's Presence

This advice was given to me years ago, and I followed it. I walked into GOD's PRESENCE, battered, bruised, broken, angry, hurt, depressed and confused. I sat in God's presence and I told Him all about my pain, sadness, loneliness, insecurity, bitterness, heartaches, breakups, abuse, suicidal attempts, and depression. It was in God's presence that my healing began and my life began to change. Being in God's presence gave me hope. It helped me affirm the things God said about me. It helped me understand my truth. It helped me understand that despite my brokenness, God still loved me and still had a plan and purpose for my life. I walked into HIS PRESENCE one way; but when I came out! I WAS NOT THE SAME!

Your freedom, your healing, and your deliverance is IN HIS PRESENCE. Get in GOD'S PRESENCE and grab hold of your freedom!

Mary Davis is a minister, author, and mentor. She is the founder of the Empowered Pearl, an organization that empowers women and girls to live free from the restraints of depression, low self-esteem, abusive relationships and destructive behaviors. She has traveled throughout the metropolitan area and to various international countries sharing her testimony of **Healing, Deliverance, Restoration and Freedom**.

Email: Theempoweredpearl@gmail.com
Facebook: @EmpoweredPearl and @MaryDavis
Website: EmpoweredPearl.com

January 7
Theresa Head

Do the things needed to reach your goals! When you see the dream and write it out this become a Goal.

A goal put into steps is a Plan. A step by step plan done consistently by ac leads to Realty.

I am the CEO of Head Art Works family business. I am a wife, mother and grandmother. I have a bachelor's degree in business management. I also am a legal secretary, medical assistant and Emergency Medical Technician. We make scented hand craft items.

Website- http://www.headartworks.online
Social Media- Head Art Works- Facebook,
Instagram- Twitter- Pintress- LinkedIn

headartworks@gmail.com

January 8
Dien Neubauer

Proverbs 22:1 – "Choose a good reputation over great riches; being held in high esteem is better than silver or gold." (NLT)

Your Crown Speaks. It speaks so loudly, that we can't hear what you're saying. People will remember your appearance, behavior, what you say, and how you made them feel to paint a complete picture of you. And, rightfully so, because a crown is made up of so many different pieces, fastened together to become a thing of beauty. May we strive to be a thing of beauty that others see, in what we say and do. May your crown speak so loudly that many are inspired when they see or hear of you.

Dien Neubauer; wife to I.J. Andrew Neubauer, is an Educator, having received her B.Sc. degree from Trinity Baptist College, in Jacksonville, Florida. Dien is also CEO of Crowned Divas Remy Collections, LLC, but for her it's more than just hair. She is also an Author and Speaker, and refers to herself as 'your Motivational Crowned Diva.' Dien uses her platform to empower and inspire women as she communicates the power of 'Your Crown.'

www.facebook.com/crowneddivasremy
www.instagram.com.crowneddivasremy
www.crowneddivasremy.com
email: info@crowneddivasremy.com
www.facebook.com/yourcrownspeaks
www.instagram.com/yourcrownspeaks
www.dienneubauer.com
email: dienneubauer@gmail.com

January 9
Sharon M. Hyman

"Nothing happens until something moves." - Albert Einstein

Often times we put off doing the things that are necessary to accomplish our goals, waiting, hoping and praying that somehow things will miraculously fall into place, without much effort, on our part. The truth is, without action, nothing will happen. So, in order for our goals to materialize, we MUST take action.

Today, I'm encouraging you to quit waiting and take the first step, regardless of how insignificant it may seem. Commit to doing, at least one thing every day, that will bring you closer to your goals. THEN! and only then, everything you've been hoping and praying for, will start to fall into place.

Sharon M. Hyman is a Canadian Entrepreneur, Founder & CEO of HYMAN Realty Inc, real estate career advisor, trainer and coach. Beyond real estate you can find her doing what she loves best—-mentoring young entrepreneurs. She is an interior design enthusiast who enjoys travelling, entertaining and spending quality time with family.

CONTACT:
Website: sharonhyman.ca
Instagram: sharon_real_estate
Twitter: sharon_hyman
Email: sharon@hymanrealty.com

January 10
Latasha "WOP" Williams

Jeremiah 29:11 11 "For I know the plans I have for you, declares the LORD, plans to prosper you and not to harm you, plans to give you hope and a future."

Today, in the midst of difficult situations, God wants us to know he has a plan and PURPOSE.

He also wants us to know that as we submit to his plan, he will use us to bless the world around us.

The key still remains during both good and difficult times: *You will seek me and find me when you search for me with all your heart.*

God has not forgot about you.... He Has Plans For You Far Greater Than Your Own Plans.

Latasha "WOP" Williams
Wife, Mother, Sister, Friend, -
CEO- Women Of Purpose

January 11
Candace Wilkerson

You are designed and destined for greatness. Don't be discouraged when others don't believe in your dreams or support your goals. Remember to keep looking up! Look to heels for which cometh your help, and put your trust in God. When you feel like you are sinking, like quick sand, just remember on Christ the solid rock, you will forever stand. David said about him:

"'I saw the Lord always before me.
Because he is at my right hand,
I will not be shaken".
Humble Servant, Candace L. Lynch-Wilkerson, Ed. S

January 12
Charmaine E. Betty-Singleton

John 11 v42-43 "Come Forth. God will, at times, place you in situations that appear to be stagnant or dead. And still yet, not come to your aid to render immediate assistance. During times like this, don't give up hope. Our God is a restorer. Remember his specialty is in the resurrection. Jesus keep your ears open and wait, for Him to call out your name and say come forth. His delay is not for your benefit, but for the benefit of those watching, so that they will know that it was only God that could have brought you out of a dead situation."

Charmaine E. Betty-Singleton aka CBS, author, advocate, veteran, entrepreneur, attorney, and transformational speaker extraordinaire, is the CEO/Owner of PTK Enterprises LLC, a business focused on supporting other business owners, community activism, and empowering individuals to greatness. Additionally, she is the owner of Victorious Vibes radio station housed on SIBN. Charmaine is an avid lover of God and all people. She attributes her success first to God, and then to her parents and mentors, one of which is the late Dr. Myles Munroe. Charmaine strongly believes that with God ALL things are possible and wishes to "die empty" successfully fulfilling ALL that God has called her to do. Charmaine is a native of Kingston, Jamaica and refers to Queens, New York as home. Charmaine currently lives in Sacramento, California.

You may connect with Charmaine at:

ptkenterprisesllc@gmail.com https://www.ptkenterprises.com

www.facebook.com/CharmaineBettySingleton

January 13
Pamela Davis-Ghavami

"A hot-tempered person stirs up conflict, but the one who is patient calms a quarrel" (Proverbs 15:18).

Today's scripture speaks to the negative effects of a hot-tempered person versus the positive effects of a patient person. Proverbs 15:18 states that conflict can occur when a person is hot-tempered. This scripture points out how a patient person has the power to calm a quarrel. Would you consider yourself to be a hot-tempered person, a patient person or both at times? There is no right or wrong answer to these questions. There is only an opportunity to evaluate where you fall on the spectrum of hot-tempered or patient. The bible has several scriptures that speak to the importance of having self-control and keeping your distance from people who are quick to anger. Reading the scriptures can help you develop patience in your spiritual journey and a closer relationship with the God. God has a purpose and a plan for your life. Building patience in your character is part of God's perfect plan. There are additional scriptures in Proverbs that give the believer insight about hot-tempers.

For example: Proverbs 19:11 states that *"Good senses makes one slow to anger, and it is his glory to overlook an offense"*; Proverbs 29:11 states that *"Fools give full vent to their rage, but the wise bring calm in the end"*; and Proverbs 22:24 says *"Do not make friends with a hot-tempered person, do not associate with one easily angered"*. There are also scriptures that tell how God managed hot-tempered people. A few examples are: Jonah was eaten by a whale when he refused to obey God's will to help the Ninevites; Moses did not get into the promise land because of his frustration and anger towards the very people he freed from slavery; Sarah and Abraham created conflict with the slave girl Hagar because of their disbelief that God could give them a child in spite of Sarah being barren. When Hagar fled to escape Sarah's anger an Angel reminded her of God's promises and purpose for her life and the child she carried for Abraham as Sarah's surrogate. Sarah's mistreatment was no longer Hagar's focus, only Gods purpose for her life and that of her child. If you find that you are hot-tempered more often than patient, you need to ask God to help you manage these emotions and help you find your life purpose. You will need to search your heart and ask yourself the question, why am I so angry? Some of you may have discovered you were bullied, mistreated by a parent, sibling or friend. Some of you could also be dealing with a form of mental illness.

No matter what causes you to be angry you will need to pray, study the scriptures and/or get help from a professional. God wants you to have an attitude that will allow you to live peacefully. The "Beatitudes" (Mathew 5:3-12) and the "Fruit of the Spirit" (Galatians 5:22) are specific instructions in scripture about the right attitude for God people. With God's love and the help of the holy spirit you can have these characteristics even when you are being mistreated or falsely accused. Evil forces that you may encounter in life will require Gods help to stay optimistic. Mastering these qualities in the mist of spiritual warfare allows God to build your character in preparation for a greater purpose. Once you have succeeded or passed these life tests with a good attitude, God is able to builds your faith. God can give you a testimony that allow you to help someone else. God can help you overcome the fear when you encounter the next challenge in life. No matter the challenge trusting in God will help you to live a victorious life while on earth just as Jesus did in his 33 years. When you accept Christ as your Lord and Savior you have the power of the holy spirit to overcome any bad behavior that will cause you to sin.

Pamela Davis-Ghavami is a Washingtonian with 30 years of federal service working in the Computer Science field and the Information Technology and Project Management field. She has a Bachelor of Business Administration (BBA) from the University of the District of Columbia in Business Administration and Computer Information Systems Science, a master's degree in the Information Technology and Project Management field from Capella University and is a certified Project Management Professional (PMP) from the Project Management Institute (PMI). She enjoys learning new things about technology and how to help people manage the technology changes. She takes pride in sharing her knowledge with Montgomery County Maryland public school students, family and friends. She is married with one son and enjoys being an active member in her Toastmaster club, the Montgomery County Maryland Tennis league, participating in the Grace Community Church of Howard County services and reading the latest books on conflict resolution best practices, change management and emotional intelligence. Spending quality time with her family are also high on her priority list.

Location:
10957 Bucknell Drive
Silver Spring MD 20902

Email Address:
pdghavami@aol.com

Psalm 46:5 NIV "God is within her; she will not fall; God will help her at break of day."

In life there are times when you will face many obstacles and challenges but every step of the way God is with you. There are times when you'll feel like God is not going to show up and that there is no hope for my situation. But we serve a miracle working God you are not walking in this alone. There is beauty for your ashes you and pain will produce your purpose. Every day He breathes a breath of fresh air into your lungs SPEAK LIFE back into yourself.... I am beautiful, I am fearfully and wonderfully made, I am the apple of His eye, I am unbreakable, I am a warrior, I am amazing, I am more than a conqueror, and I am unstoppable! Don't allow the enemy to get the best of you fight a good fight.....You've got this! Be you! Be free! Be empowered!

Shacre Bennett domestic violence advocate and survivor. She was nominated by and selected as the National Spoke person for the Allstate Foundation and National Network to End Domestic Violence (NNEDV) in April 2015. In October 2016 Bennett became an ordained Evangelist. As the National spokesperson Bennett was featured in Glamour Magazine January 2017 to bring awareness to domestic violence all across the world. In early 2018 Bennett became ordained Chaplain. In 2016 Bennett was selected as the Domestic Violence liaison for Empowered Women Ministries and as of 2018 she's serving as the CEO for the organization. Bennett has spoken on many platforms to bring awareness to domestic violence & she mentors all across the country.

shacrebennett@gmail.com purposedtoempoweryou18@gmail.com
https://www.linkedin.com/in/shacre-bennett-3428a48b/
https://www.facebook.com/authorshacre.Bennett
https://www.facebook.com/shacrerbennett
https://www.instagram.com/authorshacrebennett/

Psalms 34:4 *"I sought the Lord, and He answered me, and delivered me from all my fears."*

Trust and believe that everything will work out according to God's plan for your life. Keep smiling and keep your mind on Him, for He sees you struggling and will work things out in your favor. Don't give up on God. He will brighten your darkest moments and guide you to your victory. We must understand that sometimes we have to go through the fire to become refined and made new. God wants a deeper relationship with you and He will forgive all our faults and sins. I encourage you to stand and keep your mind on God.

ANDREA MAINE
Facebook: Andrea Maine
Email: spellbnd@gmail.com

January 16
Minister Sonya Arrington, LMSW

"Finally, brethren, whatsoever things are true, whatsoever things are honest, whatsoever things are just, whatsoever things are pure, whatsoever things are lovely, whatsoever things are of good report; if there be any virtue, and if there be any if praise, think on these things."- Philippians 4:8

Countless adults have unresolved childhood issues. However, as an adult we must identify, evaluate and rid ourselves of any negative dysfunctional thinking (core beliefs). Otherwise it can lead to feelings of failure, worthlessness, abandonment, emotional deprivation etc. These feelings have the potential to make us become angry, resentful and/or bitter. Let's Practice "cognitive restructuring" meaning if we practice changing the way we think, we can unlearn negative thought processes & behaviors. Let's intentionally change our atmosphere by thinking & speaking Gods word & feel well. Out of your heart your mouth speaks. Be transformed by operating from a sound mind.

Minster Sonya Arrington is a wife, daughter, mother, entrepreneur, singer, preacher and a licensed social worker. Sonya received her formal education in the Fairfield County school system, subsequently attended Springfield College in Springfield Mass, attained her Bachelors in Human Services and latterly obtained her Master's Degree in Social Work. God redeemed her life approximately 30 years ago from a horrific drug and alcohol addiction consequently she continuously gives God glory!

Sonya currently pursues her LCSW, Doctorate Degree & chaplaincy while simultaneously seeking more of "Her Lord & Savior Jesus Christ" as He develops, molds and perfects the prophetic anointing within.

Email: Evenmeaa@yahoo.com Instagram: wisdomspks Facebook: Sonya Arrington Bookings: 203 397-6705

January 17
Gina R. Brown

Matthew 9:20-23

"If he touches it, it has to change. Be encouraged, knowing God is a Healer, a Deliverer, a Way Maker. Take the initiative like the woman with the issue of blood. Position yourself for a touch. He is a game changer. You may be hurting, exhausted and bleeding from the thorn in your side, but don't give up. Your faith will draw you before him. It will give you strength to endure, to step forward and reach for his touch. Move like you believe his word. If he touches it, it has to change."

Gina R. Brown is the Founder and Executive Director of Exploits International Ministries. She is a Licensed Minister who has been serving in ministry for over twenty-five years. Professionally she is a proven Project Manager, Administrator, Motivational Speaker and Mobilizer who strongly believes the word of God and is on a personal mission to fulfill the call on her life. She passionately serves in the area of missions and outreach and uses that passion to fuel her and others as she works to enlighten, train, mobilize and pray. As a Missionary, she has traveled to multiple countries for overseas mission work. As a Mentor, she shares her education and life experiences to motivate and empower women, youth and young adults to live their best life. As a cancer overcomer and warrior, she uses that experience to bring awareness, support and encouragement to those who are affected by that disease. #takingcancerdown

Email: gina.brown1000@gmail.com

January 18
DeShonda Monique Jennings

Philippians 4:13
"I can do all things through Christ which strengthened me"

As you face challenges, don't lose sight on the end result. Remember that as long as God is in your life, you will make it. Sometimes you may feel weak or don't know which way to go. You can do it, keep going. Set your daily goals... If you face a challenge or a situation comes up, you may feel it is too much or too hard to keep going. You may even feel weak. Remember that you can do ALL, not some, but ALL things through Christ. Don't stop, keep pushing yourself.

She is the epitome of what a strong wife, mother, daughter, grandmother and woman of faith is. She grew up in a small rural town of Kenbridge, VA. She serves as an advocate for children and a mentor. She is the owner of Save On Travel which offers people discounts on everyday travel at www.DeeJTravel.org

Website: deshondajennings.com
IG: deshonda_j
FB: DeShonda.jennings
Twitter: DeShondaMonique   Chesterfield, VA
Email: deshondajennings@outlook.com

And it came to pass, that, when Elisabeth heard the salutation of Mary, the babe leaped in her womb; and Elisabeth was filled with the Holy Ghost:"
Luke 1:41

When the two women pregnant with greatness meet, as soon as Elisabeth hears Mary's voice she is filled with the Holy Spirit and so was her unborn child. The sound of Mary's voice made Elisabeth's baby Leap!

Throughout my life I have had so many great women speak into my destiny and they seem to always have a word or connect with me at the right time!! As women, we need a Mary in our lives who will make our baby leap, ones who will make the vision come alive, or motivate us to become better at what we do! So today, go out and Make another person's baby leap! or pray and ask God to send your Mary to awaken the sleeping Giant on the inside of you!

Facebook- Taskministries
City/State: Wake Forest NC
Email: khall777@live.com

January 20
Audrika Danielle

Financial Freedom

DO NOT ever be ashamed of where you've been. Keep on & win. They mock & lie about your story but will never understand your glory.

I am ever so thankful for words of wisdom, a knowledge of love & minds of infinite positive energy flowing with momentum along with having developed the ability to positively affect hearts & mindsets for generational prosperity one family at a time...and then some.

Born Audrika Walton in North Carolina and raised in Michigan. The eldest of three children she developed many skills & discovered many gifts along life's journey. Audrika Danielle is a mother of eight children 7 girls & 1 boy.

At a young age Audrika Danielle learned how to braid hair and was interested in crafts. Her first finished project was a latch-hooked rug and from there she learned many others such as crochet, weaving, repurposing furniture pieces, clothing and more. Audrika Danielle enjoyed having her creations in local downtown Decatur, Georgia boutiques. She specializes in unique handmade creations.

Audrika Danielle attended Bauder College & learned Fashion Design in the early 2000's and went on to become a nurse in 2012. Audrika Danielle then moved to Florida where she discovered that she had a passion for helping people to destress as well as a natural knack at listening & problem solving which gave way to both a career as a Full Specialist in 2014 which consists of Manicure/Pedicures, Facials, Foot Detox, and even learning how to do henna tattoos as well as Facial Threading. Audrika Danielle along with opening up a mini spa in Florida enjoyed becoming a Transformational Life Coach and putting together workshops along with mini pampering sessions. Audrika Danielle looks forward to what is next...

Feel free to contact Audrika Danielle @
321-339-8984
artisticsouljah@gmail.com
artisticsouljah.com
facebook.com/artisticsouljah
facebook.com/audrikadanielle

January 21
Michelle Bae Prewitt

Live

"You are the salt of the earth, if salt has lost its taste, how shall it's saltiness be restored? It is no longer of value except to be thrown out and trampled under people's feet.

Regardless of any obstacle one may face let go and love God!
No battle is yours alone and there is someone; somewhere who truly cares....
Peace be with you my SISTER'S in CHRIST.
I love you if no one has told beautiful.
Life begins with Y-O-U!!

Facebook: Michelle Bae Prewitt

Instagram: FitGang_Bae

Fitgangbae@gmail.com

January 22
Kyla M. Neil

"Stretched Toward Your Purpose" – Phil. 3:12-14

Purposed woman, you never know what you can do until you are forced to stretch beyond your limits. It is the stretching, through trials and struggles, that helps you see all that lies within you. Stretching has a purpose, which leads you to your purpose. Just like a rubber band is not really usable until it has been pulled a few times; neither are you. Your challenging moments may stretch you more than you would like them to at times, but that is only because you're being made to look like the One who created you to do great things.

Philadelphia, PA

Kyla M. Neil is an aspiring writer. She also leads the women's ministry at Jones Memorial Baptist Church, mentoring women on how to live fearlessly for the Lord. Kyla has a Bachelor of Science in Behavioral Health Counseling from Drexel University and a Master of Theological Studies from Palmer Theological Seminary.

Facebook: Kyla Myrick Neil
LinkedIn: linkedin.com/in/kylaneil
Instagram: kylaneil71
Kneil4371@gmail.com

January 23
Avice Burchett

"Have I not commanded you? Be strong and courageous. Do not be afraid; do not be discouraged, for the Lord your God will be with you wherever you go."- Joshua 1:9.

Often times in life, we are faced with giants that seem impossible to defeat. During these moments we must remember God's promises in His Word that we already have victory in Jesus. It is during these darkest hours that we must put our trust and Faith in Him. These storms and challenges have purpose. God allows certain situations to arise so that our faith in Him will grow.

Email: burchettavice@yahoo.com

January 24
Brenda Freeman

"Brethren, if a man be overtaken in a fault, ye which are spiritual, restore such as one in the spirit of meekness; considering thyself, lest thou also be tempted." Galatians 6:1 KJV

There are many scriptures that I think speak to women. When I see the word "man," I think it refers to "woman." We as women believe that we hold "our" world in our hands, and that we control the joy, success, and future of our family and friends. If we take this scripture to heart, we would hold our sisters up! We could tell our sisters, "You can't control everything that happens." We could be the ladder the ladder that helps each other overcome and see the rainbow after the storm.

City/State: Victoria, VA

Email: brendafreeman91358@gmail.com

"Therefore, since we are receiving a kingdom that cannot be shaken, let us be thankful, and so worship God acceptably with reverence and awe, for our God is a consuming fire."-- Hebrews 12:28-29 (NIV)

I start every morning singing along loudly with "For Every Mountain" by Kurt Carr because I need the reminder. It's easy to praise Him when everything is going right. It's real hard to remember to praise him when my world is shaking! It's so good to know we have a God that gives us "a brand-new mercy along with each new day". Praise him now for what He is about to do! Trust Him to conquer and consume the enemies without - and within - that are greater than you. Start your day with praise and watch Him work!

Chantaine is a powerful speaker with an incredible message. As a result of the travel strategies she teaches in her Experience Rejuvenation™ seminars and private coaching, people have epic experiences and amazing memories for years to come.

Connect with Chantaine at www.LettzChat.com

https://www.facebook.com/ChantaineBulluck

https://www.linkedin.com/in/chantainerhoebulluck

Email: crb@rejuvenateyourlife.biz

Habakkuk 3:17-19

The Message Bible and The King James Version

Firstly, Habakkuk, absolutely knew how to Praise our GOD. Moreover, one writer said fig tree and the other said cherry, however, all Habakkuk saw was a tree. We must realize that the "housing" or "container" for our Blessing is already in place. In as much as, no fruit on the vine, remember the vine (housing) is in place! In addition, "Oh Glory" I feel a definite leap in my spirit!!!! Good GOD Almighty....We must have a come what May existence, because our GOD, Has the Stage Set, even when we can't physically see it. Instantly, start shouting, the more desolate a situation seems to be, shout and Praise harder. Thusly, like that deer, Habakkuk speaks about and do cartwheels, and wave your hands in the air and dance like you don't care if someone sees you ..." Oh Glory"

Let me stop writing and dance right NOW! Love you and keep Soaring!

Gwen Smith Ministries, River of Live Inc.
FB Gwendolyn V Davis Smith
Email: gwendolyn4718@att.net

January 27
Sheila Morton

Romans 8:35 (NIV)

Who shall separate us from the love of Christ? Shall trouble or hardship or persecution or famine or nakedness or danger or sword?

How many times have we disappointed the Lord?
It has been so many times that we have no fingers to count.
Our heads hang in shame. We plead for mercy.

Living with disappointment is hard. We move away from others.

We do not want to get involved in anything. But that's not what God wants. He wants us trusting Him and knowing that we are loved.

Hold your head up, dear sister. God's compassion is great!

Let Him guide you through every disappointment. His love assures us that everything will be alright. Recite with me, *"God's Love is Amazing." God's love is Amazing; God's love is Amazing*!

Sheila Morton is a mother of 4 and grandmother of 14. She is a retired teacher, an online business owner, wife of a retired pastor and active in her woman's ministry at her church. She has her view set on writing more books soon.
Email: smorton28@hotmail.com

Facebook: Sheila Brice-Morton
Facebook: Financial Lifestyle Coach
Website: http://www.iwantitallback.com/

January 28
Linda Latrice Ranson

"Every day won't be the same, You will have good days, bad days, trying days, overwhelming days, tired days, invigorated days and days you feel you cannot go on. No matter what day you are having today decide to still show up. Show up and Keep going!" @commandingline

Finding the strength to endure is sometimes the hardest thing and most times you feel defeated. We don't see what GOD has for us and don't understand some of the trails and valleys he puts us through to strengthen us. We fall victim to our circumstances and at the brink of a breakthrough we give up never seeing our destiny. One thing you must remember GOD has a perfect plan and everything we go through has a purpose. So, those days that you feel like giving up, remember all things work for the good of the Lord. Show up and perform in excellence; see all that GOD has for you.

www.uptowndivaaccessories.biz
uptowndivatx@outlook.com
uptown_divaaccessories - Instagram
Uptown Diva Accessories - Facebook

January 29
Tocha Moore

Ecclesiastes 3:1-8
"To everything there is a season, and a time to every purpose under the
heaven: 2 A time to be born, and a time to die; a time to plant, and a time to
pluck up that which is planted;
3 A time to kill, and a time to heal; a time to break down,
and a time to build up;
4 A time to weep, and a time to laugh; a time to mourn, and a time to dance;
5 A time to cast away stones, and a time to gather stones together; a time to
embrace, and a time to refrain from embracing;
6 A time to get, and a time to lose; a time to keep, and a time to cast away;
7 A time to rend, and a time to sew; a time to keep silence,
and a time to speak;
8 A time to love, and a time to hate; a time of war, and a time of peace." (KJV)

There is a time for everything! No matter where life takes us or what happens there is a reason for it all. When we find ourselves in the rough places in life, we can take refuge in the fact that it will not be forever, the hard times will end. Purpose is the reason something is done or created, everything has a purpose remembering that will help you deal with anything! There is always a lesson to be learned as long as you are willing to be the student. It all Serves a Purpose. You have a Purpose!

Email: yourtochamoore@gmail.com

January 30
Tijera Moseley

Romans 4:17
"(As it is written, I have made thee a father of many nations,) before him whom he believed, even God, who quickeneth the dead, and calleth those things which be not as though they were."

Remember who you are, what you are purposed to do and the power that lies within you to complete the work. You have the power and ability to speak your dreams and visions into existence. Have faith and only believe that God is the power that works on the inside to manifest His glory through you. It's not too late to awaken what seems to be dead. Now speak life to what you see until you see life in what you speak!

"**You may encounter many defeats, but you must not be defeated. In fact, it may be necessary to encounter the defeats, so you can know who you are, what you can rise from, how you can still come out of it.**"
~ Maya Angelou

You are a woman of many strengths, jewels and gifts. Throughout life you will go through trials and tribulations. You may feel the weight of the world on your shoulders and it just will not let up. Just remember life is not happening to you, but for you. Do not lose focus. You were made for this. Your story is shaping you for your divine purpose. Your divine purpose is to help you fulfil the assignment God has called you to complete. Please hold on a little bit longer. The reward for patience and obedience is great favor and blessings.

Ashante Smallwood is the Founder/Owner of Princess Asia's Collection, LLC and Co-Founder of Avva's Production. I perform as an Entrepreneur, designer, mentor, author and administrative director. My mission is to empower female youth, by promoting self-love, self-care, character building and confidence.

Social media links:
FB: Princess Asia's Collection, LLC
Instagram: princess_asiascollection
Website: www.princessasiacollection.com
Email: Ashante@princessasiacollection.com

February 1
Nateshe Williams

Joshua 1:9

Don't Fret! PRAY! Did you know that was a command? GOD is always with us on this battle field ready to take action! Do you feel as if you can't handle it all? Well GOD - our knight in shining armor positions himself as our rescue from distress. See, I was HER in distress, DEPRESSED, living a LESBIAN lifestyle and GOD – DELIVERED me on the spot! Now, how amazing is that? So, don't Fret! Today is your day of deliverance! Lay it all, at the feet of the one who paid it all. Go ahead! It's your turn to trust!

Nateshe Williams is a Philadelphia native who is in love with the Lord. She is a mother, actress, advocate and an outreach liaison. She loves having worship at the beach and helping anyone in need. Like her mother Renee would say, "You never know, you may be entertaining an angel."

Facebook: https://www.facebook.com/nateshe.williams
Instagram: http://www.instagram.com/nateshe

nnwilliams1108@gmail.com

February 2
Tamala Coleman

Hebrews 11:16- "But without faith it is impossible to please him: for he that cometh to God must believe that he is, and that he is a rewarder of them that diligently seek him."

Faith is the substance or the guarantee that those things which you are waiting for will come to pass. Faith is the evidence when we cannot see the Manifestation. Faith begins when you drown your doubts, cast off fear and anchor in the truth.

God is a rewarder of those who diligently seek him. If you don't have grace or deliverance, seek Him again.

Social Media:
https://www.facebook.com/tamala.coleman.1
https://twitter.com/tamala_coleman
https://www.instagram.com/iam_tamalacoleman/
https://www.iheart.com/podcast/966-spiritually-speakin-29260154/

Email: tcpraise14@gmail.com

February 3
Tschanna Taylor

Jeremiah 29:11

Every year, I am required to have an eye exam to monitor the accuracy of my vision and if necessary, make the proper adjustments. If I miss my appointment, my vision could potentially become unclear and out of focus. Without a clear vision, you may have difficulty getting to your destination. You must have a clear vision to reach your purpose. While on your journey of purpose, don't allow distractions to advert your attention from your primary vision. Why? People, places and positions are waiting for you? Take a moment and check your vision. Do you need a new prescription?

Tschanna Taylor, MBA, aka, THE Purpose Engineer, is a Wife, Mother, Author, Entrepreneur and Teacher, who enthusiastically teaches individuals how to take life's mess and turn it into a masterpiece, unapologetically.

www.facebook.com/tschannataylor
www.instagram. com/tschannataylor
www.twitter.com/tschannataylor
linkedin.com/in/tschannataylor

February 4
Charlisa Herriott

"Where is Your Faith?"

NOW FAITH is the substance of things HOPED for, the evidence of things NOT YET seen according to Hebrews 11:1. Can you place your TRUST in believing in something that you cannot see? Can you have FAITH in something that is intangible, unforeseeable but yet believable? IF you said, "yes", then your level of FAITH is strong. Bu if you struggle with what you believe to come true or manifest within your life, then I ask you this, "Where is your FAITH?"

Charlisa Herriott is an Author, Minister, Speaker, 2x Cancer Survivor and Survivor Coach. She empowers women who experience the frails of life to rise from their ashes to Live on Purpose, Live with Passion and Live Life Full!

Website: www.CharlisaHerriottASurvivorsVoice.com

Instagram.com/CharlisaHerriott

Facebook.com/CharlisaHerriott

Linkedin.com/inCharlisaHerriott

Twitter.com/CharlisaHerriot

February 5
Crystal Bodie Smith

Matthew 6 verse 33. NKJV

"But seek ye first the kingdom of God, and his righteousness; and all these things shall be added unto you."

I, Crystal Bodie-Smith am driven by this lifeline scripture. I learned that my way didn't work. Although I have hope and faith, Seeking God First is necessary! We can't achieve anything without God in the forefront mentally, emotionally, and spiritually! No other formula works! Meditate on Him and understand that God or any Higher Power must be the source. Everything else is a resource! Daily we should Seek God, relinquish control and Stop trying to figure things out! Believe the Bible. Read and say it. Believe all in our hearts. Then keep hope alive every day and watch God move!

Crystal Bodie Smith is Co-Founder of Capital City Hope Foundation, a 501 C3 Non-Profit, in Raleigh, NC. She is the Hope Catalyst and is recently known for her Book on Amazon called Final Wishes "A Transition from Life to Death. She has appeared on television, radio, and in print.

Facebook: Crystal Bodie Smith
Linked In: Crystal Bodie Smith
Instagram:Shoutcrystal
Twitter:Shoutcrystal
Websites: www.Iamcrystalbodiesmith.com
www.capitalcityhopefoundation.com

February 6
Brenda Colter

We all experience moments when we just don't feel good enough. Much too often, we allow the thoughts and opinions of others govern the way we assess ourselves. Today I pray that you know that no matter your failings or shortcomings... you are one of a kind! You are beautiful, you are loved and you are blessed with something that God wanted to give to no one besides YOU! That thing is called Purpose. Seek it, live it and love it.

"But the Lord said unto Samuel, look not on his countenance, or on the height of his stature; because I have refused him: for the Lord seeth not as man seeth; for man looketh on the outward appearance, but the Lord looketh on the heart." 1 Samuel 16:7 KJV

HER Beautiful Mind merges Brenda's role as life coach, mentor and public speaker with the Word of God to present it in a way that makes it clear and practical to others. Her mission is to show the world that no matter where you've come from, no matter how you've been burned, it's always possible to rise up from the ashes and begin anew.

Facebook: @HERBeautifulMind220
IG: @HERBeautifulMind220
Twitter: @HER_BeauMind220
Website: brendacolter.com
Email: info@herbeautifulmind220.com

February 7
D'Tondja M. Foster

Forgiveness for The Little Girl Inside

Forgive me for not protecting you when I could.

Forgive me little girl for believing you could have done any better than you did with what you were given.

Forgive me for stealing your childhood away and making you grow so fast.

Forgive all the times I told you, you weren't enough because of your size, your color, disability.

Forgive me for starving you on so many levels I almost took your life.

Forgive me for beating you mentally, suffocating you physically that I took away your will to just Be.

February 8
Erica Hicks

Romans 8:38-39
"For I am convinced that neither death nor life, neither angels nor demons, neither the present nor the future, nor any powers, neither height nor depth, nor anything else in all creation, will be able to separate us from the love of God that is in Christ Jesus our Lord."

I love this scripture with all I have. This shows me that no matter what I do or what is done to me, God will never leave me, he is here for me int the trenches. If all that I have is taken, I will still have the love of the Lord God. I am grateful that his mercy, and his loves endures thru all that we go thru on this earth. God reminds us in the little blessings, so I am grateful that no demon, no powers, no fire, can take his love from me.

A bouquet of exotic flowers defines Erica Hicks; mother of 4, and always a friend. She's an avid supporter of the Autism movement as her 10-year-old son was diagnosed at two. Her compassion for community is the driving force for the birth of her non-profit, UMAD, United Mothers and Daughters. She has overcome hurdles & endured the loss of her husband of 23yrs in 2017. The word according to Erica Hicks is a resounding yes! "Life is powered by who you choose to be." She was a young mother who once upon a time struggled until she began to help others outside of myself". Her endeavor is to be that 'one' to help another spring free

Mserica.Hicks@yahoo.com
LinkedIn-https://www.linkedin.com/in/erica-hicks-0106aa174
Facebook-erica.hicks.980

Jeremiah 17: 7 - 8 New International Version (NIV)

7 "But blessed is the one who trusts in the Lord, whose confidence is in him. 8 They will be like a tree planted by the water that sends out its roots by the stream. It does not fear when heat comes; its leaves are always green. It has no worries in a year of drought and never fails to bear fruit."

Woman of purpose, you have been blessed, chosen and set apart to accomplish the tasks assigned to you. Sometimes we tend to experience waves of self-doubt because we haven't achieved perfection. We are all familiar with the heat of tribulation as we concern ourselves with things that are out of our control. It is then that you must recognize that these obstacles are here to distract and keep you from moving forward. Be confident that your trust in God has you right where you belong. Bask in the knowledge that you are strong, beautiful and you are making a difference in the world.

Linda A. Feliciano is a Strategic Change Agent, a Marketplace Minister, and mother of three she has overcome many obstacles, and is a successful entrepreneur known as the Small Business CFO in some circles. Linda is a keynote speaker and has been featured on a National radio show. She is the founder of Asher Business Group, LLC a full-service tax practice and accounting consultancy firm. Where she has helped small businesses save millions of dollars. Her mission is to teach stewardship in finances, health, and Spirit to the glory of God.

Social Media: Facebook: @AsherBiz @TeamPFF4Life Twitter: @AsherBiz @SmallBizCFO_ABG LinkedIn: https://www.linkedin.com/in/linda-a-feliciano-3aa12441/ Yelp: @AsherBiz Website: Asherbusinessgroup.com Location: Jacksonville, FL Email: info@asherbusinessgroup.com Aidez@live.com Laidez@yahoo.com Linda@asherbusinessgroup.com

February 10
Toni Garvin

Luke 17:5 (NKJV)
"And the apostles said to the Lord, "Increase our faith."

Without faith it's impossible to please God. He desires to bless us. If we walk in doubt and unbelief, how can God bless us? Faith is the catalyst that opens the door to God's promises. It doesn't matter what it looks like because by faith IT'S ALREADY DONE! By faith you must believe, knowing that God's word is true. You must have faith knowing you are more than a conqueror and you are victorious. You are a Royal Priesthood. You are an heir to the throne. This is your inheritance. Walk in it!!!

Toni is a devoted wife and mother, born and raised in Brooklyn, New York, currently living in Denver, Colorado. She is the CEO of Royally Scent LLC. She enjoys spending time with family. She also enjoys cooking and converting everyday recipes to vegan friendly dishes.

Social Media/Website

Facebook: www.facebook.com/toni.garvin.3

Website: www.royallyscent.com

Email: mstgarvin1@gmail.com

February 11
Wyetha Renee' Cairns

Acts 16:25-26 "And at midnight Paul and Silas prayed and sang praises unto God and the prisoners heard them. And suddenly there was a great earthquake so that the foundations of the prison were shaken and immediately all the doors were opened and every one's bands were loosed."

What are you faced with today? Do you feel like you are in your midnight hour? Well, start praising the Lord! Praise confuses the enemy – he doesn't understand how we can praise God when everything looks hopeless. No matter the circumstances, your praise can shake foundations causing chains to fall and bands to be loosed. Your praise should not be predicated by outward circumstances, but on the fact that God is good and worthy to be praised! Stop what you are doing, lift your hands and Praise the Lord and just like Paul and Silas, watch the chains that hold you bound be loosed, Selah.

https://www.facebook.com/wyetha.cairns
https://www.linkedin.com/in/wyetha-renee-cairns-993ab9123/
https://www.facebook.com/pearlsofwisdim/ reneecairns@yahoo.com

Wyetha Renee' Cairns resides in Winterville, NC with her husband Jim. Renee' is an Ordained Minister, and is the host of Pearls of Wisdom, a Live Facebook Broadcast. Renee has ministered on countless platforms for over 25 years. She mentors, disciples and serves as a role model for many women desiring to live an on purpose, dedicated Christian life. She is passionate about seeing the Body of Christ living a victorious life in Christ Jesus. Her purpose driven scripture is found in Philippians 3:10 "...That I may know Him, and the power of His resurrection, and the fellowship of His sufferings, being made conformable unto His death..."

February 12
Latasha "WOP" Williams

"You did not choose me, but I chose you and appointed you so that you might go and bear fruit — fruit that will last." John 15:16a (NIV)

How has God chosen you?

In John 15:16a, Jesus said, "You did not choose me, but I chose you and appointed you so that you might go and bear fruit — fruit that will last."

Wherever you live and work, He has gifted you with a particular genetic makeup, traits, mind, talents and spiritual gifts. And, when God calls you, He doesn't waste the gifts He's given you.

Dear God, I praise You that You have created me with gifts to make a difference. I ask that You open the way for me to use them in extending Your kingdom. In Jesus' Name, Amen.

Latasha "WOP" Williams - Wife, Mother, Daughter, Sister, Friend and The Unapologetically Purposed Woman

February 13
Camesha S. Williams

Lamentations 3:22-23, 25
"The faithful love of the Lord never ends!! His mercies never cease. Great is his faithfulness; his mercies begin afresh each morning. The Lord is good to those who depend on him, to those who search for him."

My sisters remember that God's love never fails!! Even When we fail him, his love, Grace and Mercy never wavers. You can depend on God even when everything and everyone else may fail or fall short, rest assured that God's love will prevail!! Try Him, Trust Him and Depend on Him!! He is Faithful!!

Camesha Williams was born and raised in Pine Bluff, Arkansas. She is an aspiring evangelist, author and mentor. She Works as a Psychiatric Counselor where she strives to improve the lives of others through mentorship, advocacy, and empowerment. She is also the founder of the " The Cam Project" that encourages others to Come and Mend on Purpose!!!

Email: cameshawilliams11@gmail.com

February 14
Vernita Stevens

Ephesians 6:13-17 (KJV) – "13 Wherefore take unto you the whole armor of God, that ye may be able to withstand in the evil day, and having done all, to stand.14 Stand therefore, having your loins girt about with truth, and having on the breastplate of righteousness;15 And your feet shod with the preparation of the gospel of peace;16 Above all, taking the shield of faith, wherewith ye shall be able to quench all the fiery darts of the wicked.17 And take the helmet of salvation, and the sword of the Spirit, which is the word of God."

Allow these words to inspire you today. He never said you will not face trials and tribulations, instead he has equipped you with everything you need to get through them. Today, like every day remember just before you walk out that door, look in that mirror and smile. Walk in your purpose with your head held high not to look down on others but rather to see the next level of greatness he has been preparing you for. Walk confident today knowing that you are loved, you are special, and you do make a difference!

Vernita Stevens is a retired United States Marine, Professional Trainer, Motivational Speaker, and Owner of 2p – Paradigm of Possibilities, LLC. She has a passion for helping others embrace that "ANYTHING IS POSSIBLE". She uses an inspirational approach to convey positive results to empower others to live in health and happiness.

Huntersville, NC
2p.paradigmofpossibilities@gmail.com

February 15
Leticia Hicks

Season of Adversity

"Often times God demonstrates His faithfulness in adversity by providing for us what we need to survive. He does not change our painful circumstances. He sustains us through them." -~ Charles Stanley

We will encounter adversity in different seasons of our lives. I pray, you are coping with the current challenges in your life. God will help you overcome the struggles, pain and negative thoughts. Shed tears of sorrow and joy, knowing God is there to comfort you. Your testimony will be greater than the adversity that you encounter. You are on the path to the manifestation of God's promises. Trust him on the journey. Release and allow God to do a greater work in and through you. Remember, God is in love with you.

Letitia Hicks is an women empowerment strategist, entrepreneur minster and author. I help women transform their lives with a renewed sense of power, passion and purpose.
Letitiahicks.com

Email: letitiahic63@hotmail.com

February 16
Sayra Kohen

"For assuredly, I say to you, whoever says to this mountain, 'Be removed and be cast into the sea,' and does not doubt in his heart, but believes that those things he says will be done, he will have whatever he says." Mark 11:23 (NKJV)

You are powerful beyond measure and the words you speak have the ability to lead you victoriously into the Promised Land or tragically derail your future into turmoil and bondage. Boldly declare that all of the promises of God over your life are yes and amen. Nothing is impossible for you! Use your words coupled with consistent and corresponding action to take you from where you are to where He has called and positioned you to be. You have greatness dwelling on the inside of you. Speak to the mountains in your life and command them to be removed.

Sayra Kohen is a home-based business entrepreneur, lifestyle design strategist, and success coach. She specializes in helping ordinary people get extraordinary results using simple step by step systems. Sayra is a revolutionary voice in a failing world system that is equipping men and women to break free from the status quo and live the life of their dreams!

Phone: 623.533.8788 Email: sk@sayrakohen.org
Website: www.SayraKohen.org
Facebook: https://www.facebook.com/SayraHKohen
Instagram: https://www.instagram.com/sayrakohen/
Twitter: https://twitter.com/sayrakohen
Pinterest: https://www.pinterest.com/sayrakohen/
LinkedIn: https://www.linkedin.com/in/sayrakohen/

February 17
Dr. Margareth Reed

Arise Woman of God, you were created to shine.

Isaiah 60: 1-2.

Arise, shine, for your light has come,
and the glory of the LORD rises upon you.
See, darkness covers the earth
and thick darkness is over the peoples,
but the LORD rises upon you
and his glory appears over you.

Today, allow me to remind you that God got you and every area of your life where you stumbled so many times. Darkness no longer has power over you. This year is your year to see the light that God has declared over you to shine so all can see it. Your light can no longer be hidden. I speak life into you now, his glory now appears over you.

A multilingual speaker, Dr. Reed is known for her abilities to move the audience with her contagious vivacity. The mantle on her life is to serve God's people to: Enhance, empower & equip leaders with strategies to be efficient and effective in life, business, and ministry through writing, publishing & products development. www.mrenterprisesbiz.com

She can be reached at speaker@maggyreedspeaks.com or info@mrenterprisesbiz.com
Dr. Reed is The Intentional Woman of the 21st Century.
See her on all social media and visit her site mrenterprisesbiz.com

February 18

Consuelo McAllister Colvin

"For I am the Lord your God, who holds your right hand, who says to you, 'Do not fear, I will help you." Isaiah 41:13

Life can appear overwhelming at times, but not today. God has giving you overwhelming victory. Today you have no fear. On this day you remembered. The Lord your God is escorting you through life. He is holding your right hand with all his wisdom, knowledge and power. You are lit. Your inner Shego is on fire. Filled with all the confidence and assurance of almighty God himself. Your kicking down doors. Presenting your business like you have never presented it before. You are your business. Renovate that business you call your LIFE. Never be afraid to dream. Never Fear to make that dream a reality. God is holding your right hand.

Consuelo McAllister Colvin is created faith working. She provides many services. From being the Broker in Charge over Re/Max Homestead New Bern, NC. To her home-based business LOLA Design print shop. Is her created space of faith. Consuelo is a seasoned Toastmasters Speaker. She specializes in helping people see their created faith at work. While being stylish at the same time. Shego Lash and brow business is her next step in created faith working.

Phone: 252-658-0156
Website: www.consuelocolvin.com
Facebook: https://www.facebook.com/consuelo.colvin
Instagram: https://www.instagram.com/realtorconsuelocolvin/
Twitter: https://twitter.com/RealtorConsuelo

February 19
Karmelita Stevens

"But those who trust in the Lord will find new strength. They will soar high on wings like eagles. They will run and not grow weary. They will walk and not faint." Isaiah 40:30 NLT

God chose to compare His trust and strength to that of an Eagle. The special thing about an Eagle is they don't mix with other birds and fly higher than any other bird. Eagle wings are so strong and wide that instead of seeking shelter from the storm it flies into the storm allowing the storm to lift it higher. When you trust in God there is no other direction to go but UP, taking you above what you are facing in life. Trusting in God elevates you higher than your current situation. You can guarantee that trusting in God gives you strength to face the chaos that seems to be tearing your whole world apart. Trusting in God allows you to see adversity and know there's hope in the end. Do not faint beloved, look at your mountain and command it to move through your faith and trust in God.

FB: www.facebook.com/hairrehab2014 Instagram: @hairrehab2014

Linkedin: https://www.linkedin.com/in/hair-rehab-studio-98a10884/

Karmelita dedicates her time to educating within Cosmetology schools while imparting into future Beauty Professionals. She continues to educate "beyond the walls" by teaching her clients, mentoring & speaking at seminars. For more information email hairrehabstudio@gmail.com

February 20
Donna White M. Ed

Psalms 23

This scripture is saving my life to this day. From childhood to this day for reasons only God knows, stay with me know matter how much I study the Bible. For all the times my life was in serious danger this scripture would play in my head and the danger would go away literally. I now know that this is my scripture from my Father Jesus Christ because whenever I have had fears or doubts, Psalms 23 always plays in my head. I know that God gives everyone a special word you just have to remember.

Donna White M.Ed., 51-year-old single mother of two handsome young men. I work at an early learning school in Michigan, I do a variety of thing there from enrolling to teaching preschool.

donnamew@yahoo.com
Facebook- Donna White
Instagram- artsandcraftsjunkie
Twitter-@Donnamew46White

February 21
Basheba Maiden

YOU ARE CALLED TO MORE...

Your life was predestined before the foundation of the world. Before He formed you in your mother's womb, He knew you. You are created in the image of God, fearfully and wonderfully made." Greatness is a part of your DNA. You are a natural born winner. Where ever you are in life, God has called you to more... More of His Glory, More of His Provision, More of His Peace, More of His Joy, More of His Anointing, More of His Power, More of Presence. There is another level for you and He is beckoning you to go Higher...

Today, purpose in your heart that you will allow God to birth MORE in you than where you are now and watch Him blow your mind...

Jeremiah 1:5, Genesis 1:27, Psalms 139:14

Basheba Maiden is a multi-faceted individual, from ministry, to relationship strategist, to addiction professional, and downright fun-loving individual. Through the word of God and the power of the Holy Spirit--she breaks down walls of brokenness, insecurity, and

rejection. In relationships and/or marriages, she equips men and women with a spiritual and natural action plan to not only restore relationships but to foster a relationship that thrives. As an addiction professional, she provides knowledge and real-life, no nonsense techniques to catapult patients with addiction on the road to recovery. Lastly, as an individual – Basheba is witty, compassionate, and make everybody feel special.

Basheba Maiden has overcome many obstacles in life, including rejection, brokenness, promiscuity, divorce, low-self – esteem and self-worth, and destructive behavior patterns— she has overcome them all through the power of Christ and His agents on earth.

God has utilized her pain to promote her to her purpose. Basheba utilizes the same premise with the clients she serves. There is purpose in pain, happiness after bitterness, and victory in all situations.

Basheba Maiden is a native of Lafayette, Louisiana, but currently resides in Denham Springs, LA. She is a graduate of Southern University, Baton Rouge Campus with a Bachelor's Degree in Rehabilitation Services, a Master's Degree in Rehabilitation Counseling, an Associate's Degree of Divinity Christian Education from the Don Bradford Bible College, Baton Rouge Campus. Basheba is a Licensed and Ordained Minister, Relationship Strategist, Addiction Professional, and Self-Proclaimed Comedian.

In her spare time, Basheba loves to spend time studying the word of God, spending time with family and friends, especially with her host of nieces and nephews, Serving as an example and mentor for them. She loves to travel, read books, and enjoy lots of self-care.

Social Media Tags

www.Facebook.com/BashebaMaiden

www.Instagram.com/IamBasheba

www.Twitter.com/IamBasheba

EMAIL: basheba.maiden@me.com

February 22

Mary Beasley

Numbers 23:19

"God is not a man, that He should lie, Nor a son of man, the He should repent. Has he said, and will He not do? Or has he spoken, and will He not make it good?"

He will Do It!

This scripture speaks me when doubt comes knocking at my door. God has promised me some things concerning my future and family. The Devil wants me to believe if it hasn't happened by now, it won't happen. Don't believe it! God is not a Man! He doesn't lie and he won't change His mind! If He said it, He will do it! There are over 3000 promises in the Bible. God's promises reveal his character and his eternal purposes to which he is committed to and upon which believers can absolutely depend on!

Mary Beasley is a Licensed Clinical Pastoral Counselor, Published Author and CEO of LewMar Innovations, we offer Christian counselor's licensing and degree programs. To provide quality training for pastors and mature Christians who feel God's call to counsel and make available credential that the community (Christian and non-Christian) will recognize.

Website:
lminow.com
Email:
maryb.lewmar@gmail.com

February 23
Naomi Roe (Shaffer)

It is possible!

"What do you mean, 'If I can'?" Jesus asked. "Anything is possible if a person believes." Mark 9:23 NLT

As I walked through the doors of my senior classroom, I knew this would be my last chance to prove to myself and my Teacher that I could complete an assignment. I was graduating a year behind my fellow classmates and the pressure was on. You see I didn't have a track record of finishing strong, in fact just about all of my past work was either incomplete or missing however, on this day something was different. I don't know if it was the pressure of time catching up to me or the fact that my classmates had moved on without me.

As the final hour approaches my teacher walks over to me and quietly kneels down to whisper in my ear "you only have 30 minutes left; you're not going to make it." Something inside of me almost broke into pieces as she settled there with a serious look in her eyes. Yet I knew that I've come to far to give up now! I began to find comfort in a tiny voice inside my head that said "keep going!" The thirty minutes had passed and I'd finished the test. I knew I could do it. You see all things are possible to them that believe. I pray that you take from this story the courage to go on even when the clock is winding down because anything is possible if you believe"

Naomiroe30@yahoo.com Facebook Naomi Roe

February 24
Tunda Wannamaker

Luke 2:52 New King James Version (NKJV)

"And Jesus increased in wisdom and stature, and in favor with God and men."

Every day is a day filled with new opportunities for increase.

What you believe and speak is creating your reality.

Today awake and arise in a spirit of increase, use the most powerful weapon you have your tongue:

Affirm:
I am increasing in favor
I am increasing in knowledge
I am increasing in love
I am increasing in wisdom
I am increasing in stature
I am increasing in wealth
I am in tune with my destiny
I am grateful
I am healthy
I am in direct alignment
I am creating my best life!

Tunda Wannamaker is a mother of two, Speaker Coach and Prophetess. She is passionate about teaching women to face fears, remove blocks, to speak life and step out of their comfort zone. She is the Founder and creator of Nurturing Our Women (now) and Balance Lyfe Coaching.

Email: Tundawan17@gmail.com

Instagram: Www.instagram.com/instabundance
Facebook: https://www.facebook.com/tunda.wannamaker/
LinkedIn: https://www.linkedin.com/in/tunda-wannamaker-98b2bb13/
Twitter: https://twitter.com/TundaWannamaker
Website: https://www.mybalancelyfe.com/

February 25
Nikki Denise

Matthew 19:26 NIV Study Bible (2011).
"With GOD all things are Possible".

Jesus looked at him at them and said, with this is impossible, but with GOD all things are possible.

Everything has a time and a season in our lives. However, dont ever give up on yourself, your goals or your dreams because God is always on time. In your planting season you will endure many things but remember that you will never be alone. God will always show up and show out on you each day. When things look impossible to your naked eye understand that it is possible for you today and always. Never mind what others will say or think. In the scripture God reminds you that he looked at them and said with this is impossible but with God all things are possible. Matthews 19:26NIV (2011). Study bible. When faced with adversity that is the primary example of when God is shaping and molding you for greater. Do not ever think that you cannot Win. Because all things Are Possible. "FAITHFULNESS with the strength to believe.

Social media tags: Facebook:Nikkidenise IG: Nikkidenise7

February 26
Latasha "WOP" Williams

"Be still before the LORD and wait patiently for him; fret not yourself over the one who prospers in his way, over the man who carries out evil devices!"
Psalm 37:7 (ESV)

If you're worried or troubled today by another's vengeful actions, don't try to fix the outcome or control the situation. Trust God to move, and then give yourself a little three-word pep talk: Fret not yourself.

Lord, whenever I begin to feel anxiety rising up in me over the harmful words or actions of another, help me to stop. To pray. To trust in Your plan and leave the fretting behind. In Jesus' Name, Amen

Latasha "WOP" Williams - Wife, Mother, Daughter, Sister, Friend and The Unapologetically Purposed Woman

Genesis 1:1KJV "In the beginning, God created the heaven and the earth."

"In the beginning, God created the heaven and the earth." This first powerful line of the Holy Bible opens the door to faith. There are no variations, or pre story. It just is. No saying we think, or maybe. The reader steps out on faith by choosing to continue the journey or close the book. I remember when I first read those words for the first time as an adult. I didn't question Why? or How? I didn't scoff and say impossible. I chose to believe, I chose to continue the journey towards faith. Dedicated to Steffond, Adrian, Jordan, Tiara and Dejah .
Love and Favor, Mom

Lisa is Southern at heart. Raised in Rutherfordton North Carolina She grew up playing 4 squares and beating the street lights home. Graduating from R-S central, she pursued a career as a Registered Nurse. Lisa enjoys reading and silent auctions in her spare time. She resides in Asheville NC with her Husband Mark and teenage daughter Dejah

lisagray5058@gmail.com
http:www.facebook.com/lisagray
Instagram oilynursern
YouTube Lisa Gray MyGodlife

Jeremiah 29:11 CSB Version
"For I know the plans I have for you"- [this is] the Lord's declaration-"plans for [your] welfare, not for disaster, to give you a future and a hope."

Your future only hears your voice! So, if you're not saying anything, your future has no instruction nor directions to follow. So, nothing changes or occurs! Everyday say to yourself that you expect good things to happen for me, to me and with me. Many people will be offended at how aggressively you must defend your time and space. If you're accessible to the wrong people, wrong focus and wrong things, it will in turn expose you and jeopardize your goals. Cherish and reposition yourself. Go after and possess what is already yours! You owe NO ONE apologies and if they're offended, so be it, they will be fine.

Every day is an opportunity to restart, (refocus) if the mark was not met. It's important to not wallow in defeat, but learn and keep forging ahead. Therefore, keep speaking into the atmosphere and the future will be made manifest. #SpeakToSee

I am a single mother that raised three children to adulthood, though not easy I prayed for wisdom to do my best! Now a grandmother of three children, Two-young adults and one-grade schooler, A brand new Great-Grandmother of one little precious baby girl. I've had the pleasure of raising great children, one who is a Stanford graduate and was a professional NFL player, retired now, which made me proud. I am a servant/leader as a Praise/Worshipper team member, when I serve. Singing and sewing are my greatest passions, I love them tremendously I am a Psalmist/Professional Gospel Artist, A Professional Designer/Seamstress for Full-Figured Fashion, GlamaZonly Beautiful D'Zigns, Sewpreneur/Sewernista, Craft and DIYer Preneur and Braid/WeavePreneur and Travelpreneur~ love to travel too

glamazique28@gmail.com, www.myvortex365.com/DominionaireTravel, www.ytbtravel.com/DominionaireTravel, www.Surge365.com/DominionaireTravel

March 1
Gwendolyn Arnette

Ezekiel 37:3-5 King James Version (KJV)
"3 And he said unto me, Son of man, can these bones live? And I answered, O Lord God, thou knowest. 4 Again he said unto me, Prophesy upon these bones, and say unto them, O ye dry bones, hear the word of the Lord. 5 Thus saith the Lord God unto these bones; Behold, I will cause breath to enter into you, and ye shall live:"

We all have had challenges asking ourselves "Is this thing going to live or will I let it die?" You have to make the choice to speak life and breath on every situation that you are faced with, no matter how big or small. Where there is a dry valley in life...seek the word. Be determined that you have the authority to SPEAK LIFE. This is how we overcome, by SPEAKING LIFE and the BREATH OF THE WORD causes it to LIVE. Go to those dry valleys and see those bones rising up and shaking together until they have LIFE.

Gwendolyn Arnette is an entrepreneur and owner of GiGis Creations an Innovative Branding Solution, focused on Branding Photography while also providing other brand solutions. She is a mother of three and a grandmother of three. Her motto passed down from her grandmother is "TRUST IN THE LORD AND TREAT EVERYBODY RIGHT" the key to longevity.

www.instagram.com/gigis_creativeshots
https://www.facebook.com/gigis.creativeshot
Https://gmacollins.comhportolio.com www.instagram.com/elitequeen72

http://linkedin.com/in/gwendolyn-collins-7b00825https://gdmacollins.myportfolio.com gdmacollins@gmail.com\

March 2
Key Bentley

"Don't be Afraid, He's Got You!"

"Have I not commanded you? Be strong and courageous. Do not be afraid and do not be dismayed, for the LORD your God will be with you wherever you go" (Joshua 1:9 English Standard Version).

You were offered an opportunity to become a business partner with three ex-colleagues. The proposal does not require a monetary investment from you. The venture consists of running offsite human resources and payroll for privately held companies. You're highly suited, because of the knowledge and expertise you have acquired in HR. Excited about the opportunity, but you allow doubt to boggle your mind. So, the first thing you do is share with others instead of praying. After speaking with a circle of friends, you are now in fear of accepting the venture opportunity. Not because of bad advice; however, different perspectives were brought to light. When we allow doubt and fear to enter our thoughts in decision making confusion can easily take control.

This scenario can resonate with many because sometimes we seek the direction from others first rather God. I want you to consider, he awaits us to recite scriptures and seek him first. For example, the Sermon on the Mount Jesus tells us to "But seek first his kingdom and righteousness and, all these things will be given to you as well" (Matthew 6:33 New International Version). This means, seek God's kingdom, first, in all we do, as its sovereigns throughout the universe. Therefore, when an opportunity opens its doors to excel your life, fear not. Fear and confusion limit courage. Which are negative tricks from evil spirits; however, with God you have the power in prayer, actions, language and faith.

When people kept asking Key, "What is your line of work?" With a career background in Human Resources Recruitment, she took the lead and founded Key The Careerologist. She believes there is a new rhythm in onboarding. KTC is set to offer – Resume Writing, Interview Coaching, Resume Storytelling, Career Coaching, and Corporate Travel. The surplus of services is to bring *candidates and employers* up to speed with innovative recruitment. Throughout Key's Recruitment career she prioritized to solve modern day recruitment inefficacies; by bridging the gaps in candidate and employer onboarding experiences. What she found is they are not speaking the same language. Geared with a professional background ranging 20 years KTC aims to solve this problem. Key has served on planning committees with local non-profits like Goodwill and the Lutheran Social Services to produce mega career fairs in Phoenix, Arizona. In addition, as a Special Project Producer Intern, to NBC 12 News "You Paid for It" franchise. While there she wrote weekly online web articles to collaborate the reporter's aired story for AZCentral.com. Key is a woman of many trades: She states, "In life, we are gifted with more than one talent. So, don't hide them its evolution for all to evolve."

You can contact Key at:
rhimehire@yahoo.com
www.keythecareerologist.com
https://www.linkedin.com/in/keybentleyambassador

March 3
Teresa Robinson

Romans 14: 22 KJV "Hast thou faith? Has it to thyself before God? Happy is he that condemneth not himself in that thing which he alloweth."

Summary: Sometimes, God places us in positions in life to make us stronger or to be a testimony unto someone else. As human nature, when something is unfamiliar to us, at times we begin to fear and have doubt. But, I'm here to tell you, fear and doubt is not of God. Do you not trust God enough and believe that what He say he'll do, that its already done? He said that if you have faith the size of a mustard seed, you can say to the mountain move and it shall be done. You must remember when taking any position or whatever the situation may be, you are in control of what you allow in you. Don't doubt nor condemn yourself. Stand firm and you shall do great things.

Facebook: @Teresa Robinson
　　　　　@Sweet & Frosted
　　　　　@ S.I.S.T.A.S FYC
Instagram: ladiit_rachelle
　　　　　Sweetnfrosted
Email: t.rachellerobinson@gmail.com

Teresa R. Robinson is a very outgoing, strong-willed, and loving mother of two. Teresa is also an inspiring author, entrepreneur and owner and founder of Sweet & Frosted Custom Confectioners and Savory Foods LLC and founder of S.I.S.T.A.S. FYC a non-profit organization encouraging females of all ages to smile and take hold of life. Teresa is a firm believer in Fabienne Fredrickson's quote, "The things you are passionate about are not random. They are you're calling." So, she spends her time encouraging family and others to find something that they love to do and make a difference.

Psalm 34:4-5(KJV)

"I sought the Lord, and he heard me and delivered me from all my fears. They looked unto him and were lightened: and their faces were not ashamed."

Today is a new day! Seek the Lord in the good and the bad. He wants to be there to deliver you out of anything that may cause you harm or fear. When you have a conversation with him, he will not only deliver you from any fears but he will continue to lighten your path. Don't be ashamed of your past failures or experiences or even what happened yesterday. God cares all about what you care about and will keep you in peace no matter the situation. Your testimonies of victory will help others to overcome.

Sharice Rush is a Mother, Wife, Author, Entrepreneur, Mentor and Counselor. C.E.O of Sharice Rush Enterprises as well as Signer's Touch of Paparazzi Jewelry. She also serves as a Minister, Youth leader, Prayer Intercessor and Community Outreach Leader for her local church. Among other endeavors she is a Co-Author of Upcoming Book collaboration H.E.R. Extreme Makeover: Reflections of Healing, Equipping and Restoring Life's Messes into Masterpieces. Sharice is a Lover of God and truly has a heart for people.

sharicerush@gmail.com

https://www.facebook.com/signerstouchofpaparazzi/

https://www.facebook.com/sharice.rush

March 5

Tameka Bowens

Don't Panic, Detour Ahead!

When I'm traveling, I am one of those people who wants to get where they are going with no issue. "I plan it all out" to a tee. I even ensure that there is a Plan B in place. My smart phone voice automated GPS app navigates me through every turn just in case!

No matter how much I plan, there are times when my plan fails. I run into a detour. For whatever reason, I begrudge detours. I always have. They slow me down, it causes me to make U-turns, or even take alternate route. I waste energy in getting upset, frustrated, and complain. There is absolutely nothing I can to change what's happening in that moment. I just have to change my attitude & trust the process. God showed me something& I truly get it! His ways are not my ways, his thoughts are definitely not my thoughts.

HE spoke suddenly and softly. Truth of the matter is:
HE has to slow us down.
HE needs my undivided attention.
Lastly, HE needs me to trust in Him.
I must take the alternate path because he knows what lies ahead. I simply want to encourage you my sister not to begrudge detours. Cease your moment. It's necessary for your new journey! Beloved, HE'S GOT YOU-DETOUR STRAIGHT AHEAD!

March 6
Dr. Christine Handy

Above Only Living

Deuteronomy 23:13 tells us - And the LORD shall make thee the head, and not the tail; and thou shalt be above only, and thou shalt not be beneath- Let's stop right there! Take a moment and think about your life. What are examples of your Above Only Living? Are you the lender or the borrower, are you the employee or the employer, are you fed or do you feed? Reflect on how you are living and set your goal to live "Above Only". Pay off your debts, plan your dream vacations, fly first class, live where you want, drive what you want, control your time, bless your family, bless your community, live the life that the Lord intended for you! You have God's permission to live Above Only.

Dr. Christine Handy is an educator, entrepreneur, life coach, and author. A respected high school principal and leader, she is also a Senior Manager and Relationship Marketing expert with Send Out Cards and a leader with a health and wellness company. Additionally, she is a collaborating author in the Amazon Best Seller – Dear Fear Volume II and It Takes Money Honey. You can connect with Dr. Handy on Facebook under Christine Handy or by email christine@aboveonly.ws.

March 7
Maria L. Perryman

I want to share this revelation with you. Whenever you're going through something go to the word of God and read scriptures pertaining to that situation. I did just that for my business. I went to the word of God for financial growth! I looked up prosperity and wealth. Wealth is mentioned 27 times and Prosperity is mentioned 17 times. This scripture will be a blessing to you!

"Save now I beseech thee O LORD O LORD I beseech thee send now prosperity" Psalm 118:25

You shall have what you say! Now speak this verse out loud over your business!

amperryman7@gmail.com

"You're going to rise higher, accomplish more than you thought possible and reach the fullness of your destiny"

"To instruct, empower, and equip individuals with the skills and resources needed for a prosperous Christ-centered enriched life".

"Trust in the LORD with all thine heart; and lean not unto thine own understanding."

"In all thy ways acknowledge him, and he shall direct thy paths." Proverbs 3:5-6

Instagram – mperryman_55

Facebook Personal Page - https://www.facebook.com/maria.perryman.5

FB Group Page - Social Networking Academy with Maria Perryman
https://www.facebook.com/groups/108386819831153/

Twitter – Maria Perryman @pedcompany

Maria L Perryman is a wife, mother, grandmother, woman of God. educator and entrepreneur.

She has been married to her college sweetheart for 36 years and together they have 3 grown children, a daughter in law and 2 grandsons. As a woman of God Maria has served in numerous capacities, First Lady, Scholastic Motivation Ministries Leader and Youth on a Mission team leader.

Maria taught for 31 years before retiring in June 2017. During her teaching career she served as a regular classroom teacher, schoolwide Literacy Coach, Citywide Reading Coach, Assistant Principal and 6th grade teacher. Maria achieved National Board Certification in 2004 and renewed in 2013. She had extensive training in Reading & Writing Workshop from Lucy Calkins Teachers College Columbia University. She is an America Achieves Fellow and a TeachingChannel.org Teacher Laureate. Maria has been a conference presenter citywide, state, national and international.

An entrepreneur for 3 years! With the first company Maria rose to the leadership position in a year. She is now with a different business and in less than 2 months has double status advanced.

March 8
Margareth "Maggy" Reed

Psalm 46:5
"God is within her; she will not fail."

Woman of God,

How many times people have spoken negative words over you?

How many times even family members don't see how you will overcome your situation now, see, they only see your now, but have no clue what God has for you, and the blessings that are about to flow in your life. I have come to remind you that what God has for you, eyes have not seen. Your focus needs to be on the Almighty, the author and finisher of your faith. When no one sees a way out for you, I'm persuaded that God has something amazing just for you. On woman's day know that God is within you, you will have testimonies, you will not fail in the matchless name of Jesus Christ the messiah.

A multilingual speaker, Dr. Reed is known for her abilities to move the audience with her contagious vivacity. The mantle on her life is to serve God's people to: Enhance, empower & equip leaders with strategies to be efficient and effective in life, business, and ministry through writing, publishing & products development. www.mrenterprisesbiz.com

She can be reached at speaker@maggyreedspeaks.com or info@mrenterprisesbiz.com

Dr. Reed is The Intentional Woman of the 21st Century.
See her on all social media and visit her site mrenterprisesbiz.com

March 9

Rhonda Wilson

"Trust in the Lord with all your heart and lean not on your own understanding" - Prov. 3:5 NIV

Situations during our life journey can seem overwhelming. In October 2011, my family experienced an overwhelming situation. Doctors diagnosed my 18-year-old daughter with an enlarged heart, and she needed a heart transplant. My daughter clung to her love for the Lord and this scripture, finding courage, strength, and peace to face her journey. She trusted and flourished through the loss of her second child, the transplant itself, and the battles with organ rejection and health complications, even when her kidneys failed and the end was near. So, I encourage you to trust Him no matter what you're facing. Trust His unfailing, never-ending love. Trust that Hos Grace is sufficient. Trust Him because He will bring you renewed faith, renewed hope, renewed strength, and even renewed joy.

March 10
Cathy Harris

Romans 12:2

"Mind Management"

"A woman has Gods ability to control her thought life. It is hidden in her usage of divine authority and in her usage of the blood of Jesus. When a woman has faith, her authority flows stronger. When she has faith, her authority is more vocal and verbal, she can speak to mountains in her mind. She can speak to issues in her heart and she can destroy the atmosphere of Satan with her words. A woman must protect her mind, for this is the object that Satan will attack most."

Author: Prophet Joshua Holmes
Book: Increasing Your Anointing as a Virtuous Woman

March 11

Janae Black

Psalms 51:10

"Create in me a clean heart, O' God and renew a right spirit within me."

This scripture speaks to me because I once struggled with feeling as if I wasn't worthy of God's promises and his blessings. I struggled with forgiving. I held on to every negative thing someone done to me and would throw it in their face every change I got. I prayed for God to renew a right spirit within me. To create in me, a clean heart. It was then when I realized the power in forgiving. I forgive people and move on. I no longer hold on to the negative but say "I forgive you and may God bless you".

Bio: my name is Janae Black. I am a Cleveland, Ohio native currently residing in Atlanta, Georgia. I am also the founder of BAlive (Be Alive) a non-profit organization geared towards suicide awareness and prevention for adolescents. I am an actress and enjoy writing and bringing things to life. I am a firm believer that there is a purpose for your pain.

Instagram @imjusnae @BAlive
Facebook: Nae Black
BAlive

Cecellia Hall

2 Corinthians 6-18 NIV
" And, I will be a Father to you, and you will be my sons and daughters, says the Lord Almighty."

I went through life without a Father. I always wondered if my life would have been different for me if he was in my life. I feel that being fatherless affected my life in a great way. I grew up seeing one side of love and it dimmed my vision to recognize real love from a man. I suffered from low self-esteem, rejection and feeling I wasn't pretty enough. I had no positive male in my life to love me and pour into my life and give me direction for my life. Later in life I had to woman up and learn to love and forgive and to love who God created me to be and I had a Heavenly Father that loved me unconditionally. God is my loving Father like no other. In him I was made complete. It's a blessed assurance that our Father God will never leave us nor forsake us.

FB: Beauty4ashes
Email: rountree45@me.com

Teesbeauty4ashes.wixsite.com

March 13

Cheena R. Headen

Philippians 4:8-9

"Finally, brothers, whatever is true, whatever is honorable, whatever is just, whatever is pure, whatever is lovely, whatever is commendable, if there is any excellence, if there is anything worthy of praise, think about these things."

Your living is determined not so much by what life brings to you, but by the attitude you bring to life! 100% of your ATTITUDE contributes to you surviving a trial in life. It helps with keeping a healthy outlook on life. Here is a mathematical formula to the word: A-T-T-I-T-U-D-E would be 1+20+20+9+20+21+4+5 which equals 100%. Each of these letters are numbered by their position in the alphabet. Practice daily what Philippians 4:8-9 says when faced with adversity and watch how the peace of God guards your heart and mind.

Cite: https://www.motivationalmemo.com/100-mathematical-reasons-for-developing-a-great-attitude/

Certified Emotional Healing Life Coach and founder of Breakout Mindset Mentoring and Coaching, focusing on helping women strategically develop the mindset that will change the dynamics of their life Spiritually, Mentally, Emotionally, and Physically. Cheena is the 2018 recipient of the ACHI WSWA Magazine Awards Charlotte/Triad Chapter Woman of the Year Award and the 2018 recipient of the Trials to Triumph Award. She has been seen on many platforms sharing her huge vision and passion to impact the lives of women, young ladies and girls for Christ. Encouraging them all to have faith in the power they possess within to take back their life and OWN IT! Cheena is also the founder of Triple Empowerment Network,1000WomenInMotion, and PINK4CHEE Inc. She is the Author of Spiritual Steps to Surviving a Triple-Negative Diagnosis, Until

Further Notice Celebrate Everything the Journal and Compiler of the Anthology Unleashed Travails: From Pain to Purpose.

Cheena is a friend to many, a mother of two and a caring sister to four brothers and one sister. She enjoys availing herself to opportunities to know and serve others as a Certified Mentor for the American Cancer Society, program called Reach to Recovery in Greensboro, NC. She is a Moses Cone Systems Volunteer at the Wesley Long Cancer Center. An active member of Lambda Tau Upsilon Christian Sorority and also an active member of NCNW, Inc.

Cheena's motto: "I may not captivate my whole audience, but if only one person, then I've done what I was purposed to do". So, Until Further Notice CELEBRATE Everything!

cheena@cheespeak.com
www.facebook.com/cheenarheaden
www.instagram.com/cheenarheaden
www.linkedin.com/in/cheenarheaden
www.twitter.com/cheespeaks
www.breakoutmindset.com
www.unleashedtravailsbook.com
www.cheespeaks.com

March 14

Jahmia Jackson

"Show me the right path, O Lord; point out the road for me to follow."
(Psalms 25:4)

All paths and journeys in life lead back to experiences that involve a point of learning. Your choices affect what outcome will be experienced. Turn to God for spiritual direction and trust the process. What you are currently experiencing may be for the benefit of you sharing your testimony with someone else. The experience is not to destroy you but, the test that you share through your testimony shows your reverence and honor to God that his grace and mercy is sufficient. Your purpose is preparing room for you to live a life of gratefulness! Push through and bless him today through prayer!

March 15

Pastor Osita S. Osagbue

Joshua 1:3

"Every place that the sole of your foot shall tread upon I have given you, as I said to Moses."

Go and Possess the Land!

The year of 2019 is a season of unique launching, especially for those who have been preserving for many years. As 19 is the number of faith, I know many of you have been tested beyond belief. However, God divinely states this is your season of rest. As Moses laid the foundation for his mentee Joshua, someone has already laid the foundation for you. It is time for you to walk into your destiny and inherit the path that has already been placed before you. Therefore, do not ponder upon your past weary season, but launch forth into your inheritance.

Osita Osagbue is an ordained Pastor serving at risk populations in Washington, DC. As President of Violet Glory Ministries, she delivers effective community outreach ministries.

Services offered include coaching/mentoring, leadership training, and dance ministry. In addition, we offer the "Are You a Visionary" Conference to assist non-profits attain 501c3 status.

https://violetglorymin.org

violetglory96@outlook.com

March 16

Jennifer J. Bryant

Psalm 34:18

"The Lord is near to the brokenhearted and saves those crushed in spirit."

Disappointment is the first seed of doubt that can impact our faith. Think of disappointment as a test permitted by God to see if you'll continue trusting Him, obeying Him, and believing that He is good. Disappointment sounds so harmless, but it can stagnate our spiritual growth and makes us bitter and defeated towards people and our circumstances. Gain a new perspective, and tell yourself this situation is a lesson that could've been much worse...and ask yourself what specifically about this am I grateful for? Reach within, look for opportunities of growth, and believe in God's promise that He'll never forsake you.

Reach within to regain your power to live your life confidently, victoriously, and successfully!

Reachingwithin2017@gmail.com

Facebook, Instagram, LinkedIn, and Twitter: ReachingWithin

www.ReachingWithinEmpowerment.com

March 17

Stephanie Shelling

"Casting down imaginations, and every high thing that exalts itself against the knowledge of God, and bringing into captivity every thought to the obedience of Christ;" ~ 2 Corinthians 10:5

The voices in our head are real.

Voices of those we held in some regard. A school teacher, an aunt or uncle, a mother or father – a bully. We play those voices and their words over and over again in the mind – a fortress where we hold all recorded, we've experienced, consciously and subconsciously. But if it isn't in line with the Word of God, is it truly real? Be encouraged in this moment to pull down those voices. Saturate your mind in God's word. You are made in His image! Remember - You are who HE says you are!

pearlsofagreatprice@gmail.com

March 18

Yolanda Sinclair

"No one has ever become poor by giving." Anne Frank

What is giving? Giving is freely presenting something to someone without expecting anything in return. Giving can be done monetarily, by performing Random acts of Kindness (Smiling, paying for someone else's meal, Helping the environment by picking up trash), Volunteering (working with non-profit organizations, homeless shelters, or nursing homes) and Donating (giving away clothing that you don't wear, books you don't read, donating blood).

When you think of giving, people look at the size of the gift or the goodness of the cause. But Jesus measures generosity by the condition of the giver's heart. Giving is more than an obligation for followers of Christ; it is an opportunity to lay up treasure that will last for all eternity. Jesus said: 'It is more blessed to give than to receive'. Our attitude in giving matters much more to God than the size of our giving. Giving freely and with a good heart, will never go unrewarded. Don't expect your reward from man; your reward will come from God. Everyone can experience the joy and blessing of generosity; because everyone has something to give. The more you give the more you will receive. Give for the sake of giving and give in secret. God loves a cheerful giver.

Matthew 6:3-4 (NLT) "(3) But when you give to someone in need, don't let your left hand know what your right hand is doing. (4) Give your gifts in private, and your Father, who sees everything, will reward you."

2 Corinthians 9:6-7 (NLT) "(6) Remember this—a farmer who plants only a few seeds will get a small crop. But the one who plants generously will get a generous crop. (7) You must each decide in your heart how much to give. And don't give reluctantly or in response to pressure. "For God loves a person who gives cheerfully.""

I am Yolanda Sinclair, a Certified Event Planner with over 8 years of experience planning weddings and special events. I am also a travel professional with over 2 years of experience planning and booking travel. I have a Master's Degree in Business Administration with a Concentration in Accounting and have worked as an administrator within several State agencies in North Carolina for over 19 years.

Yolanda A. Sinclair, MBA CWP, CEP
A Red-Carpet Affair, LLC
http://aredcarpetaffairllc.com/
https://www.facebook.com/pg/ARedCarpetAffairllc
http://redcarpetexcursions.traverusglobal.com
ARedCarpetAffairLLC@gmail.com

March 19

Tia Kennebrew

Thessalonians 5:18 NIV

Give Thanks in Circumstances, for this is God's will for you in Christ Jesus Give Thanks to good in all circumstances. Circumstances being good or bad. It seems so easy to thank God when things are going good but more difficult when things aren't going so well. The word says, "These are God's will". There is reason for our struggles, tragic, losses, gains and wins. It could be to test our Faith, prepare us for what is coming or we may never know. Thank God every day for all circumstances in your life today and everyday all blessing, unseen blessings, future blessings and even things we don't consider blessings.

Email: tia_knnbrw@yahoo.com

March 20
Gwendolyn Demby

Discovering the Benefits of Joy

Joy is a position that we must possess at all times. My brethren, count it all joy when you fall into divers' temptations James 1:2. This is why it's important to remain in a state of joyfulness,

"There will always be strength present, even though trials. Thou will show me the path of life & being in His presence brings us fullness of Joy" Psalm 16:11.

"No matter what we go through make the Joy of the Lord your first priority. The Joy of the Lord is my strength" Nehemiah 8:10

Gwendolyn is first a woman that loves and fears the Lord, married 33 years and has one biological son, two stepdaughters, one adopted daughter who is her biological niece. She was also a guardian to her youngest nephew, who is now an adult. She has returned to school, aspiring to become a licensed professional counselor.

"She's learned that whatever state she's in therewith to be content."
Philippians 4:11

March 21
Mary Harris

Matthew 5:14-15 NIV

**"You are the light of the world. A town built on a hill cannot be hidden.
Neither do people light a lamp and put it under a bowl. Instead they put it on
its stand, and it gives light to everyone in the house."**

Live Out Loud - this seems like a simple phrase, but we tend to not live full out, center stage, front and center especially women. We support others' dreams but aren't as passionate in pursuit of our own. Your vision matters! You diminishing yourself to make others feel important does a disservice to you & God! He creates us to be peculiar & bold not to shrink & crumble. So be the bodacious bold and beautiful   Y-O-U who can change lives, spread hope & shape nations! Decide to live each day intentionally on purpose. Living Your Life Unapologetically Out Loud!

Mary Harris is a domestic violence and sexual abuse advocate through her foundation; Dvine Beauti, a minister, speaker, contributing author to the bestselling book Faith for Fiery Trial, social media personality, host of From Trial to Triumph Facebook Live Show, and her greatest accomplishment of being proud mother and grandmother.

www.dvinebeauti.com; www.facebook.com/realdvinebeauti;
www.instagram.com/realdvinebeauti; www.twitter.com/realdvinebeauti;
https://www.linkedin.com/in/realdvinebeauti/

positivae@yahoo.com

Romans 8:28 - "And we know that all things work together for good to those who love the Lord, to those who are called according to His purpose."

To be in the sovereign will of God, means regardless of every situation that happens in our lives, we are confident that if we put our trust in God, it will work for our good and God's Glory.

The plan of God is not to hurt or harm us, but to give us good success. Remember, God is Omniscient and is in control. He is All Knowing. Therefore, He might be saying just wait on My timing.

I believe there is divine purpose for every battle that you may have to fight. We must trust God believing that all things are working together for good to them who love Him.

Jacqueline L. Knowles (Mrs.)
Principal
P. A. C. E.
East Street opposite Deveaux Street
Phone: 356-0943/676-5944

Email: Jackie_Knowles@hotmail.com

March 23
Doral Rolle

Philippians 4:19
"But my God shall supply all your need according to his riches in glory by Christ Jesus!"

Have you ever felt like your back was against the wall, and you were going under, and even though you prayed, it looked like the end? You are not alone, I can tell you from personal experience where my husband and I were having a major financial crisis, we began to seek Jehovah Jireh, our provider with all sincerity, and I can tell you that God made a way out of no way, and He opened doors that no man could have opened, and closed doors that no man could close, I truly believe that God is waiting for us to remind him of his promises He has made to us, He is waiting for you to speak his word.

Freeport Grand Bahama, Bahamas
Facebook: Doral Butler-Rolle
Instagram: Doral Butler-Rolle

March 24
Danielle Mo'nae Worth

James 4:7
"Be subject therefore unto God, but resist the devil, and he will flee from you."

No matter what troubles you may endure, keep your focus on God, as he will see you through all things. God has the power to get you through sickness, divorce, financial hardship, death, healing, and an abundance of challenges you may face in your lifetime. The key is to remain obedient, and keep your trust in God. Through storms your FAITH in God will be challenged, but I promise you the devil will flee if you just trust God. You must believe that whatever you are facing you are strong enough to bear, and know that God is always with you.

Danielle Worth, New Jersey native, was born and raised in Jersey City NJ. Danielle earned her Bachelors of Arts in Communications from Howard University and her Masters of Business Administration from Kean University (honor graduate, Cum Laude). Danielle is the founder and CEO of Up Rising Stars Incorporated, a nonprofit organization that provides scholarships to high school seniors that plan to attend a four-year University. Danielle takes on the big screen in her spare time as an actress; she has been seen in feature Television, and Films projects throughout the world. Danielle motto is change starts from within.

Facebook: https.//m.facebook.com/Danielle.worth
Instagram https;//Instagram.com/Danielle_mo_nae
Email: daniellewoth@hotmail.com
Website: www.uprisingstarsinc.org

March 25
Sabrina Jones

2 Kings 6:17-20 King James Version (KJV)

"17 And Elisha prayed, and said, LORD, I pray thee, open his eyes, that he may see. And the LORD opened the eyes of the young man; and he saw: and, behold, the mountain was full of horses and chariots of fire round about Elisha."

Sometimes just because we have the corners all finished to a puzzle, we think that we can make out the entire picture. Today, look to the END. It may start off shaky, and even now it may not look like it is coming together, but know that Jesus is waiving the box with the finished picture. Open your eyes and look beyond yourself to see that HE has equipped you with everything you need to complete the task. What HE needs of you will take HIM to complete it. No matter how it all began, know that in the END, you have a victory celebration awaiting your arrival.

Sabrina Jones is the founder and director of "The Transformation Experience "which is a deliverance and equipping program for women. She has also recently launched "The Berean Equipping Center" which is a weekly online intense bible study, she holds a Bachelor of Science from N.C. A&T State University in Greensboro, NC. Her gifting within the fivefold are Teacher and Evangelist. Sabrina has a passion for seeing those in bondage find freedom to live as Jesus lived, serve as He served and do as He commanded us to do. She has been married to Terence Jones for thirty years and they have three awesome children. Sabrina Jones is a trail blazer and has a genuine love for the people of God.

Website: www.Transformation4you.com
Email: Sabrinajones88@yahoo.com
Transformation email: Transformationkingdom88@gmail.com
Twitter: @Transformedsj

Rest

"For the Lord God, the One of Israel has said this, 'In returning (to me) and rest you shall be saved, in quietness and confident trust is your Strength.'"
Isaiah 30:15 AMP

I have a tradition of going away by myself every year. My goal is to disconnect from my normal activities and find time to reconnect with God and Myself. This scripture sums it up so clearly for me by reminding me that in returning to God and Rest; we are saved. And that is where we find our strength.

Return my sister HE is waiting!

March 27
Argentina Harris

2 Timothy 1:7

"For God hath not given us the spirit of fear; but of power, and of love, and of a sound mind."

Fear is an emotion that will surely cripple you if you allow it. Overcoming fear often takes practice in the area you are most fearful. God has gifted us all with the ability to use our minds to overcome doubt and fear through the power of prayer, persistence and perseverance. Jesus endured persecution on the cross so that we, as God's children, can fearlessly move in faith and power. Go forth today without fear and claim what is rightfully yours. You have been given everything that you need in order to become who you are supposed to be!

argenharris@gmail.com

MARCH 28
Miriam M. Wright

"The biggest adventure you can take is to live the life of your dreams!"
-Oprah Winfrey

Remember when you were A child you had dreams of how you wanted your life to be? Remember the question "what do you wanna be when you grow up?" Are you living that life now? Many people say they try but life happens and they get side tracked.

Dreams cannot become reality without action, take the first step today; everything is possible in this life if you try! Remember the heart of that child and the dream they had. Get started on your adventure trip today, there is no time like the present God bless you on your journey.

Miriam M. Wright
Dream Life Coach/Network Marketing Consultant, Orlando, Florida

www.mmwdreams.com
livingyourdream@mmdreams.com
https://www.facebook.com/wrightwaytoyourdreams/

March 29

Ruby La-Nice Garner

LISTENING FOR A LIFE CHANGING WORD

John 5:1-17

"Today is a new day, everything that happened yesterday has passed away. FORGIVE the past, LIVE NOW, in the present and PLAN your future." ~Ruby La-Nice Garner

During my life's journey many incidents occurred where I constantly found myself reliving those moments. riveting on the why's and why not's, or the wish I coulda, shoulda, woulda. Yet building a wall of unforgiveness, regret and instability while yet serving under Christian faith this simple battle was flowing through my heart and mind. Imagine that, attending family gatherings acting as if nothing ever happened having a joyous time, the whole day may go well and every now and then it doesn't. That's when you build up more rage and want to expose the family member about passed actions to everyone one not caring about how it will affect their current situation. "How'd you like those green apples...not so good huh?" Would be the thought I'd have. After many episodes of this continues cycle of inner rage, because in my family you better NOT let that foolishness roll off of your tongue that was trouble for sure, no matter how old you were.

I asked God, one night as I worked alone cleaning a school in my home town, to provide me a word to live by that will help me with dealing with past hurts that I would no longer harbor those thoughts. Within 30min I began to hear those words " Today is a new day everything that happened yesterday has yesterday has passed away, FORGIVE the past live now in present and PLAN your future. That word immediately resigned in my spirit. I ran to the nearest classroom, grabbed a piece of chalk and began writing what I heard. And have used it as a guide to carry me through. There's always going to be a time where forgiveness is needed or learning to be ok with your current situation and even planning ahead is key to a better future outcome. It's the best word I could have ever received. Similar to the man at pool of Bethesda, who had an infirmity for 38 years. Jesus told him to "Rise, take up your bed and walk." A word that changed man's life forever.

Email: <rubygarner71@gmail.com>

March 30
LaTasha Alex

Matthew 17:20 KJV

"And Jesus said unto them, Because of your unbelief: verily I say unto you, if ye have faith as a grain of mustard seed, ye shall say unto this mountain, Remove hence to yonder place, and it shall remove; and nothing shall be impossible unto you."

Dear sister, start your day with Prayer! Prayer is the seed needed to strengthen your faith. When you water that seed with confidence in our God, you will watch your faith grow and blossom into a beautiful understanding for things unseen. We may not see it but we must believe it. I could not see myself passing an important exam because of the two attempts of failure. God whispered to me; my child have faith the size of a mustard seed. Pray, trust in God, never lose faith and always remember God is in control.

LaTasha was born and raised in Shreveport, LA. She obtained her Associates of Science Degree in Surgical Technology from Southern University at Shreveport and Bachelors of Science Degree in Nursing from Grambling State University. She's a member of Delta Sigma Theta, Inc. She is a woman of God who loves telling others about his works. Her life motto is live your best life because tomorrow is not promised. She's been through many obstacles in life. Her faith in God is what keeps her going, fueled and motivated.

Facebook- Tasha Alex
IG @ohitsjusttasha and @plannernursenmore
http://linkedin.com/in/latasha-alex-b65b2767
Email: latashadalex@yahoo.com , tashada03@gmail.com

March 31
Lena Payton-Webb

"The purpose of life is to believe, to hope, and to strive."- by Indira Gandhi

Often times we as women become consumed with our roles as mothers, sisters, wives, caregivers and even providers. Our everyday roles leave little or no time to dream and hope. We push aside our own hopes and dreams we set aside our pain and hurts. It's hard to imagine life without hope. We all strive to be better, to love more, to live with purpose, to heal and not hurt. Each day is yours to believe in your dreams, wants and desires.

Lena Payton-Webb
Blu Horizon Travel
Southfield, Michigan
Email: mswebb711@gmail.com

"Too often we underestimate the power of a touch, a smile, a kind word, a listening ear, an honest compliment, or the smallest act of caring, all of which have the potential to turn a life around." — Leo Buscaglia

April 1
Rasheeda George

Psalms 2:8-

"Ask Me, and I will make the nations your inheritance, the ends of the earth your possession."

ASK, and these are the "consequences" of your asking. I don't know about you, but I like these consequences. It doesn't stop at asking though, it takes faith and work. You have to have faith to back it up and work at what you want. So, those of you who have dreams in your heart; don't allow your dreams to die with you. If you don't know where to start; start by Asking God, then Ask Yourself. What's meant will come to pass, but in what way do you want it to come to pass. Do you want someone else manifesting your position? Take your position. It's yours, take possession of it and act like it belongs to you, just like you would take ownership and responsibility of a child. GIVE yourself permission to be GREAT.

Rasheeda George, Owner of Breaking Chains Now, loves the Lord and has a love for people. She's dedicated her life in helping others grow and discover themselves as she went through the journey herself. Rasheeda has a BA in Sociology with a minor in Human Resources and a MS in Human Services Administration with a concentration in Negotiations and Conflict Management. She also became a Certified Mediator and Certified Professional Life Coach and Speaker. Rasheeda discovered that there was not peace inside of her so she decided to make peace within herself and start fulfilling her "calling" in life. She has NOW made it her mission to help people experience that beautiful feeling of freedom, fulfillment and fun by **Breaking Chains NOW!**
www.breakingchainsnow.org
www.facebook.com/breakchainsnow
www.instagram.com/breakchainsnow

April 2
Lakisha Harris, MA, LPC

Healing is Power!

For years we have heard that "Money is Power" and then "Knowledge is Power" but yet we have seen those with both money and knowledge succumb to depression, low self-esteem, poor decision making, and even suicide.

Your true living happy power comes from healing! Healing emotionally, mentally, and physically. We are not able to pick our upbringings, or why things affect us negatively but we can gain healing from them both. This often means exploring difficult times and taking a deep understanding on what brought you to this point. Exploring and correcting negative thoughts.

It is possible to be heal and it is possible to be truly and consistently Happy!

You must however seek out your healing process! Find a therapist or a group and do the work to Heal! You Got This!

Is a mental health therapist specializing in trauma, a parent coach and author of "Every Woman's Little Black Book - Heal. Date. Thrive!"
www.HarrisCandC.com
www.healingispower.net
Facebook: @HarrisCandC and @HealDateThrive
Instagram: @HarrisCandC
YouTube: @HealingIsPower
Twitter: HarrisCandC

April 3
LaToya O. Guion (Olivia G.)

"And the day came when the risk to remain tight in a bud, was more painful than the risk it took to Blossom..." Anais Nin

The Process

In a world of instant Everything, Process is always avoided. How you ask? We are always looking for the quick fix, instant opportunities, instant relationships, all of which waste time, money, and lead to the land of disappointment. Or maybe you avoid Process out of FEAR, so you never start, or give up before the Process is complete. God, is a God of Process. God has written your story, but it's up to you to fulfill it. The Process may hurt or even be scary, but go ahead and try your Blooming Process, you will Love the Beautiful Flower you become!

LaToya O. Guion (Olivia G.) Wife, Mom, and Global Entrepreneur in the Financial Literacy space. Health, Wealth, and Organic Beauty are my passions! Born to Eugene and Doretha Peterson, October 3, 1978. As a small child I often daydreamed while prancing around carrying my dad's briefcase, imagining myself as Owner and CEO of my own company. Thank God I'm fulfilling that Dream! Stay Tuned!

Email: LGuion@OliviaG.org
www.myfes.net/LGuion
www.facebook.com/OliviaGsFitnessandFinance
www.instagram.com/LaToyaOliviaG
www.twitter.com/LOliviaG1
www.Linkedin.com/LaToya(Olivia G)Guion

April 4
LaTasha Jones, MSW, ASW

Ezekiel 37:1–14

Dear Tired Teresa,

I speak restorative power over the dry bones of your fatigued body and mind in a world that tells you that you must be "STRONG." In a life space that rewards busyness and financial gains oppose to spiritual healing; *UNPLUG* today. Tired Teresa be honest; *YOU* can't take it anymore; another break up, another NSF fee hitting your bank account, an insane boss, a health crisis and the kids that seem to have lost their mind. Yet you keep pressing daily with a fake smile hoping it will all go away someday soon. Remember there is a reward on the other side of your obedience. Stop Stressing walk in your Blessing!

Website: www.talk2tasha.com
FB: Talk2Tasha
Instagram talk2tash
YouTube talk2tasha
Twitter; tashatalk2
email: hello@talk2tasha.com

LaTasha Jones have served in human suffering for more than 20 years in both child welfare and California correctional facilities as a Social Worker. Empowering people is something she has been gifted and born to do. She transformed from Section 8 public housing to the first in the family to obtain a Master's Degree in Social Work; buy housing units, yet still found herself stressed, tired and unfulfilled. She dived into her own self-discovery and found freedom. She currently serves as a motivational coach that serves career women impacted by stress. Talk2Tasha provides real convos and solutions for women to walk in their truth while redefining their success. As she candidly defines success as; "the ability to be who you are without lying about it."

LaKel Farley

"Suppose you wanted to build a tower. Will he not first sit down and estimate the cost to see if he has enough money to complete it? For if he lays the foundation and he is unable to finish it, everyone who see it will ridicule him, saying, 'This fellow began to build and was unable to finish."

LUKE: 14:28-30(NIV)

At some point in life, We ALL, will experience the feeling of being confused, disgusted, disorganized and in disarray. At this such appointed moment, we must become transparent about our thoughts and our objectives by becoming placid. Search within your hearts for Gods answer by first writing down your heart's desire. After you have received his/your resolution and or answer you shall be able to categorize your own foot-steps to start building your own solid foundation. Don't feel pressured in the process of building, make sure you have thought through all of the components to lay your solid foundation. Find your own channel of life, remember life is built on dreams and ambition never give up on both.

Website:www.la-kel.com
Email:lakellyfeintervention@mail.com
Phone: 404-223-9995
IN:Lakel Lyfe Intervention
IG: iamla_kel
FB: Author Lakel Farley

April 6
Brenda Brasher

2 TIMOTHY 3:1

Considering what the future holds, we find many uncertainties but also certainties. Because of the magnitude of the individual events I will sum them up into two categories, good and evil.

The times Paul warned Timothy about in his letter recorded in 2 Timothy, chapter 3 are here now. We are living in the last days. I came to this conclusion by observing the spiritual perils listed in 2 Timothy chapter 3 and the perils of occurrences of nature in Matthew chapter 24. The perils are sent by God to remind man that God is in control. Perils perpetrated by man are spiritual perils which then cause carnal problems because of man's disobedience to God. We can't control nature but we do control our spiritual attitude.

Life here is temporary but eternity is forever.

April 7
Natasha Saunders

Romans 8:28

"And we know that God causes everything to work together for the good of those who love God and are called according to his purpose for them."

So, my windows were jammed shut for a year... Could not open them for the life of me. Until one afternoon – God showed me a vision. I prayed, got the tool out and viola, the windows opened!

Amazing how we can struggle to do things on our own for YEARS and yield poor results. But when we call on Jesus, no matter how silly we feel that He has us doing what we have done before; it is SUCCESSFUL & FRUITFUL. When we wait on God and His perfect timing, it always works out for our good in the end!

Natasha Saunders is Co-Founder of TRIFECTA, an enterprise and social movement empowering youth, individuals and communities through economic and community development. TRIFECTA's mission's to "Guard it, Nurture it and Reveal it," strengthening community collectivism while creating cultural shifts and eliminating disparities. Saunders' passion is to help others actualize their potential.

Natasha Saunders, MS
Trifecta Inc.
CEO | Co-Founder | Motivational Speaker
https://www.trifectainc.org/

https://business.facebook.com/TRIFECTAinc/

April 8
Sheila E. Morton

Psalm 71:18

"Even when I am old and gray, do not forsake me, my God, till I declare your power to the next generation, your mighty acts to all who are to come."

Purposed Woman: There were times when we cherished the counsel from our elders; the founders and keepers of our heritage. There was a time when we valued their opinion and were esteemed by their spiritual presence in every situation. Through prayer, they guide and protect us. We are their hopes, dreams, possibilities and expectations. For they have been where we yearn to go, seen what we yearn to see. Their truths are more than a moment in time. They are the link that connects us. We honor their names, and we should never forget their wisdom and contribution to our lives.

Sheila Morton is a mother of 4 and grandmother of 14. She is a retired teacher, an online business owner, wife of a retired pastor and active in her woman's ministry at her church. She has her view set on writing more books soon.

Email: smorton28@hotmail.com
Facebook: Sheila Brice-Morton
Facebook: Financial Lifestyle Coach
Website: http://www.iwantitallback.com/

April 9
Brunette Kirtdoll Smith

Job 15:17-And now where is my HOPE
Who shall see it?
What do you hope for?
HOPE for a Superior Correlation with our Savior?
HOPE for a better existence?
HOPE for tranquility?
There is competence in HOPE. HOPE is related to a positive outcome. If you
have HOPE you WILL bloom!

Brunette is a Mother of 4 Brieanna, Robert Jr., Briearra & Brittnee Toeran. Kyree is her only grand. Brunette has been on her Purposed Journey for many years. She finds enjoyment in being and giving as A Server, Philanthropist, Health Ambassador, Creating Cozy Atmosphere's for Refuge and Relaxation. She amateurly writes music and children's books. Brunette has volunteered and donated to countless Outreach Ministries throughout The Atlanta Metro area, Alabama and Beyond. My Purpose is to provide knowledge and a Safe Haven for all.

Brunette's 21 Day Spousal Survival Abandonment Book is set to release in 2020.

FB- Brunette Kirtdoll Smith-Greensboro, AL.
Twitter@Prosperity6
LinkedIn-B&B Legacy Building

April 10

Sharmaine M. Moore

John 14: 12-14 (NIV)

12 I tell you the truth, anyone who has faith in me will do what I have been doing. He will do even greater things than these, because I am going to the Father.

13 And I will do whatever you ask in my name, so that the Son may bring glory to the Father,

14 You may ask me for anything in my name, and I will do it.

When your faith is more significant than your situation, your faith makes you BOLD enough to ask Jesus to do the impossible. Once you ASK for the impossible, you need to TRUST that the impossible will be done. You see, Jesus will take your need to the Father. In order to get to the Father, you need to go through His Son. When your faith is unshakeable, there is NOTHING He will not do for you, in His name. I've seen Him do it. JUST ASK!

Sharmaine Moore is the CEO of Framework Consulting, a Minister, Speaker and Mentor encouraging women, men and children how to love themselves the way God sees them.

smoore@frameworkconsulting.org
Instagram: Purebrowngal
Facebook: Sharmaine Moore

April 11
Edie Price

Upon sitting & reflecting on us as Women, Mothers, Wives, Sisters, Daughters, Aunts, Grandmothers, & Friends. I can only say that we wear many hats throughout our lives. No hat is greater than the other & no pain or heartache is felt any less.

Our strength & determination is Phenomenal. Our strength is not just for ourselves but for our children & families. It allows us to deal with challenges. My question to you ladies is "How do you handle unexpected challenges "?

I gain encouragement & strength from this scripture from:

Philippians 4:13
"I CAN DO ALL THINGS THROUGH HIM WHO STRENGTHENS ME."

Ms. Edie Price is native of Detroit. She is a loving Mother of one daughter. She is an Entrepreneur in a few Businesses, a Professional in the Automotive Industry. Ms. Price loves the Lord & enjoys helping others. Her goal is to start a Nonprofit organization that helps Single Moms & children.

Facebook - Edie Price
Instagram - Edietravelsprice
LinkedIn - Edie Price
Facebook Business Page - Wholesale Travel and Financial Freedom

April 12
Sharlene Peters

II Timothy 1:7 NKJV
"For God has not given us a spirit of Fear, but of power and of love and of a sound mind."

There are so much in life that causes us to be fearful. God has not given us the spirit of fear, so when it creeps up on you, I want you to tell the fear that you are Not Afraid. Tell the Fear that you will Not overcome me, and I will get through this. Know that you are Not alone, God is with you and will guide you through this. You have the Power and the ability to do anything that you put your mind to. Walk in The Power, Love, and the Strong Mind that God has given to you.

April 13
Chou Hallegra

You Are It!
"I took you from the ends of the earth, from its farthest corners I called you. I said, 'You are my servant'; I have chosen you and have not rejected you."
Isaiah 41:9 NIV

Stop saying, "I don't have what it takes!". There are people who are more talented and who have more experience, but God still called you. YOU ARE IT! God knows what you're made of. He knows your past experiences, present weaknesses, and future mistakes, and He still says, "I've chosen you!" You're chosen in spite of yourself. Therefore, put the excuses, the fear, the shame, the guilt, and everything else aside. It's time to rise up to your calling. Seize it and embrace it, but most importantly live it out and enjoy every moment of it because YOU ARE IT!

Chou Hallegra is a Board-Certified Christian Counselor and Certified Spiritual Life Coach. She is passionate about helping individuals and families live out the abundant life that is theirs in Christ. Through her writing, speaking, counseling, and coaching, she empowers others to achieve emotional wellness and reach their full potential.
Website: www.graceandhopeconsulting.com
Facebook: https://www.facebook.com/ChouHallegra/
Instagram: https://www.instagram.com/chouhallegra/
Twitter: https://twitter.com/GHConsultingLLC
LinkedIn: https://www.linkedin.com/in/chouhallegra/
Poscast:https://anchor.fm/chouhallegra

April 14
Celestine Davis

Isaiah 55:8 (ESV)

"For my thoughts are not your thoughts, neither are your ways my ways, declares the Lord."

As children of an omnipotent divine creator, blessed with intelligence and the ability to communicate, we can start to believe that whatever we imagine is His will. Even Jesus focused on the Word and the Holy Spirit to stay in His Father's will. Do not let human pride lead you astray to fall into the pit set by the enemy. Pray and seek God in all your comings and goings. What may seem foolish to man may just be your deliverance. Trust His intentions for your life. Wait on Him and He promises that you will never be ashamed.

Celestine is a writer, visual artist, emerging filmmaker, speaker, and community arts promoter. She is the Director of the annual Down East Flick Fest held in Greenville, NC and the creator of the visual journaling workshop, "ReCreations: Rewriting Your Life Script ™" and facilitates writing-to-heal workshops.

https://www.linkedin.com/in/celestine-davis-75147422/
https://www.instagram.com/faithdame/
http://celestinedavis.com/
https://www.facebook.com/4thecreator/
downeastflickfest.org

"When there is no enemy within, the enemies outside cannot hurt you." - African Proverb

Sit back and think about what it means to have an enemy. An enemy can cause disturbances in your life and have you feeling powerless. What if you have been an enemy towards yourself and causing your own blockages? What if these blockages prevented you from growing in your own truth? You can overcome this! Finding peace within your mind will take you on a journey that is uncomfortable and it comes with a price. Peace will cost you discomfort, unlearning and learning new behaviors, however you will gain knowledge of self and start to cater to your values and beliefs.

Shawnee Palmer is a therapist and owner of Alpine's Empowerment Agency. She is also the Co-Owner of Bj's Bookstore with her son, Bryant. The online bookstore provides books to help the youth overcome various issues. Shawnee's mission to assist others with overcoming barriers to become a better version of themselves.

EMAIL: shawnee@alpinesempowermentagency.com
SOCIAL MEDIA TAGS: @AlpinesEA @BjsBookstore (Facebook, Twitter & Instagram)
WEBSITES: www.alpinesempowermentagency.com & www.bjsbookstore.com

April 16
Cassandra F. Ward

Proverbs 18:21
"Death and life are in the power of the tongue, and those who love it will eat its fruit"

Speak life my daughter, the Power of Life and Death are in the Power of the tongue. Do you truly comprehend what that really mean? Words Kill, Words give LIFE, they're either poison or fruit. Which will you choose? You can't talk negative and expect positive results. You can't speak defeat and expect victory. You can't speak lack and expect abundance. Words are like seeds, what you plant, you give life too. My challenge to you is that you speak things as if they were. Begin your day with this set of affirmations:

I will hear the voice of the Holy Spirit

I will Lead and not Follow

I will create and not destroy

I am the head, not the tail

I am above, not beneath

I am the lender, not the borrower

I am loved by God,

I am chosen by God

I am protected by God

No weapon formed against me shall prosper, and every tongue

That rises against me in judgement shall be condemned.

I'm healthy, I'm humble, I'm happy, I'm wealthy.

I (state your name) will never be broke another day in my life, and

I will live the fullness of life and all

God has for me.

Cassandra F. Ward, was born and raised in Rich Square, North Carolina. Cassandra currently resides in Greensboro NC and is the mother on one adult son, Shaquis' Jaquon. Cassandra is a graduate of East Carolina, with a Master's Degree in Middle Grades Math and Language Arts. She is employed as an educator with Guilford County Schools. One of her greatest accomplishments is becoming a Co-author of an Amazon Best Seller in 2017. Cassandra strongly believes in the Power of your words. It is her prayer, that you will use your words to change your life.

April 17
Kimberlee Bilbrew

Psalms 56:3 "Whenever I am afraid, I will trust in You"

Have you ever been in a storm and felt you had no anchor? No sense of direction, the territory unfamiliar and the atmosphere uncomfortable. Will you trust him through health concerns, turmoil, conflict in your home, the unknown on your job, and through uncertainty. You are a daughter of the King who knows ALL things yet will you trust him? Will you allow him to lead you? Will you trust him for all that HE has promised? Know this area of uncertainty can only be temporary. When you have a navigator who owns the territory, is the creator of living beings and knows all things. He is the ALPHA, the OMEGA, the Prince of Peace, the OMNIPOTENT, and the King of Kings. You shall not be afraid. You are Being Led by our Father. Ask for his Will and he will direct thy path.

Kimberlee Bilbrew has been working in the child welfare sector for twenty years. She also is a speaker and Realtor in Los Angeles, CA.

April 18
Janet French-Cannedy

Ruth 3:11

"Now, my daughter, do not, fear. I will do for you whatever you ask, for all my people in the city know that you are a woman of excellence."

As I travel this amazing journey called life, I find fulfillment in encouraging others along the way. Having survived six major back surgeries, I have come to realize that becoming a woman of excellence, may involve many obstacles (including pain), but it should not prevent us from inspiring others to live their full potential. Even through our pain we must remember that we can do all things through Christ who strengthens us, in our pursuit towards excellence.

*"God sees the Broken as the Best and He sees the Best in the Broken
And He calls the Wounded to be the World Changers."*
~Ann Voskamp

On this day, be encourage my sister! God will use your brokenness to change the world of around you. It may not appear today that your brokenness can be used for anything; but now that it has a divine purpose. Your brokenness is designed to bring hope, healing, deliverance and a solution to others on how to overcome. Never be ashamed of what you had to endure, overcome, or currently going through. Just know the brokenness will be used to bring others out. Choose today to walk in healing, forgiveness and peace! Know all things are working out for your good!

Candice P. Simpson, PhD is a Life Strategist Coach and Faith-Based Consultant. She is called to equip, empower, and impart into women, families, leaders, faith-based ministries to break through barriers that are preventing them from changing the world around them.

Email: info@candicepsimpson.com or
Website: www.candicepsimpson.com
Facebook: www.facebook.com/candicespeak
Instagram: www.instagram.com/candicespeak
Twitter: www.twitter.com/candicespeak
LinkedIn: linkedin.com/in/befreeandspeak

April 20
LaToya O. Guion (Olivia G.)

Ephesians 6:11-17 VS 16

"Above all, taking the shield of faith, wherewith ye shall be able to quench all the fiery darts of the wicked."

Faith a small yet powerful and profound word, a word we do not activate enough. We think it should only be used in certain situations and circumstances. Fact is, Faith can be used for any trial or tribulation. You see God pointed out in verse 16 how the Shield of Faith, was the most important piece of your Armor. So, no matter what your mind or the Enemy tells you...You can't write that book, you will never be debt free...You're not good enough, it's All a Lie! Activate and Raise your Shield of Faith, because when you do you activate God himself! I believe the report of the Lord...Do you?

LaToya O. Guion (Olivia G.) Wife, Mom, and Global Entrepreneur in the Financial Literacy space. Health, Wealth, and Organic Beauty are my passions! Born to Eugene and Doretha Peterson, October 3, 1978. As a small child I often daydreamed while prancing around carrying my dad's briefcase, imagining myself as Owner and CEO of my own company. Thank God I'm fulfilling that Dream! Stay Tuned!

LGuion@OliviaG.org www.myfes.net/LGuion
www.facebook.com/OliviaGsFitnessandFinance
www.instagram.com/LaToyaOliviaG
www.twitter.com/LOliviaG1
www.Linkedin.com/LaToya(Olivia G)Guion

April 21
Nakiya Jackson

1 Corinthians 16:13
"Be your guard, stand firm in the faith, be courageous; be strong "

(Repeat) I am, I can, and I will! You are worthy! Be confident with your self-worth and know your abilities. This creates value in your life. Gain the confidence and assurance needed in whatever you may be going through. Trials and tribulations from our past such as limiting beliefs about ourselves, family and financial issues can be healed with the decision to trust in God and do the work required for you to reap the fruits of your labor as you journey through life. If you stand firm in what you believe in as far as goals and aspirations; then your faith and courage has already answered your prayers. Know your worth and let no one take what you've worked so hard for away.

April 22
Gaylin Munford

Ecclesiastes 3:1-8 King James Version (KJV)
"To everything there is a season, and a time to every purpose under the Heaven:"

My biological clock is ticking !!!!", rings often through my head. I think of my life and my anticipated timeline. College, Career, Marriage, Children and Happily Ever After. Unfortunately, this timeline is still incomplete. "My biological clock is ticking !!!!", This phrase often rings through my head. I think of my life and my anticipated timeline. College, Career, Marriage, Children and Happily Ever After. Unfortunately, this timeline is still incomplete. It's easy to become discouraged by what seems like our turtle timeline. Remember that God has ordained the seasons for our lives. When doubt and discouragement creep in we must walk by faith believing that our season is ordained in his perfect timing.

Dear Lord,

Teach me how to patiently wait for my season, without doubt, and to trust that you are my time keeper.

Gaylin Munford is a business woman and educator. She owns Jennifer Rose Co., a concierge service that offers event, travel planning and decor services. She is a graduate of Loyola Marymount University and Cal State Dominguez Hills University where she earned degrees in Communication and Education.

https://www.facebook.com/jenniferroseeventandtravelboutique/
https://www.instagram.com/jenniferroseeventdesign/?hl=en
Jenniferroseco@yahoo.com 323 497-3135

April 23
Erica L. Brasher, M. Ed

Romans 12: 1 (New International Version)

Therefore, I urge you, brothers and sisters, in view of God's mercy, to offer your bodies as a living sacrifice, holy and pleasing to God—this is your true and proper worship.

We often focus on turning away from worldly ways and taking on holy ways. I challenge you to expand your thinking and to consider that a living sacrifice also includes taking care of the body that God has entrusted you with. Not only should we "study to show ourselves approved unto God." We should sit up, push up, run, jump, walk, breathe, and exercise to show ourselves approved unto God. Say it loud: "I'm on a journey to wellness and I'm Proud!" Well, that last part isn't in the bible, but we should get excited about our journey to wellness.

Erica L. Brasher, M.Ed., is a Certified Master Health and Wellness Coach, Certified Life Coach, Certified Laughter Facilitator, Mini Me Yoga Ambassador, and Arbonne Independent Consultant. Her mission is to help women obtain optimal happiness, health, and wealth using holistic methods that align mind, body, soul, and spirit.

Website: mywellness.coach
Website: ericabrasher.arbonne.com
e-mail: Erica@mywellness.coach
Facebook.com/mywellnessnow
Instagram.com/4mywellness
Twitter.com/4mywellness Pinterest.com/4mywellness

April 24
Debra Reed

Be encouraged! You are not alone. You might be in a painful situation but know this. There is no place that God is not. He sees all, knows all and He sees you. God is there with you and hears your softest cry. With everything in you, hold on to your faith in God. Don't give up! If you have asked God to show you the pathway to go, be still so that you may hear where He is leading you. No matter how hard, how tough or how much you think you can't. Know right now that you can make it, can survive it, and can conquer it!

Deuteronomy 31:6:

"Be strong and courageous. Do not fear or be in dread of them, for it is the LORD your God who goes with you. He will not leave you or forsake you."

Debra Reed is a PlanNet Marketing Representative and an Independent Travel Agent. Providing an effective way for people to create entrepreneurship opportunities in the largest industry in the world, TRAVEL.

Ms. Reed also has over 25 years of diversified clinical social work practice offering psychotherapy, supervision, training and consultation. Her areas of expertise include childhood trauma, grief and loss, and domestic violence. Ms. Reed's educational background includes a Bachelor of Science Degree in Health Education and a Master's Degree in Social Work from Howard University.

www.plannetmarketing.com/dfreed88
www.debrareed.inteletravel.com

April 25
Deanna Murphy

"Do you not know that your bodies are temples of the Holy Spirit, who is in you, whom you have received from God? You are not your own;"
- 1 Corinthians 6:19 (NIV)

The most high, living God, lives inside of you! How incredible is that. I used to think about my body as a temple only in a healthy physical sense. Over the years I came to realize it's also about being healthy mentally, emotionally and spiritually. Recently I discovered how to access the power and the characteristics of the Holy Spirit. One example - there is no sickness only health. My allergies were non- existent this year after a 25-year struggle with them. Tap into the power and characteristics of the Holy Spirit. Your life will be changed!

April 26
Dien Neubauer

Proverbs 22:1

"Choose a food reputation over great riches; being held in high esteem is better than silver or gold." (NLT)

Your Crown Speaks. It speaks so loudly, that we can't hear what you're saying. People will remember your appearance, behavior, what you say, and how you made them feel to paint a complete picture of you. And, rightfully so, because a crown is made up of so many different pieces, fastened together to become a thing of beauty. May we strive to be a thing of beauty that others see, in what we say and do. May your crown speak so loudly that many are inspired when they see or hear of you.

Dien Neubauer; wife to I.J. Andrew Neubauer, is an Educator, having received her B.Sc. degree from Trinity Baptist College, in Jacksonville, Florida. Dien is also CEO of Crowned Divas Remy Collections, LLC, but for her it's more than just hair. She is also an Author and Speaker, and refers to herself as 'your Motivational Crowned Diva.' Dien uses her platform to empower and inspire women as she communicates the power of 'Your Crown.'

Social Media Handles:

www.facebook.com/crowneddivasremy

www.instagram.com.crowneddivasremy

www.crowneddivasremy.com

email: info@crowneddivasremy.com

www.facebook.com/yourcrownspeaks

www.instagram.com/yourcrownspeaks

www.dienneubauer.com

email: dienneubauer@gmail.com

April 27
Allison Braham

**"It Appears that Vulnerability is also the birthplace
of joy and creativity, of belonging, and of love."
... Brene Brown**

Stop, take a minute and breathe in and out slowly and understand that the word vulnerable does not mean you are weak. It means that you are human and its okay to be able to feel hurt, to feel pain. The most important outcome of being in a vulnerable state, is your ability to express how you are feeling. The joy in that is, by doing so, you then embark on an opportunity to create a new sense of self. When you open up yourself and share how you feel, the possibilities of helping are endless. Release your vulnerabilities.

Allison Braham, Jamaican -American author is a passionate writer and blogger who has worked in various multi- faceted areas such as, Media, Marketing and Public Health. Her forthcoming book 'The Happy Black Daughter' will debut in the Spring of 2019. As a writer and avid reader, she has written plays and short stories, one of which "No, Woman Don't Cry", has been showcased at her Alma Mater, Brooklyn College. Her Monday, Friday motivational thoughts posted weekly has inspired many on her social media handles. She holds a BS., in Broadcast Journalism and Theatre Arts. Allison was born In Jamaica West Indies, and grew up in Brooklyn, New York. She currently resides in Columbus, Ohio.
www.allisonbraham.com
Instagram @allybraham
Twitter @allyblogger

Inspirational Post

Jeremiah 29:11 – "For I know the plans I have for you, declares the Lord, plans to prosper you and not harm you, plans to give you hope and a future."

I am the Founder of SISer's In Stilettos. The purpose of this organization is to empower, motivate and encourage women to walk in their "Purpose". This organization encourages a Sisterhood of Women to "Walk in their Destiny" by enjoying life, traveling, and making a difference in our community, wearing Stilettos.

Ladies, I could not have been successfully in life without God's grace, mercy and direction. I have HOPE and FAITH" I can do all things through Christ that strengthens me", and so can you. I am determined to walk it out by empowering, inspiring, uplifting, supporting ALL Women, one pair of Stilettos at a time.

Kim B. Wells is a Woman of God who wears high heels, walked up many high mountains and made several detours in the valley wearing my Stilettos. She has been featured in a Christian magazine and hosted Women Conferences globally, encouraging and motivating women to live their best life, wearing their Stilettos.

Facebook Kim Wells
Email kimbwells80@yahoo.com

April 29

Teara Q. Booker, MA, CNP

We are all entitled to live a mindful and content life. We deserve wellness, peace, and happiness. Many people struggle with discontentment, trauma and pain. It is our purpose to help them become, Well Within Themselves. We believe as people we must cultivate a life of contentment for ourselves. Contentment is simply defined as a "state of wellness, happiness, and satisfaction". We are deserving and worthy of this state. Love what you have, change what you dislike, and embrace what is sure to come.

Teara is an accomplished health and wellness practitioner, author, professor, and the founder of Well With Her Soul. Well With Her Soul is a movement that demonstrates the truth that all women are entitled to live a healthy, thriving and well life. Teara is the owner of the Vagina Lounge, a vaginal steaming spa and She's So Well Box, a monthly subscription box that delivers a tranquil, stress relieving, fulfilled experience to the doorsteps of women all over the world. Teara is a graduate of Notre Dame of Maryland where she earned an MA in Nonprofit Management and Social Entrepreneurship. She also holds a graduate certification in Negotiation and Conflict Management and many health and wellness related certifications. Teara resides in Baltimore with her daughter.

tearaqbooker@gmail.com / teara@wellwithhersoul.com

She knew she could so she did! It is WELL WITH HER SOUL!

Psalm 46 1-3 (It is Well With My Soul)
"God is our refuge and strength, an ever-present help in trouble. Therefore, we will not fear, though the earth gives way and the mountains fall into the heart of the sea, though its waters roar and foam and the mountains quake with their surging."

Instagram @Wellwithhersoul_ / @Tearathegoalslayer
Facebook @WellWithHerSoul / @TearaBooker
Twitter
@WellWIthHerSou1
WEBSITE
www.wellwithhersoul.com

April 30

Jessie C. Love

"Forget the Past and Press Forward in God's Compassion"

Isaiah 43:18-18 (NIV)

"Forget the former things; do not dwell on the past. See, I am doing a new thing! Now it springs up; do you not perceive it? I am making a way in the wilderness and streams in the wasteland."

Did you "fail" at something yesterday? Great! So what! "Failures" aren't permanent. See them as gains to recognize how to change and do better. Do not persecute yourself over your "failures." "Failures" are lessons to learn what steps must be taken to get you to the "success" that God has planned for you. God's compassion is new every morning to uphold you as you press toward your expected end. Your steps are ordered. Forget the past and walk forward. Hold your head high! Breathe! Smile! Trust! Believe! Experiment! Grow! Woman, God's with you! Receive your BLESSINGS! (Also see Lamentations 3:22-23.)

Jessie C. Love

Email: jesslovenaturally@gmail.com

May 1
Danielle Mo'nae Worth

Jeremiah 29: 11
"For I know the plans I have for you, declares the Lord, plans to prosper you and not harm you, plans to give you hope and a future."

Although life presents us with challenges, it is imperative to have a strong faith in God, and understand that he has a plan for your life. When faced with trials and tribulations such as; the loss of a job, mental illness, anxiety, bankruptcy, depression, and a host of other adversities, put your faith in the God, as he will guide through your life challenges. Adhere to, and Rely on the word of God for direction and instruction as no one but God can turn your sorrows into a Testimony of joy. Pray without ceasing! Trust and believe in God's plan for your life.

Danielle Worth, New Jersey native, was born and raised in Jersey City NJ. Danielle earned her Bachelors of Arts in Communications from Howard University and her Masters of Business Administration from Kean University (honor graduate, Cum Laude). Danielle is the founder and CEO of Up Rising Stars Incorporated, a nonprofit organization that provides scholarships to high school seniors that plan to attend a four-year University. Danielle takes on the big screen in her spare time as an actress; she has been seen in feature Television, and Films projects throughout the world. Danielle motto is change starts from within.

Facebook: https.//m.facebook.com/Danielle.worth
Instagram https;//Instagram.com/Danielle_mo_nae
Email: daniellewoth@hotmail.com Website: www.uprisingstarsinc.org

May 2
Dr. Christine Handy

Becoming

Former First Lady Michelle Obama's book, "Becoming" really made me think about "me". Even in my 50s, I am still "Becoming". We hear people say, "I may not be where I want to be but Thank God I'm not where I used to be." Think about that. Are you where you want to be? Do you still have dreams of a better life, a better job, a better business, home, spouse, love? The bible says, "Faith without works is dead" so you can't "become" without action. So, if you are still "Becoming" remember that you must "work" on it! So just say to yourself, "I am Becoming" and then plan your work and work your plan.

Dr. Christine Handy is an educator, entrepreneur, life coach, and author. A respected high school principal and leader, she is also a Senior Manager and Relationship Marketing expert with Send Out Cards and a leader with a health and wellness company. Additionally, she is a collaborating author in the Amazon Best Seller – Dear Fear Volume II and It Takes Money Honey. You can connect with Dr. Handy on Facebook under Christine Handy or by email christine@aboveonly.ws.

May 3
Teneisha Robinson

"The cave you fear to enter holds the treasure you seek". Joseph Campbell

Imagine standing on the shore alone, peering through the entrance, and being able to see a flicker of light. You need that light but are afraid to enter. You need the light as a guide, for nourishment. You are not physically bound by anyone or anything, yet, your feet are cemented firmly in place. What's in your cave? A business? A new relationship; letting go of an old one? Believing in and loving yourself unapologetically? Your feet will follow when you make up your mind that you are ready for bold and courageous action. *Enter. That. Cave.* There's freedom there.

Linkedin.com/in/teneisharobinson Facebook: @msmagnoliacoach Twitter: @magnoliacoach

Teneisha Robinson is the founder of Magnolia Coaching, LLC; an integrative coaching provider that works with clientele looking to improve interpersonal and professional communication and conflict resolution skills. A native Mississippian, Ms. Robinson, earned her undergraduate degree at Delta State University. She went on to earn her MACR from Bethel University. Currently, Ms. Robinson serves as a coach mentor for LITE Memphis, an entrepreneurial innovation program for high school students. Ms. Robinson also sits on the board of a local fatherhood organization and is co-creator of a small business professional development program. Her education, training, and natural ability for communication contribute to clients being able to create and maintain healthy, vibrant relationships within their families and professions. In her spare time, she loves to read, binge-watch Criminal Minds, travel, and drags her Mom to estate sales.

May 4
Brittnee Toeran

"Faith is taking the first step even when you don't see the whole staircase" Dr. Martin Luther King Jr

In this quote the staircase reminds me of progress and that's exactly what comes after having faith and taking that first step. In a situation where you have to walk out on fish you may not understand why at that moment, you're making a move, you'll have doubts, fears, and even bad thoughts about failing. Maybe you've been in situations before, and you're afraid of trying again because of your terrible experiences in the past, however when you let faith be your guide and make that first step, you will be led onto the journey of success. Next time when you're second guessing a decision in life, remember that the staircase is already built for you, you just have to reach your destination.

Name: Brittnee Toeran
Hometown: Greensboro, Alabama

Social media tags
Facebook: Brittnee T. Smith
YouTube: Keyana's Life
Instagram: t.keyana
Twitter: keyanaways
Email
Brittneesmith82@gmail.com

May 5
Renee Dantzler

Proverbs 24:5 (NASB)
"A wise man is strong, and a man of knowledge increases power."

Be STRONG!

Strength is withstanding life's challenges, obstacles, trials and storms and still getting up, still standing, still believing, still trusting, still encouraging, still praying and sometimes simply just being still. Never mistake a feeling of weakness as not being strong. We all have moments, we are human. God is the one and only omnipotent one! The first step to being strong is thinking that you are. Next, start saying, "I am Strong." Regardless of how you feel, repeat it to yourself over and over again. Lastly, start to believe it! Think Strong, Speak Strong, Be Strong!

Renee Dantzler is a woman of God, loving wife of over 30 years and mother of 3 sons. Certified Personal Trainer and business owner, Renee is a transformation artist who is passionate about helping others overcome challenges physically, emotionally and spiritually. Her motto is, "Be the best you, you can be!"

FACEBOOK Renee Taylor Dantzler INSTAGRAM: coachreneedantzler TWITTER: Coach Renee @ReneeDantzler
LINKEDIN: linkedin.com/in/reneedantzler
City/State: Rockville, MD
email: CoachRenee@reneedantzler.com

May 6
Geanell E. Robinson

Psalm 5:3 NIV
"In the morning, Lord, you hear my voice; in the morning I lay my request before you and wait expectantly."

Are you following the example of David who was considered "A Man After God's Own Heart? Are you communicating with God daily? My Sisters God desires a real relationship with us not some ritualistic way of life. God knows you and He wants you to get to know Him. In any relationship no one wants to be ignored until they are needed.

Take time daily to talk to God. Not only does He hear, God answers.

geanellrob@gmail.com

May 7
Linda A. Feliciano

Philippians 4:12-13 & 19 New International Version (NIV)

"12 I know what it is to be in need, and I know what it is to have plenty. I have learned the secret of being content in any and every situation, whether well fed or hungry, whether living in plenty or in want. 13 I can do all this through Christ who gives me strength. 19 And my God will meet all your needs according to the riches of his glory in Christ Jesus."

As women we wear many crowns (mother, sister, friend, wife, minister) and often bear the burden of not enough money, time, milk, you name it. We experience difficulties and barriers that keep us from accomplishing our goals/mission. Whether you're trying to visit the sick and shut in, lose that extra 20 pounds, finish that presentation or close that sale, this scripture encourages you to know that YOU CAN DO IT. Regardless of the obstacle or circumstance allow your Spirit man to strengthen your resolve because God has already provided you with All you need to accomplish your mission. Go forth on purpose!"

Linda A. Feliciano is a Strategic Change Agent, a Marketplace Minister, Minister of the Gospel and mother of three she has overcome many obstacles, and is a successful entrepreneur known as the Small Business CFO in some circles. Linda is a keynote speaker and has been featured on The Community Spotlight Hour Cox Media Group. Her desire to help others succeed led her to obtain her degree and establish Asher Business Group, LLC a full-service tax practice and accounting consultancy firm. Her mission is to teach stewardship in finances, health, and Spirit to the glory of God.

Social Media: Facebook: @AsherBiz @TeamPFF4Life
Twitter: @AsherBiz @SmallBizCFO_ABG LinkedIn:
https://www.linkedin.com/in/linda-a-feliciano-3aa12441/
Yelp: @AsherBiz Website: Asherbusinessgroup.com
Location: Jacksonville, FL
Email: info@asherbusinessgroup.com Aidez@live.com Laidez@yahoo.com
Linda@asherbusinessgroup.com

May 8
Alice M. Jarman

Colossians 3:13 (NLT)

**"Make allowance for each other's faults,
and forgive anyone who offends you.
Remember, the Lord forgave you, so you must forgive others."**

We've all been hurt by someone; be it in word or deed. Relationships end horribly, children act disrespectfully, coworkers do not respect boundaries. Our nature tells us to hold a grudge or get one up on the other person; but the Word commands us to forgive. Genuine forgiveness is difficult to achieve. Qualities like kindness, patience and love help to make it easier to pardon the offenses. Deciding to forgive, truly forgive, frees you from anger and allows the healing process to begin. Relinquishing your hold on anger will release unimaginable blessings in your life. Try it and see!

I am a woman of God; wife to Leo; mother of 5; grandmother of 5 and serial entrepreneur! "Some succeed because they are DESTINED but most because they are DETERMINED!" - unknown

Social Media Tags:	https://www.facebook.com/amreid.williams
City/State:	Creedmoor, North Carolina
Email:	amreid-williams@hotmail.com

May 9
Debbie Ann Andrews

"And we know that all things work together for the good to them that love God, to them who are called according to his purpose." Romans 8:28

Those who love God, are in fact, called by God when they encounter our risen Lord and are baptized by His spirit. This is when their divine purpose for their lives is unlocked. Our birthing seeds were planted with fertile soil and essential nutrients so that our dreams will manifest. Therefore, Beloved, stay focused and don't allow immorality of the world's systems to deter you from reaching your "divine destiny." Always dream big, cultivate faith and pray so the Lord can commune more intimately with you. He will give you immeasurable faith to do what He has called you to do. You are a mighty instrument in the hands of God!

Debbie is a breast cancer survivor, advocate and contributing bestselling author for "Faith for Fiery Trials." Debbie is a speaker on the topic of "Living with and Beyond the Breast Cancer Diagnosis." She openly and transparently shares her journey in an effort to encourage and inspire others as they walk through what can be a very "dark night of the soul." She infuses her talks with how she incorporated positive affirmations and indomitable faith to survive breast cancer. Debbie is a woman living on purpose, in purpose and committed bringing breast cancer awareness to women, one woman at a time. Debbie is a member of Greater Mount Calvary Holy Church in Washington D.C., under Bishop Alfred A. Owens and Co-Pastor Susie C. Owens. She serves in several ministries and a graduate of Bible Calvary Institute with a certificate in "Biblical Studies."

prayer1@rcn.com Facebook, Debbie Ann Andrews IG, Debbie A Andrews Twitter, Debbie Ann Andrew www.DebbieAnnAndrews.com

May 10
Keni Fleming

Joshua 1:6-9 New King James Version (NKJV)
"Be strong and of good courage; do not be afraid, nor be dismayed, for the
Lord your God *is* with you wherever you go."

We are to keep the Book of the Law always on our lips; meditate on it day and night, so that we may be careful to do everything written in it. Then we will be prosperous and successful. The Lord tells us that He is with us wherever we go so we don't have to be afraid or discouraged. When what we ask for in His name lines up with his Will it will be done

Corona, Ca
facebook.com/kenifleming

May 11
Dr. LaToya Wiggins

Luke 10: 40-42

"Lord, do you not care that my sister has left me to serve alone? Tell her then to help me. But the Lord answered her, "Martha, Martha, you are anxious and troubled about many things, but one thing is necessary. Mary has chosen the good portion, which will not be taken away from her."

How often do we get upset, frustrated, or angry when taking care of our household and other responsibilities, while our family sits back and enjoy themselves? We have to make ourselves a priority and ensure we enjoy ourselves, too! Let us take time to enjoy what the Lord has given us, just like Mary did. Take time to relax, read or listen to something enjoyable, spend quality time with your loved ones, or do absolutely nothing. Do not frustrate yourself like Martha when those things you deem important are not more important than your well-being.

Dr. LaToya Wiggins is a physical therapist in the inpatient hospital setting and a wellness coach for moms. As a busy mom herself, she enjoys helping other moms prioritize self-care. Dr. Wiggins is a wife and mother of 2 sons. She enjoys SocaRobics, dancing, step classes, comedy shows, and traveling.

www.facebook.com/essenceoflivinghlc
www.instagram.com/essenceofliving_hlc
www.essenceoflivinghlc.com www.linkedin.com/in/latoya-wiggins-578033158

May 12
Pastor Margareth "Maggy" Reed

Psalm 139:13-18

Knitted for a special mission.

Woman of God, who knew you would make it this far for everything you have been through?

I'm persuaded that on this special day, this is the word for you. God prepared you for such a time like this. You are here to instruct and serve others on how to do it also in their situation. You are an overcomer so you can guide others to overcome. God prepared you for this season, and it's a special mission, it's a special calling, special oil is being poured over your head for this task. Will you answer the calling on your life? God knitted you perfectly in your mother's womb.

A multilingual speaker, Dr. Reed is known for her abilities to move the audience with her contagious vivacity. The mantle on her life is to serve God's people to: Enhance, empower & equip leaders with strategies to be efficient and effective in life, business, and ministry through writing, publishing & products development. www.mrenterprisesbiz.com

She can be reached at speaker@maggyreedspeaks.com or info@mrenterprisesbiz.com
Dr. Reed is The Intentional Woman of the 21st Century.
See her on all social media and visit her site mrenterprisesbiz.com

May 13
Jessie C. Love

"Go Out In Joy"

Isaiah 55:12 (NIV)

"For you shall go out in joy and be led forth in peace; the mountains and the hills before you shall break forth into singing, and all the trees of the field shall clap their hands."

God has blessed you with a new day of this gift called life. The way that you perceive what happens FOR you will determine what transpires WITHIN you. You were not buried, you were covered. Take account of every ability that has been blessed into you and push through. The struggles that you've survived gave you time to stretch forth and thrive. Since God is for you and will never leave you nor forsake you, stay courageous in your faith journey. Look in the mirror, feel God's love surrounding you, smile, and go out in joy today. Listen...nature is singing.

May 14

Sandra Hardy

1 Chronicles 29:11-12

"11 Thine, O Lord, is the greatness, and the power, and the glory, and the victory, and majesty; for all that is in the heaven and in the earth is thine; thine is the kingdom, O Lord, and thou art exalted as head above all.

12 Both riches and honor come of thee, and reinvest over all; and in thine hand is power and might; and in thine hand it is to make great, and give strength unto all."

There are times when we go through so many challenges in life. Our first response is to try and handle everything without assistance. If we fail or if we succeed the results is credited to ourselves. 1 Chronicles 29:11-12 is a constant reminder to not only give our test and trials to God but that the results will be due to is power and majesty. I get so much comfort knowing God is in control my life!!! Just understanding that nothing you can ever encounter is outside God's control is the peace of God.

Sandra Hardy is the founder of Bootz to Heelz, a retired veteran, a federal employee, and entrepreneur of two multilevel marketing companies. Master's in Human Resources, son Marcus.

www.facebook.com/BZ2HZ

sandra.hardy44@gmail.com

May 15
Valerie Woodard

Romans 8:38-39

"38 For I am convinced that neither death nor life, neither angels nor demons, neither the present nor the future, nor any powers, 39 neither height nor depth, nor anything else in all creation, will be able to separate us from the love of God that is in Christ Jesus our Lord."

Even before I was formed in my mother's womb, you knew the enemy would come to try and steal, kill, and destroy the very treasure you had placed inside of me - the breath of life that you breathed into me before the very beginning of all time. But even before I knew you were -you were. You covered me, you carried me, you protected me. and for that reason, you will always be my first love. Despite every obstacle, you have sustained me and I will always give you Glory, honor, and praise.

Email: woodardv1@yahoo.com

May 16
Melinda Wynn

"No one has the power to shatter your dreams unless you give it to them."
Maeve Greyson

Many times, we allow people's thoughts and opinions to dictate our decisions about our dreams. Do not give people total power of the choices you make in your life. You and only you have the power to make your dreams happen. I say the recipe of God+ self-belief +self-determination+ self+motivation = your dreams. The only way someone can stop you from dreaming or fulfilling it, is if you give them the power too. So, keep and hold on to your power. Speak life and truth into all of your dreams.

email: veryblessedone@hotmail.com

May 17
Rhonda "Ro" Solomon

"Be fearless in the pursuit of what sets your soul on fire." ~ Unknown

At times the challenges of "Adulting" spiral our lives into a world of doubt, despair and depression. There may be times we feel undervalued, or that our life serves no purpose. Listen, God does not make mistakes! You were divinely and uniquely created for your sole purpose. So, rise from the darkness of despair and the ashes of self-doubt. Emerge renewed through faith!

Cultivate a Phoenix mindset in the pursuit to live in your purpose. Never doubt your journey, always let your passions ignite your focus allowing you to proceed fearlessly through life.

Rhonda Solomon, affectionately known as "Ro" (and most recently nicknamed "The Phoenix), is a Media Personality, Life Coach, Speaker and Author. She was born in the United States but spent her formative school years in St. Ann, Jamaica with her Aunt and Uncle. She later returned to the USA to complete her education. As a media personality Ro is able to ignite her community on current events and issues. Ro hosts 'The RoSolo Show" on www.106LiveRadio.com every Tuesday. She works as a host with Caribbean Life TV Network. She is also a cast member of "Women on the Rise Atlanta", which airs on Comcast in the Fall of 2018.

As a Certified Life Coach, she has mastered the art of helping individuals uncover their true identity by cultivating a love affair with their passions and turning their passions into their life's purpose. Driven by her passion to provide the support to at risk teens that was not provided to her, Ro created "The Phoenix Foundation". The Phoenix Foundation provides a nurturing program, which allows teens to know they are not broken. The focus of the organization is to provide the support young teens often do not receive because society is too busy judging. Ro's organization encourages young women to cultivate a phoenix mindset by rising above their current challenges, brushing off the dust, and becoming a Phoenix. Ro's driven by her purpose to mentor, uplift and walk others through their distractions into their transformation. Her various platforms provide outlets for women to come together and discuss life's challenges in a safe, secure and judgment free environment.

Facebook: Rhonda Fleming-Solomon
Instagram: @rosolo71 and @therosoloshow
Website:
www.rosolo.net
Email Address:
therosoloshow@gmail.com

May 18
Krystle Bradley

Psalm 23:4 NLT
"Even when I walk through the darkest valley, I will not be afraid, for you are close beside me. Your rod and your staff protect and comfort me."

God's promises are guaranteed. They WILL happen. While waiting on the promise we have to go through a process. The process is where your faith (trust) is put to the test. No matter how rough, there is purpose in this season. You need to become weighted. It is the time where you pray, fast, read, study, grow, change, develop and reflect and become spiritually mature. Remember the teacher is always quiet during the test. He has entrusted you with silence for a greater reason. Don't allow what you see to forget what God said. I was picked on purpose!

Krystle Bradley is the founder of Brave University, a nonprofit organization that aims to end the bullying epidemic. She is an author, mentor, public speaker, educator, graduate of North Carolina A&T and member of Delta Sigma Theta Sorority, Incorporated. She believes in seeing the good in everyone she meets.

Instagram: KMilli84 and BraveUniversity3
Facebook: KMillionaire Bradley and Brave University
Twitter: b_krystle and @BraveUniv3
E-mail address: bravebradley3@gmail.com

May 19
Terri Sharmaine

Get Up, Get Going

"I press on toward the goal to win the prize for which God has called me heavenward in Christ Jesus." – Philippians 3:14 (NIV)

As my son began to walk at 9 months old. He didn't quit after he fell, he got up and he kept going. You can get up too! When we fall, we focus on our failures. That failure is potentially a blessing in disguise because God has something greater prepared for us. During your prayer time ask God for continued guidance so that you can press on toward the goal and GET UP!

Terri Sharmaine, a Little Rock native, wears many hats. She is a Proud mother, Change Agent, Business Owner, and Servant to name a few. Terri enjoys working with her outreach ministry through social media ministry, hosting empowerment events, hosting and collaborating with health fairs and community outreach seminars. When she is not working her full-time job as an IT Business analyst, Adjunct professor, her new business venture TF Solutions Center, LLC and being a full-time mom. She strives to continue to share positive news and information to help her community through a servant's heart. During her free time, she enjoys reading, writing and spending quality time with her son and family. She strives each day to show her son that all things are possible through Christ, Faith, hard work and determination.

FB: TF Solutions Center, LLC IG: TeeFloSpeaks Twitter: TeeFloTweets
www.thegoaldiggersblueprint.com

May 20
LaToya O. Guion

Ephesians 6:11-17 VS 16
"Above all, taking the shield of faith, wherewith ye shall be able to quench all the fiery darts of the wicked."

Faith

Faith a small yet powerful and profound word, a word we do not activate enough. We think it should only be used in certain situations and circumstances. Fact is Faith can be used for any trail or tribulation. You see God pointed out in verse 16 how the Shield of Faith, was the most important piece of your Armor. So, no matter what your mind or the Enemy tells you...You can't write that book, you will never be debt free...You're not good enough, it's All a Lie! Activate and Raise your Shield of Faith, because when you do you activate God himself! I believe the report of the Lord...Do you?

LaToya O. Guion (Olivia G.) Wife, Mom, and Global Entrepreneur in the Financial Literacy space. Health, Wealth, and Organic Beauty are my passions! Born to Eugene and Doretha Peterson, October 3, 1978. As a small child I often daydreamed while prancing around carrying my dad's briefcase, imagining myself as Owner and CEO of my own company. Thank God I'm fulfilling that Dream! Stay Tuned!

Social Media/Websites:
Email: LGuion@OliviaG.org
www.myfes.net/LGuion
www.facebook.com/OliviaGsFitnessandFinance
www.instagram.com/LaToyaOliviaG
www.twitter.com/LOliviaG1 www.Linkedin.com/LaToya(Olivia)Guion

May 21
M.Latea Newhouse

Proverbs 18:21 (NKJ)
"Death and Life are in the tongue, And those who love it will eat it's fruit."

As I ponder on the scripture, I find it to be profound. To Encourage or Destroy one's own circumstance or future by words we speak is astounding. I'm reminded of a story, The Little Engine Who Could. All the other trains that were better equipped to pull the toys the smaller train accepted the challenge. With odds against her. She spoke "I Think I Can" not once nor twice, until she accomplished the mission. Then spoke "I Thought I Could". I invite us to speak Life to ourselves by applying affirmations then believe. Despite the odds I Think We Can.

As a woman who has endured yet overcome many obstacles with the Love and Support of God, Prayer, Family and Friends please remember God uses ordinary woman to do extraordinary things. You may reach me at latea.newhouse@yahoo.com or Facebook under Latea Foreevah Newhouse.

May 22
Angelica Lassiter

Proverbs 4:25
"Let your eyes look straight ahead; fix your gaze directly before you."

STOP ALLOWING PEOPLE AND THEIR OPINIONS OF YOU TO DISTRACT YOU FROM YOUR PURPOSE AND BRING YOU DOWN MENTALLY. REMEMBER GOD IS THE ONE WHO WAKES YOU UP EVERY MORNING WITH A PURPOSE AND HE DOES NOT CONSULT WITH OTHER PEOPLE AND THEIR THOUGHTS OF YOU WHEN CHOOSING YOUR JOURNEY OR THE DAYS OF YOUR LIFE. JUST STAY DETERMINED AND IF MUST BE AVOID NEGATIVE PEOPLE AND SURROUND YOURSELF WITH POSITIVE PEOPLE WHO WILL HELP LIFT YOU UP SO THAT YOU CAN GET ALL OF YOUR RESPONSIBILITIES DONE AND ORDAINED PURPOSE ACCOMPLISHED.

Angelica Lassiter was born in Providence, Rhode Island. She is the author of 2 other books of inspiration, Confidence in God and Uplifting Quotes for Trusting in God. She enjoys spending her time with her 2 children and empowering others.

Website
www.Gracedinspirations.com
Facebook
https://www.facebook.com/angelica.lassiter   Email: Gracedinspirations@gmail
.com

May 23
Destiny Amanda Johnson

Psalm 136:26

"Give thanks to the God of Heaven, For His lovingkindness (graciousness, mercy, compassion) endures forever"

As an only child, I am always reminded of God's unfailing, unending and constant love through the love my mother has for me. No matter how many times I fail to listen, I disappoint and I make the wrong decisions, she just never seems to love me any less.

Our failures, our missteps and even our inconsistencies do not cause God to change his mind about how much He loves us. Like every parent, He hurts and sometimes He punishes but His Love is and will always remain constant.

Know today, that no matter what you are Loved!!! AMEN.

dajj2591@gmail.com

May 24
Carmelesha Matthewson

Give God the Same Time You Give Your Cell Phone

Put that cell phone down and spend some time with me. I heard God so clearly that morning. I asked for forgiveness immediately. I knew he was right. I was spending more time on my social media than with him. It's so easy to do five minutes turns into thirty. Then you have wasted more than an hour watching useless videos and reading a negative post. We are so quick to watch and listen to things that add no value to our lives.

But then we will call it just entertainment when it is only one more thing to distract you. Count how many times you pick up your phone in a day. Then count how much time you spend with God. That cell phone can't answer prayers, heal your body, give you peace, or give you divine protection. Spending time with God will provide you with that. Plus, it's FREE!

City/State: Knightdale N.C.

Email: info@carmelesha.com

May 25
Demetria Burren

Philippians 4:6

Is there something in your life that has you worried? Worry derives from fearing what we cannot control. I used to worry about my daughter when she'd walk home from school, because I couldn't control who had access to her along the way. Philippians 4:6 tells us that God's antidote to worrying is prayer. Prayer places our trust in the one person that can be everywhere at all times and has all power. And He loves us! So, the next time you are tempted to worry, see it as God calling you to trust Him with your life at a new level.

EMAIL: demiburren@gmail.com
Demetria Burren is an IT Support Analyst for a Healthcare IT company and also CEO of Brown Sugar Beauty Supply. She is married to Isaac Burren and has 3 children: Jonathan, Amira and Jackson. Also, she serves Social Media Manager for the Dallas Chapter of Black CEO organization.

SOCIAL MEDIA TAGS: FB and Twitter @demiburren
WEBSITES: www.brownsugarbeautysupply.com
EMAIL: demiburren@gmail.com

May 26

LATASHA ALEX

Joshua 1:9 KJV

"Have I not commanded thee? Be strong and of a good courage; be not afraid, neither be thou dismayed: for the Lord thy God is with thee wheresoever thou goest."

Sometimes life takes us through storms that we'll one day understand. Every storm is part our journey. The storms prove our strengths. God knows what you're going through. He promised to bring the good out of the storm. Are u going to shout or question God about the storm raging in your life? I want you to call out to him, uplift his holy name and praise him. After the storm there is always sunshine. Today my sister, I want you to tell your storm that you will win!

LaTasha was born and raised in Shreveport, LA. She obtained her Associate's of Science Degree in Surgical Technology from Southern University at Shreveport, and Bachelor's of Science Degree in Nursing from Grambling State University. She's a member of Delta Sigma Theta, Inc. She is a woman of God who loves telling others about his works. Her life motto is live your best life because tomorrow is not promised. She's been through many obstacles in life. Her faith in God is what keeps her going, fueled and motivated.

Email: latashadalex@yahoo.com
IG names: @ohitsjusttasha and @plannernursenmore.

May 27
Akasha Kinlock

"There is a Warrior Goddess within me. She does not expect me to do anything that does not come Naturally. Because of Her, I am no longer friendless. I no longer feel like an orphan or an outcast And I may not be foe-free, but I am fearless. I'm free to bask in the sun of my truth, count the stars, celebrate the moon and dance through my storms. I am grateful for both challenges and blessings of prosperity. I am a fierce, fabulous Black woman just loving who I am. Manifesting goodness. Becoming a Create-her!"

Ms. Akasha is a self-published author, handmade jewelry designer, a feminist scholar in social psychology and mother of two fine young men, Jarrod & Josheua. I have an eBook coming out in 2019 called: "U Gone Hear My Mouth, aimed at helping sistahs connect with their inner Warrior Goddess.

My email address: akashancharge@gmail.com. Facebook/Instagram: AKASHAZALL4UBOUTIQUE. My Website: http://ALL4Uhandmadesbymsakasha.com.

May 28
Kelly S. White

2 Corinthians 6:18

"And I will be a father to you, and you shall be the sons and daughters to me, says the Lord Almighty."

Being "Daddy's little girl" is a relationship that is sought after by every daughter. Unfortunately, the quintessential father-daughter relationship does not happen for everyone. Day after day, little girls wish and hope that the relationship with their father would change but, sometimes, it never does. Girls can become bitter, especially when feeling scared or lost, knowing that they would not receive any help or support from their father. It took me a while to realize where my help truly comes from. Father God has loved us before we even existed, and His love will NEVER fade. His love makes me stronger and better every single day, and His love will do the same for you – just ask.

(804) 571-1357

Email: paradisetravelva@gmail.com

Social Media tags: Facebook @paradisetravelllc

Instagram @paradisetravelllc

Website: www.paradisetravelva.com

May 29

Atiya Fowler-Myers

Jeremiah 29:11

"For I know the plans I have for you," declares the LORD, "plans to prosper you and not to harm you, plans to give you hope and a future."

Take comfort in God's promise. No matter what you are faced with today, you can rest in the fact that God has more in store for you. There will be times in our lives that it looks like God's plan will not come to pass. In those times, we must remember that all things work together for the good of those that love the Lord. Continue to praise God. He has an expected end planned for you if you only believe.

Atiya Fowler is a mother, wife, daughter, sister and friend to those that God has chosen. She was a high school dropout that realized after a fatal car accident that it is never too late to start over. Now a college graduate, she is an overcomer whose purpose is to encourage others to do the same. She is a "Royal Rebel".

Instagram Tag: royalrebels215
Facebook: Royal Rebels Inc.
Facebook: Atiya Fowler-Myers
Website: www.royalrebelsontherise.com

May 30

Nicole Gaines

2 Kings 4:7

"When she told the man of God what had happened, he said to her, 'Now sell the olive oil and pay your debts, and you and your sons can live on what is left over.'"

I always knew God created me for a greater purpose. I didn't always understand my value. Then the pressures of life forced me recognized that I had the ability to create more wealth for my family.

Sometimes Gods allows the pressures of life to squeeze us until we remember that we already possess everything we need to create more.
Do you want more? It's already inside of you. The instructions were written.
1. Use the skills and knowledge you already possess and sell it
2. Pay your debts
3. Live off of what is leftover.

It's your God given responsibility.

Nicole Gaines who is called the "Cashflow Queen." for her business and accounting acumen hails from Detroit, MI. Nicole specializes in helping start-up and small businesses create a solid financial foundation. Nicole is no stranger to entrepreneurship. She is the co-owner of Gaines Construction Services. Her newest entrepreneurial endeavor is Regal Tax Pros, LLC a full-service accounting and tax agency. You can reach Nicole at Nicole.gaines@regaltaxpros.com and 833-482-9249

May 31
Shanae Starnes

Jeremiah 29:11 - "For I know the plans I have for you", declares the Lord, "plans to prosper you and not to harm you, plans to give you hope and a future."

Your lessons in your journey through life tells a story. Understand that every lesson you have experienced has equipped you with hope and the very future you are experiencing now. Finding the joy in the journey is where you will find your breakthrough. Once you cast your cares to God, your life lessons will empower you and you'll see that lesson was there to build tenacity and your faith because your troubles over to God! Allow the God in you to awaken your spirit that it's time to grow on to the next lesson. The call on your life will be clear because you'll have the testimony to qualify you!

Shanae Starnes is a self-starter, mother of three who has taken every opportunity to strengthen her background. Her peers and colleagues describe her as a compassionate leader who is committed to others. With over twenty years of knowledge and training in cosmetology, public speaking, a strong background in customer relations, and a genuine desire to help others love themselves; Shanae Starnes is truly an example of what it means to live your dreams. For more information email starnesshanae@gmail.com.

FB: https://www.facebook.com/sstarnes1
Instagram: @shaanestarnes
Twitter: shanaedastylist
Linkedin: linkedin.com/in/shanae-starnes-215a05100

June 1
Lisa-Gaye Richards

Deuteronomy 1:11 NIV
"May the Lord, the God of your fathers increase you a thousand times and bless you as he has promised!"

God desires to pour into your life blessings and favor. He promises to increase you a thousand-fold and bless you beyond measure. Blessings can be stored up for you just because a family member honored Him. It could be a parent, a grandparent or someone in your family history that you may not know; but because they lived a life of faith and blessed others you are now reaping the rewards. When you see yourself receiving "surprise favor" thank God for his grace and mercy. Live a life of expectancy because your blessing is coming.

Lisa-Gaye Richards is a Jamaican native who holds a Master's Degree in Child and Adolescent Psychology. She strongly believes that her purpose in life is to be of service to others… She enjoys volunteering and giving back to her community. As a Brand Awareness Ambassador, Lisa-Gaye is passionate about spreading the "Now We No" Mission to young girls and women and a healthy lifestyle. She is a wife and a mother who loves the Lord with all her heart.

EMAIL: leeceg@live.com
SOCIAL MEDIA TAGS: Website: www.easethesuffering.com
FB:
https://www.facebook.com/NowWeNowithLisaGaye/
Instagram:
https://www.instagram.com/r.lisagaye/

June 2:

Theresa Hand

Proverbs chapter 3 verses 5 and 6.

"Trust in the Lord with all your heart, do not depend on your own understanding. Seek his will in all you do, and he will direct your paths."

This just speak for itself, if we do this our life be blessed with wisdom and knowledge.

I am the CEO of Head Art Works family business. I am a wife, mother and grandmother. I have a bachelor's degree in business management. I also am a legal secretary, medical assistant and Emergency Medical Technician. We make scented hand craft items.

Website- http://www.headartworks.online
Social Media- Head Art Works- Facebook,
Instagram- Twitter- Pintress-
LinkedIn headartworks@gmail.com

June 3
Nalema Ross

Ephesians 4:29

"Let no corrupting talk come out of your mouths but only such as is good for building up as fits the occasion, that it may give grace to those who hear."

Words are a powerful tool that can be used to build someone up or tear someone down. Remember when you are speaking to one another, that you are expressing words of encouragement, tenderness, delight, and compassion. Let the last thing you say to someone be the thing that they walk away with in their heart for goodness not for badness.

Nalema Ross (AKA "Mimi") is a plus size model, actress and writer in the NY/NJ/Pa area and is the mother of 3 wonderful grown boys. Nalema is very close to her family, especially her sister who battles Lupus, and she takes every opportunity to support those struggling with Lupus and other illness through foundations such as the Lupus Foundation of America, Autism Awareness, National Breast Cancer Foundation, HIV/AIDS Awareness and Toys for Tots. Nalema's faith in God is strong and insists "God has provided me with everything I could possibly need and I will always allow Him to direct my path."

You can connect with Nalema Ross on Facebook at www.facebook.com/nalemaross/ and Instagram at www.instagram.com/nalemaross/ website is in the works.

June 4
Candice J Arnold

Psalm 150:6
"Let everything that has breath praise the Lord"

This is a commandment, not an option for the believer. We were created to praise the Lord. In the good times, bad times, and all things in between, there should always be a praise on our lips to Him! He is the author and finisher of our faith. Praise Him!

IG: Candice J Arnold
Facebook: Candice Arnold

June 5
Nakisha Blackwell

"Her worth is far above Rubies" Proverbs 31:10

Listen, you are worthy! You're a rare jewel, a one of a kind that's worthy to be praised. It doesn't matter who you use to be, stop allowing people to validate who you are and start allowing God to use you. It's time to move forward. It's time for you to live your life, so get up and dust yourself off. Be the best version of you.

Your uniqueness is a gift. You are a virtuous woman; more precious than any jewel. You are worthy!! You are enough!!

Email: kywfashion@gmail.com

June 6
Minister Robyn Curry

Luke 9:23-24

Then He said to them all, "If anyone desires to come after Me, let him deny himself, and take up his cross daily, and follow Me. For whosoever will save his life shall lose it: but whosoever will lose his life for my sake, the same shall save it."

As we follow Christ, many crosses will be laid upon our path. These crosses are not meant to be stepped over or handed off to another, rather, we are instructed to take them up. These are the crosses we bare. My cross may not look like your cross, and your cross may not look like mine, but chances are they are both heavy, and they are both painful. For following Jesus does not mean we escape suffering, but instead we should prepare to face it. For the sake of Christ, when we lay down our agendas, our wills, and our lives, it is there that we save them. May God's grace be sufficient each and every day as you pick up your cross.

Min. Robyn M. Curry's spiritual upbringing began in the Otterbein United Methodist Church, in Altoona Pennsylvania, where she was a member for 19 years. Robyn's call to teach the Word of God, has led her, in service, to various ministries such as; Youth Leadership, Women's Ministry, Missions and Outreach, and Director of Sunday School Education while residing in Palm Coast, Florida. Robyn joined Worship World Church, after moving to Maryland in 2010, where she currently serves under the leadership of Pastor W. Andrew Best, Jr. Robyn has been married to Justin R. Curry for Thirteen years and is the mother of four children and two grandchildren. The Curry's felt the Lord was calling them back home and returned to Altoona, Pennsylvania, where they currently reside.

June 7
Nikki W. Miller

Ecclesiastes 3:1-8
"It's All In God's Timing!"

God has ordained timing for everything that happens in our lives. Sometimes we become impatient and want to rush God's timing. God is not a microwave! We even sometimes take matters into our own hands and make a complete mess! You know the story of Abraham and Sarah when they so desired to have a baby that would be named Isaac. What happened? Impatience got in the way, and Hagar, the maidservant was given to Abraham to bear a child, Ishmael, rather than trusting God's timing and the promised child, Isaac. What are you waiting for God to answer and fulfill in your life? Wait on the Lord, it is coming forth, in God's timing!

Nikki W. Miller is a passionate Educator, Entrepreneur, Christian Life Coach, and Author. She is the wife of Anthony Louis Miller of 27 years and the mother of two beautiful adult daughters Gabrielle and Moriah Miller. Nikki is the doggie mom of a gorgeous Shih Tzu Macey Ann Miller. Nikki serves in many ministries at her church in Greenville, NC Sycamore Hill Missionary Baptist Church and is an active member of Delta Sigma Theta Sorority, Inc.

Greenville, North Carolina
Facebook - Nikki Williams Miller
nikkiwmillerbiz@gmail.com

June 8

Brieanna Toeran

Romans 8:28

"And we know that all things work together for good for those who love God to those that are called according to his purpose."

Heavenly Father, I pray today if I'm comparing myself to another that I have strength to open my bible.... Romans 8:28

Heavenly Father, I pray today if I'm wrestling with all effort and strength to open my bible to Romans 8:25

God not only said that he'll make the weak strong but ALL THINGS (everything that I'm tangling with (Heavenly Father are called according to his purpose Heavenly Father for you are in control of" all things me" Not me...Amen

toeranbrienna@yahoo.com

mdaadvocate@yahoo.com

June 9

Katrina French

Galatians 6:9 "And let us not be weary in well doing, for in due season we shall reap, if we faint not."

No matter how much faith a person has in the Most High God sometimes we can allow our flesh to get in the way and grow weary. Beloved don't stay there! Let God's word be confirmation that in due season you shall REAP! In order to have a testimony, you must have a test! Some of those tests can knock you down, keep getting up! You are STRONG, FEARLESS AND PURPOSED FOR GREATNESS, THIS TOO SHALL PASS, YOU GOT THIS!!!!

Katrina French is the owner and operator of Rainbow Locs of Love Hair Studio LLC, where she is a traveling Cosmetologist and Master loctician specializing in permanent dreadlock extensions, custom units, as well as a variety of hair services, catering to relaxed and natural clientele as well as alopecia clients. She's the mother of one daughter, Zenobia , yet mothered many foster children including 2 very special young ladies Ashley and Mylandra Trinae .She enjoys reading and helping others. She's currently working on her natural hair product line as well as her memoir. She loves to make custom units at no cost for cancer patients in her spare time. Katrina also has as a passion for assisting aspiring stylists and goes to schools in her spare time in Guildford county to speak to them about their future.

Instagram: make_hairstory
Facebook: Rainbow Locs Of Love Hair Studio LLC
Facebook: PTP Travels Pain To Purpose Travels.
Facebook: Bundles By Hairstory
Wilson, NC
Email: tfrench376@gmail.com

June 10
Freida Henderson

Great Faith
Romans 4:20-21 AMP,
"But he did not doubt or waver in unbelief concerning the promise of God, but he grew stronger and empowered by faith, giving glory to God, being fully convinced that God had the power to do what he had promised."

As we go through our everyday life things don't always go the way we planned or hoped but in the mist of it all we should always remember the promises of God concerning our lives and keep unshakable faith. Not being moved by the circumstances but keep our focus on the promise not the problem. God is bigger than your obstacle doesn't get discouraged and don't complain. Even if it looked like a set back because it could be your setup for greater. While you wait don't talk yourself out of your miracle, blessings, and breakthrough but keep speaking life and the Word of God over your life.

Like Abraham grow stronger and become more empowered and give God the glory.

Apostle Freida Henderson is the Senior Pastor and founder of Faith Assembly Christian Center Word of Truth. As an Apostolic visionary she has birthed Daughters of Destiny, Women Ready 2 Win, and Faith Assembly Child Development Center. Operating in the Five-Fold Ministry Apostle Henderson is dedicated to winning souls and saving lives for Jesus Christ.

June 11
Carole Sallid-Times

"So shall my word be that goes out from my mouth; it shall not return to me empty..." Isaiah 55:11

Words Matter

God created the heavens and earth with words. My words, too, manifest as my heaven and earth, my destiny. Today, I choose my words wisely knowing they can create or destroy my world and the creation of those around me. I recognize that my words are so powerful that I must not use them to curse my life but to glorify and build upon the God given good within us all. I use my words wisely. Words matter.

Carole Sallid-Times, MHS
Pinch Me, It's Real
facebook.com/pinchmefast

June 12
Rochelle Redding

John 10:10 King James Version (KJV)
"10 The thief cometh not, but for to steal, and to kill, and to destroy: I am come that they might have life, and that they might have it more abundantly."

There are many times in our lives when we feel as though "All Hell is breaking loose" all around us. You may be going through a divorce, struggling with addiction, experiencing domestic violence, or suffering from depression. But God will use our challenges and difficulties to teach, grow, and even protect us from situations in our lives. Bishop T.D. Jakes often says "There is a blessing in your pressing". We must continue to press on and not grow weary as God will reward our faithfulness.

Rochelle Redding is an author, certified life coach, and motivational speaker. She is dedicated to helping women achieve wellness in all aspects of their lives.

Facebook – Rochelle Redding Coaching and Consulting
Instagram – Rochelleliveswell
Twitter – RochelleRedding
Website – www.Rochelleliveswell.com
Email – Rochelleliveswell@gmail.com

Jeremiah 29:11

Hello Beloved,

This is the day that the Lord has made; let us rejoice and be glad in it! Do not be consumed with digital distractions and the competing demands of your time & energy. Give yourself permission to 'UNPLUG' from the noise of life so that you can clearly hear from our heavenly Father. You do know by now that God has a plan for your life far greater than the storms that it requires of you to get to your divine life space.   #Issaplan #issappurpose #issahopefactor #issafuture #bestill

Stay Focused!

LaTasha Jones have served in human suffering for more than 20 years in both child welfare and California correctional facilities as a Social Worker. Empowering people is something she has been gifted and born to do. She transformed from Section 8 public housing to the first in the family to obtain a Master's Degree in Social Work; buy housing units, yet still found herself stressed, tired and unfulfilled. She dived into her own self-discovery and found freedom. She currently serves as a motivational coach that serves career women impacted by stress. Talk2Tasha provides real convos and solutions for women to walk in their truth while redefining their success. As she candidly defines success as; "the ability to be who you are without lying about it."

Website: www.talk2tasha.com FB: Talk2Tasha Instagram talk2tash YouTube talk2tasha Twitter; tashatalk2 email: hello@talk2tasha.com

June 14

Fredrika Sellers

Proverbs 3:5-6

"Trust in the Lord with all your heart and lean not on your own understanding; In all your ways acknowledge Him and He shall direct your paths."

"Find Your Center"

As a dance minister/choreographer there are times when I will create movements that I believe will fit with the music. That isn't always the case. I have learned not to throw things together just to get it done. I trust that God will not allow me to stumble as I move to His rhythm. And if I do, I just make it part of the dance. You may not be a dancer but I encourage you to "Find Your Center". Focus on the Lord. He is the best choreographer. As He moved over the earth creating, let Him move over you. Your movement matters.

Fredrika Sellers describes herself as a mixture of rhythm and writing. She is the youngest of four, an aunt, an author, CEO of Genesis Transition and a dance minister. More importantly she is a creative vessel for God. In her spare time, she reads, writes, and dances.

Social Media and Website:
Facebook: Genesis Transition
Twitter: @genesistransit
Instagram: genesis_transition
Website: www.genesistransition.com

Michelle Bae Prewitt

Live
"You are the salt of the earth, if salt has lost its taste, how shall it's saltiness be restored?
It is no longer of value except to be thrown out and trampled under people's feet.

Regardless of any obstacle one may face let go and love God!
No battle is yours alone and there is someone; somewhere who truly cares.....
Peace be with you my SISTER'S in CHRIST.
I love you if no one has told beautiful.
Life begins with Y-O-U!!

Facebook: Michelle Bae Prewitt

Instagram: FitGang_Bae

Fitgangbae@gmail.com

JUNE 16
Pastor Margareth "Maggy" Reed

Deuteronomy 11:19.

Teach your children.

It's an amazing opportunity to become parents, but God gave us very specific responsibility. Woman of God, what a great opportunity God has given unto you to become parent to an angel? you ought to teach your children the laws of God. If we want the next generation to have the favor of God on their life, it's a mandate we have on your life to not disobey God's laws.

Your children must know who God is, the trinity, and the Holy Spirit. They must learn how God operates, how he loves us so much that he sent his only son to redeem us and Jesus, Yahuah is that bridge of reconciliation between us and the father. God said to teach them to your children, talking about them when you sit at home and when you walk along the road, when you lie down and when you get up. Most importantly, teach your children the truth.

A multilingual speaker, Dr. Reed is known for her abilities to move the audience with her contagious vivacity. The mantle on her life is to serve God's people to: Enhance, empower & equip leaders with strategies to be efficient and effective in life, business, and ministry through writing, publishing & products development. www.mrenterprisesbiz.com

She can be reached at speaker@maggyreedspeaks.com or info@mrenterprisesbiz.com
Dr. Reed is The Intentional Woman of the 21st Century.
See her on all social media and visit her site mrenterprisesbiz.com

June 17
Jean A. Garner

"When you think you've done enough, always do a little more and a little more." 1 Samuel 1: 2, 4, 20

Have you ever felt like you never measured up? With this story, there's one woman (Peninnah) who would flaunt that fact that she had children and that Hannah didn't. So often, we really have more going for ourselves but we're too busy looking at what it appears that someone else has. Even though Peninnah had the children, Hannah was given more provision than Peninnah. Because of the sincere desires of Hannah's heart, God granted her a son, Samuel who became a vital figure in the bible and was instrumental to the building of the kingdom. But we don't hear anything else about Peninnah or her children. So, I say to you stop being concerned about what others have because, "you only need one" (a Samuel), to make a difference in the world.

Bio: Jean A. Garner is a savvy empowerment and image strategist. She is the visionary of the FierceFactor Academy and Boutique, where empowerment and style meet. Her avant-garde approach assists her clients positions them to Discover, Embrace and Ignite their FierceFactor and impact the audience that's waiting on her.

email: msjeangarner@gmail.com
Instagram : @jeanempowers Twitter: @jeanempowers
Facebook page: Jean A. Garner
Facebook: The FierceFactor Academy and Boutique
Facebook: Nae'j International Salon Facebook group: Girl, Go Be Fierce
Website: JeanAGarner.com **Raleigh, NC**
msjeangarner@gmail.com

June 18

Karshena McCain Adkins

Psalm 3:3 New International Version (NIV)

"3 But you, Lord, are a shield around me, my glory, the One who lifts my head high."

No matter what happens today, or what will happen or has happened, LIFT YOUR HEAD. I remember my mom constantly telling me to not to drop my head. EVER.

You are fearfully and wonderfully made. You are special. God has you in the palm of his hand.

Hold your head HIGH. Be bold. Be confident. BE YOU!

Email Karshenamccainadkins@gmail.com

June 19
Lisa Harris-Jones

Job 42:12A
"So, the Lord Blessed the latter end of Job more than his beginning"

Life IS Good???

I study the Word, tithe, pray faithfully, treat others right, stay in my lane and I diligently try to do what's right! Yet, I'm continuously going through and sometimes I want to throw in the towel!

Sometimes we feel that we've done all that we can and begin to question God when life gets too tough.

God being God, has to step in and remind us of exactly who He is!
God knows our heart; our intentions and we have to continue to trust Him and know that He is behind the scenes working on our behalf.

How your story ends is more amazing than you know right now.
Hold on! Trust God, it ain't over!!

Email: telicia13@gmail.com

FB: Lisa Harris-Jones
IG @teliciaj
Website:www.Hisimage.us

June 20
Nakisha Blackwell

"You alone are enough. You have nothing to prove to anybody"
- Maya Angelou

Believe in you and stop expecting for your imperfection to show up; It all starts with you. Don't lose yourself trying to be good enough for someone else. The only validation that you need is from yourself. Let your voice be heard. Don't let how someone feel about you affect how you feel about yourself because your value is far more than they will ever see. Don't let people define who you are. Stop holding your future hostage to your past. There's only one you; that alone is power. You are Amazing! You alone are Enough!

June 21
Kimberly Carter

"You may encounter many defeats, but you must not be defeated. In fact, it may be necessary to encounter the defeats, so you can know who you are, what you can rise from, how you can still come out of it." -Maya Angelou

In every aspect of my life I have encountered defeats. In school, at work, within my own business ventures and relationships. But guess what, I'm still here and every defeat has taught me something along the way. I'm still a work in progress, WE ALL ARE, but that doesn't stop me from continuing to try to be the best me I can be. So, ladies if you want to start that business, change careers, get out of that relationship that's no good for you to concentrate on yourself, have that baby, get married... whatever it is that you want to do, don't let fear hold you back. Make your plans and take that leap! We are all meant to shine so SHINE ON LADIES!

Kimberly Carter was born in Bronx, New York and raised in the Washington, DC (DMV) area. She is a published Poet, the owner of I Like it RAW, an all-natural bath and body company, and the Founder of Because We Care Network, an organization dedicated to helping the community. She is currently continuing her education at Southern New Hampshire University with a Business Management focus of study.

www.ilikeitrawbodybutters.com
rawbodybutters@aol.com
www.facebook.com/ilikeitraw
Instagram- ilikeiraw_llc kcchevette@aol.com

June 22

Hope Krystal Hood

"It's not how you fall, it's how you get back up."

-Unknown

Your crown may get twisted and need a little readjustment. You may even be a little scarred and bruised. But just like a toddler learning how to walk, don't give up until you succeed. Failure will not define who you are. Keep steadfast and push forward. Mark your will with determination and commitment. Color your path with wisdom and courage. Adjust your crown and walk again. For there is a new day to begin.

Hope Krystal Hood is a native of Faunsdale AL, and a graduate of Sunshine High school. She is also a graduate of Stillman College with a Bachelor's degree in Journalism. 2012 Hope lived in College Park GA, where she became a Paraprofessional for special needs at Atlanta Public Schools. 2015 Hope became a Paraprofessional for special needs at Tuscaloosa City Schools. Hope is working on her Masters of Journalism, and aspires to become an inspiration writer and Professor of Journalism.

Romans 12:2 (New Living Translation) "Don't copy the behavior and customs of this world, but let God transform you into a new person by changing the way you think. Then you will learn to know God's will for you, which is good and pleasing and perfect."

100 Word Summary: What can present itself as one of life's most daunting tasks is changing the way we think, especially when it comes to thoughts of negativity. Negative thoughts often serve as the catalyst for stagnation. Some of us have been holding on to negative beliefs which, often, take root early. Despite the origination, you have been equipped with the power to transform your life by the changing of your thoughts. A negative belief system does not benefit, nor does it serve, any of us. It's time to stop letting negative thoughts paralyze you and walk out God's will for your life.

50 Word Bio: I am a 34-year-old LPN from Meherrin, VA. 2002 graduate of Prince Edward Co. High, Farmville, VA. Received A.A.S. from SVCC in Keysville, VA. Mother of a 7-year-old daughter, Portlyn King. Aspiring entrepreneur with interests in starting a non-profit organization.

Facebook: Tempie Walton-Berry   Instagram: @no_comparis1

Let Go and Let God

Matthew 11:28-30 "Come to me, all you who are weary and burdened, and I will give you rest. Take my yoke on you and learn from me, because I am gentle and humble in heart, and you will find rest for your souls. For my yoke is easy to bear, and my load is not hard to carry."

Today GO! and Be the Best You that you were designed to be. God created you to wonderfully and fearfully made in his image. With God by your side on this journey today nothing is impossible. God is the great I AM and everything you put in place behind the I AM you will be!

Father Bless my sister on her journey today, give her the strength to let go of yesterday's hurt, pain, disappointment and failures and strengthen her to walk into life today decreeing and declaring that all Glory and Victories belong to you. Give her a sound mind and heart to face whatever adversity that she may encounter and give her the peace that passes all understanding, Strength, Good Health and Love Shall Follow her all the days of her life, be her God today and Guide her through, Amen

June 25

Lisa Blauvelt

Joshua 1:9

"Be strong and courageous. Do not be afraid; do not be discouraged, for the Lord your God will be with you wherever you go."

Several years ago, I had been praying about an upcoming trip to Haiti. Leaving family, friends and the fear of going to a third world country, made the decision hard, but I felt God was urging me to go. One day I shared my fear with a co-worker, she prayed with me and quoted the Scripture Psalms 91. Instantly, I felt God's peace and I knew God was asking me to go and promising to be with me.

While I was in Haiti a friend had taken a picture of a bright beautiful tap tap (their version of a taxi) for me as we were traveling back to the hotel. When we returned to the hotel, I enlarged the picture and noticed, in French Psaumes 91 on the front of the tap tap. I quickly used Google to translate it, and it was Psalms 91! The same scripture my friend quoted before my trip. This was my confirmation from God that he had called me to be his hands and feet in Haiti, and that he would protect me.

On my recent trip to Haiti, God gave me confirmation again from Joshua 1:9. There was another team from Garner at the hotel. The pastor prayed with me and quoted Joshua 1:9. Family and friends wrote me cards and letters to open each night after devotions. That night I opened a card from my daughter, and the Scripture she quoted was Joshua 1:9. Each morning in Haiti we sang "This is the Day" and prayed before going out into the community. My first Sunday back at church, our opening hymn was "This is the Day", and my devotion that day referenced Joshua 1:9. I think this was a clear message from God that he called me to do his work in Haiti and that he will be with me wherever I go.

When God asks us to do something new or challenging, God will be with us – giving us strength and courage to obey. Every time we read Scripture and ask God to help us apply it to our lives, we can watch and wait. God is faithful to encourage us along the way. Thank you, God, for giving us the strength and courage to do what you have called us to do.

EMAIL: lblauvelt@gmail.com

June 26
Nichelle B. Crump

William Shakespeare; Hamlet "This above all: to thine own self be true and it must follow, as the night the day Though canst not then be false to any man/Farewell, my blessing season this in thee."

The Original Intent of God. Let's intentionally live by our own expectations; not those imposed upon us by others. If not, we fail God, ourselves, and those that await our arrival. It is with parallel certainty, that night is followed by day; just as your *DESTINY* is connected to your *TRUTH*! Operating under false pretense, is an internal and external disservice. *Navigating daily under the microscope of "you should be" only leaves to an unfulfilled life of unnecessary disappointments. I encourage you to say "Farewell" because the blessing season lies within and can only be released when YOU come forward!*

Nichelle B. Crump is a mother of 4 (3 girls/1 son), Business Owner, Personal Trainer, Executive Administrator of a local gym and a Minister of the Gospel. Her commitment and dedication have led her to a successful career; uniquely training the "whole" personal NOT just their physical being. And she does it One Body at A Time.

crumpnichelle06@gmail.com avesselofhonor14@gmail.com
https://www.facebook.com/nichelle.crump
https://www.instagram.com/vesselsofhonor/
Email: crumpnichelle06@gmail.com

June 27

Cheyenne X. Mickey

"Many are the afflictions of the righteous; but the Lord delivereth him out of the all." KJV Psalms 34:19

In the dark places we feel lost, a heaviness on our hearts, at times it's so heavy it's hard to breathe. Feelings of intense pain, hopelessness, defeat, depression and anxiety. Suicidal thoughts of giving up on life. Homicidal thoughts of taking another's life. God knows your pain he will deliver you out of it all. Trust in God, trust in his word and the Father, the Son and Holy Spirit will be there to deliver, just as he delivered me!

Lord, today we come before you asking for your strength, while delivering us out of the dark places. In Jesus name Amen, Amen and Amen.

Website: https://beingresilientlyme.com/

June 28
Candice Davis

2 Corinthians 12:9-10
"My grace is sufficient for you, for my power is made perfect in weakness.'
Therefore, I will boast all the more gladly of my weaknesses, so that the
power of Christ may rest upon me. For the sake of Christ, then, I am content
with weaknesses, insults, hardships, persecutions, and calamities. For when I
am weak, then I am strong".

You may have endured hardships in life whether financial, with love, or health and are maybe thinking you will not see better days. God tells us that his grace is sufficient to not only see us through but to use these adversities to build us up. Seek God in everything and rest in Him knowing that He is continuously working it out for your good. The idea and visions of what you think is better are given to you by God. They are attainable if you keep the faith. You may get knocked down, you will grow weary, but it is important that in those moments you allow God to be your rock. He is solid and His love for you is everlasting.

Candice Davis is a mother of four children living in Philadelphia. A teenage mother and high school dropout, she is currently enrolled in college. Candice enjoys encouraging others to use their hardships as fuel to excel in life. The cofounder of Royal Rebels on the Rise Candice is seeking to help others build on and grow through life's curveballs.

Instagram Tag: Royalrebels215
Facebook: Royal Rebels Inc. Website: www.royalrebelsontherise.com

June 29
Stacey Florio

JESUS IS LOVE

"FOR GOD SO LOVED THE WORLD THAT HE GAVE HIS ONLY BEGOTTEN SON THAT WHOSOEVER BELIEVETH IN HIM SHOULD NOT PERISH, BUT HAVE EVERLASTING LIFE" JOHN 3:16

STACEY L. FLORIO was born and raised in PHILADELPHIA, PA in the year 1966. She was raised by her Aunt Mattie and Uncle Frank from the age of six weeks old, Stacey has been a Christian since she could walk. Stacey met her brother Keith L. Crawford and sister Ava V. Crawford at the age of 15, Stacey grew up the only child. She was very shy growing up. Acting class brought her out more and writing poetry and keeping a journal was a big part of it too. Stacey became a Actress, she was an Extra in the movie Mannequin, Former Singer of the a group called Cover Story, Modern Jazz dancer Domestic Abuse Survivor. Medical Assistant, Certified Phlebotomist She had co-authored her first book with 29 business women and authors across the U.S. called Daily Dose of Direction for Women in Business. and Sweet Matilda and her loving Ways. She has other books on their way out.

Her Media Tags are: Facebook @StaceyFlorio

Instagram@StayFlowing

Hattie Hammond

Job 13:15 – "Though he slays me, I will hope in him; yet I will surely defend my ways to his face. (NIV)

I came to live this scripture out on August 26 2014 I went to the ER with a slight fever no pain following a gallbladder surgery. Blood work was order it came back fine so a CT Scan was ordered next before the test could happen something went wrong. My body began to swell with poison from my bowel duct the room goes black and Satan walks in. He tells me if I would denounce God right now, he would save me. I begin to remind God of the word he gave me two years prior. Remember to stand on your God given Word!

Greensboro, North Carolina

Email: godsprincess63@icloud.com

July 1
Charlisa Herriott

"Surrendering isn't easy but it's healthy!"

Since the Art of Surrendering is to "Let Go". The decision to surrender may be made easy in certain situations and become more difficult to do in others. Surrendering is giving up your power or control over something or someone or "relinquishing your own will" to submit unto the "will of another. Still the question arises, "Am I willing to let go?" Well, ask yourself, what am I gaining from holding on? What am I loosing for not letting go? Or will it drain me from healthy interactions? So, what are you waiting on?

Charlisa Herriott is an Author, Minister, Speaker, 2x Cancer Survivor and Survivor Coach. She empowers women who experience the frails of life to rise from their ashes to Live on Purpose, Live with Passion and Live Life Full!

Website: www.CharlisaHerriottASurvivorsVoice.com
Instagram.com/CharlisaHerriott
Facebook.com/CharlisaHerriott
Linkedin.com/inCharlisaHerriott
Twitter.com/CharlisaHerriot

July 2
Viva Lewis-Harris

Psalm 3:3

"But you, Lord, are a shield around me, my glory, the One who lifts my head high."

Our father is our protector IN SPITE of what we experience. Once we look at what He has protected us from, HIS glory manifests; as we realize that our trials and tribulations are not in vain. The beautiful thing is, He lifts our heads high coming out. NO GUILT, NO SHAME, NO REMNANTS of what we went through. Remember, we are NOT what we did or experienced in our lives, we are who GOD says we are.

Email: only1viva@gmail.com

July 3
Eve S. Hendricks

Life can often hand out its share of hurt and pain. Our love ones pass away. Those who we thought were our friends leave us without any reasons as to why. Our marriages and relationships end and leave us hurt and heart broken. Yet, we are able to remain strong through some of the hardest seasons of our lives. While enduring so many things in the last few years, I had to remind myself "My Heal Game is Strong." We are worthy of total healing. Mind, body, soul and heart! Stay in the game. Never quit. Someone is watching to see you win.

Eve S. Hendricks is a youthful and loving mom who credits those attributes to her three beautiful daughters, Akala, Ayana and Alivia. She enjoys thrifting, spending time with her children and inspiring other women to live their best life despite setbacks. She loves God and that is her super power.

Facebook: Eve Hendricks

IG: on the_eve_lifestyle_

City/State: Graham, NC

Email: ontheevestyle@gmail.com

Rasheeda George

Matthew 7:7
"Ask and it will be given to you; seek and you will find; knock and the door will be opened to you."

Sometimes we're not mindful of when and how we should speak and to whom we should speak to. We sometimes keep our mouths closed to the right people and open our mouths to the wrong people, ignoring the "asking" bible verses. Remember the saying, "a closed mouth, don't get fed." When feeding a baby, they keep their mouths closed and sometimes spit it back at you. Don't be in a position where things are being thrown back in your face because you disclosed it to the wrong people, instead be the one who is depositing greatness into the right people. Nothing will go in or out unless the baby wants it to. Don't be like a baby making a mess. Be a person that is growing up into your destiny. Clean up the mess and feed your inner being and provide the world what's needed. Life will spit out whatever you put in it. Believe in yourself and OPEN YOUR MOUTH AND OPEN THE DOOR TO GREATNESS.

Rasheeda George, Owner of Breaking Chains Now, loves the Lord and has a love for people. She's dedicated her life in helping others grow and discover themselves as she went through the journey herself. Rasheeda has a BA in Sociology with a minor in Human Resources and a MS in Human Services Administration with a concentration in Negotiations and Conflict Management. She also became a Certified Mediator and Certified Professional Life Coach and Speaker. Rasheeda discovered that there was not peace inside of her so she decided to make peace within herself and start fulfilling her "calling" in life. She has NOW made it her mission to help people experience that beautiful feeling of freedom, fulfillment and fun by **Breaking Chains NOW!**

www.breakingchainsnow.org
www.facebook.com/breakchainsnow
www.instagram.com/breakchainsnow
443-31B-REAK/443-312-7325

Alma M. Holley

"I lift up my eyes to the mountains—where does my help come from? 2 My help "comes from the Lord, the Maker of heaven and earth." Psalm 121: 1-2

God's got it!

This scripture speaks to me when I feel my back is against the wall and need help. Sometimes I allow the issues of life to overtake me. It is those time that I must remind myself that my help comes from the Lord. All I must do is look to God for direction. He created everything and he has controls of everything. I lift a pray, praise and listen for guidance. I am learning to "let go and let God". I still need to do my part. There is no need to worry because God's got it!

Alma Holley is a Clinical Nurse Leader in Washington DC. She lives in Maryland with her wonderful, husband Joseph (Retired Military), their three lovely, daughters Holley, Joale, Jada and their dog, Autumn.

Email:
Amhol92858@aol.com

July 6
Erica Hicks

Matthew 6:34
34 "So don't worry about tomorrow, for tomorrow will bring its own worries. Today's trouble is enough for today."

One of the most prominent scriptures of the bible, and why do you think so? I can tell you, because our God is not a God that want you to worry or stress, he wants you to live for today. He has already taken care of tomorrow so it's not our job to worry about it. We are to live for today not worry. I love how, if we seek, God will give us all we need to get thru "THIS" day. As for tomorrow, he will give us what we need to get thru THAT day.

A bouquet of exotic flowers defines Erica Hicks; mother of 4, and always a friend. She's an avid supporter of the Autism movement as her 10-year-old son was diagnosed at two. Her compassion for community is the driving force for the birth of her non-profit, UMAD, United Mothers and Daughters. She has overcome hurdles & endured the loss of her husband of 23yrs in 2017. The word according to Erica Hicks is a resounding yes! "Life is powered by who you choose to be." She was a young mother who once upon a time struggled until she began to help others outside of myself". Her endeavor is to be that 'one' to help another spring free!

Mserica.Hicks@yahoo.com
LinkedIn-https://www.linkedin.com/in/erica-hicks-0106aa174
Facebook-erica.hicks.980

July 7
Nikki Goodloe

"But understand this, that in the last days there will come times of difficulty. For people will be lovers of self, lovers of money, proud, arrogant, abusive, disobedient to their parents, ungrateful, unholy, heartless, unappeasable, slanderous, without self-control, brutal, not loving God, treacherous, reckless, swollen with conceit, lovers of pleasure rather than lovers of God, having the appearance of godliness, but denying its power. Avoid such people."
2nd Timothy 3:1-17

In the words of Iyana Vanzant "It's not selfish to put yourself first, it's self-ful." It's your life. You have permission to remove yourself from any relationship, situationship, job, etc. that no longer serves you in a positive, meaningful, uplifting manner. You don't owe any explanations to anyone who has not walked a day in the life of YOU! You have one life to live and owe it to yourself to make it your best! It's time to break out those brand-new heels, lace up those sneakers and give yourself permission to walk straight into your God purposed destiny!

https://www.facebook.com/nikki.goodloe2018
https://www.facebook.com/nikkilgoodloe/
www.instagram.com/nlgoodloe

Email: nikkilgoodloe@gmail.com

Trust the process

The process of life can get crazy at times, heck it is crazy cause you don't know whether to turn left or right, go up or down, or to say yes or no, but trust it. Stay focused. Be committed. It will bring you to a better place in yourself, one of humbleness and appreciation. It takes failures and "do overs" to get it right. All the, woulda's, and coulda's, don't prepare us for the future. Nothing really does, but life itself happening. When you yield yourself in the one who made heaven and earth will all your being, things will turn around in your favor. Trust the process. He will give you, patience, strength and endurance to go through and come out as pure gold.

Proverbs 3:5-7(NKJV)

"Trust in the Lord with all your heart, and lean not on your own understanding; In all your ways acknowledge Him, and He shall direct your paths. Do not be wise in your own eyes; Fear the Lord and depart from evil."

Natasha K. Ransom is a woman of God, wife, sister, cousin and friend. Whatever God will have me to be. I love to worship and travel. My husband is my heart and my children bless my soul. I aspire to be someone who leaves a mark. This is only the beginning.

My Facebook is natashablessingsransom
My Instagram is blessings2012
My LinkedIn info is https://www.linkedin.com/in/natasha-ransom-41573b73

July 9

Pam Dorsey

Psalms 139:13-14 (NKJV)

"For You formed my inward parts; You covered me in my mother's womb. I will praise You, for I am fearfully and wonderfully made; Marvelous are Your works, and that my soul knows very well."

Today your declaration and affirmation are that you are becoming better daily. Be proud of the woman that you see in the mirror because you have fought to become her. You are Fearfully and Wonderfully made, knitted perfectly in your mother's womb. God handcrafted you into who He wanted you to be and who He needs you to be in this earth! No One can do you like you! You are an Original created by the Originator of all mankind. Embrace All of You! Trust God! Trust You! Trust Your Process! You are Needed and Necessary!

Pamela E. Dorsey was born and raised in Greenville, SC and now resides in Columbia, SC. She is a wife, mother, author, entrepreneur, and speaker. Pam is purposed to help women not only discover their God given purpose, but walk it out Authentically, Boldly & Confidently! At the core of Pam's brand are these three words, Purpose Passion and Life

www.PamDorsey.com
Facebook.com/IAmPamDorsey
Instagram.com/IAmPamDorsey
Twitter.com/IAmPamDorsey
LinkedIn: https://www.linkedin.com/in/pamela-dorsey-80a3a344

July 10
LaShaunda R. Browne

Philippians 4:13
"I can do all things through Christ who strengthens me"

Women we are like a pair of heels, we may be in pain and hurting on the inside but on the outside all you see is the beauty, grace and strength. The strongest strengths that God has given women are to withhold the shaking of walls in their life but they never fall apart. When you are in doubt and your faith is low encourage yourself that you are a woman who is unstoppable, fearless, anointed, confident, and beautiful. God is polishing your heels for empowerment for you to stand tall and proud so that you can walk in your destiny that he has planned for you. This is your turnaround season for an unexpectedly blessing from God. So celebrate your womanhood will all you have overcome and what you are about to gain. You are already blessed beyond belief.

LaShaunda R. Browne
Winston- Salem, NC
lashbrowne@gmail.com

July 11
Mary Davis

Rest in God's Presence

This advice was given to me years ago, and I followed it. I walked into GOD's PRESENCE, battered, bruised, broken, angry, hurt, depressed and confused. I sat in God's presence and I told Him all about my pain, sadness, loneliness, insecurity, bitterness, heartaches, breakups, abuse, suicidal attempts, and depression. It was in God's presence that my healing began and my life began to change. Being in God's presence gave me hope. It helped me affirm the things God said about me. It helped me understand my truth. It helped me understand that despite my brokenness, God still loved me and still had a plan and purpose for my life. I walked into HIS PRESENCE one way; but when I came out! I WAS NOT THE SAME!

Your freedom, your healing, and your deliverance is IN HIS PRESENCE.

Get in GOD'S PRESENCE and grab hold of your freedom!
Mary Davis is a minister, author, and mentor. She is the founder of the Empowered Pearl, an organization that empowers women and girls to live free from the restraints of depression, low self-esteem, abusive relationships and destructive behaviors. She has traveled throughout the metropolitan area and to various international countries sharing her testimony of **Healing, Deliverance, Restoration and Freedom**.

Email: Theempoweredpearl@gmail.com
Facebook: @EmpoweredPearl and @MaryDavis
Website: EmpoweredPearl.com

July 12
Mary ScullyD

FROM FEAR TO FAITH

"For assuredly, I say to you, whoever says to this mountain, 'Be removed and be cast into the sea,' and does not doubt in his heart, but believes that those things he says will be done, he will have whatever he says." **Mark 11:23**

What is that obstacle in front of you that seems so big that it is making you fearful?   Are you facing an illness that is causing you dis-ease? What do you do? Pray. Yes, but instead of saying "God, please heal me," do what Jesus said in this verse. Speak to your mountain and command it to go! Do not doubt. Hold on until you receive your healing. This is faith! When you truly believe in Jesus and take Him at His Word, you can live the abundant life He promised you. You can move from fear to faith!

Mary ScullyD is passionate about empowering women of faith to know their identity and authority in Jesus Christ, so that they can experience total healing and enjoy a healthy and fulfilling life. When she was diagnosed with breast cancer in 2016, Mary refused chemotherapy and surgery. Instead, she trusted God fully for her healing and has been walking victoriously, by His miraculous power and grace.

www.facebook.com/MaryScullyD

July 13
Keisha Boatwright

So, I like what I see when I'm looking at me
When I'm walking past the mirror
No stress through the night, at a time in my life
Ain't worried about if you feel it
Got my head on straight, I got my mind right
I ain't gonna let you kill it
You see I wouldn't change my life, my life's just" – Mary J. Blige

Know that loving yourself first is not an option it's a must. Know that it matters what you tell yourself your heart is listening. Give yourself permission to embrace your flaws because are enough. There are some things you can't do by yourself, stop and ask for help when necessary. Live life to the fullest by taking some chances. All that to say it's perfectly fine to love yourself unconditionally and to be unapologetic. People will have their opinions but you don't have to feed into. Silence speaks volume but know the power of hearing your voice. Most importantly breathe.

Keisha Boatwright also known as "Kesh" is a native of Newark, New Jersey. She attended Rutgers University in New Brunswick, New Jersey as an engineering major prior to entering the military. Kesh is a fourteen-year Navy Veteran.

Kesh is a certified Yoga instructor. She completed 200hr YTT in 2017 at Yoga Mindset in High Point, NC.

Kesh is also an author writing her first short story.; "The Meet and Greet" in 2015 which was published in Short Fiction Break literary magazine and co-author of Unleashed Travails - from Pain to Purpose.

Kesh a mother of three and GiGi to one grandchild currently in NC; splits her spare time between writing, teaching yoga or crafting.

<u>SOCIAL MEDIA:</u>
Facebook: soulistickesh
               kreativitybykesh

Instagram: soulistickesh
               kreativitybykesh

Twitter: MzKeshNJ

<u>WEBSITE:</u>
www.soulistickesh.com
www.mzkesh.wordpress.com

July 14
Rosalind Jones

"Does your life need some pruning?"
John 15

Continuing His parting words to His friends, Jesus explains that the way to stay connected to God is by following His example. He also warns that they will be hated and misunderstood. Pruning is the process of cutting limbs from a plant to keep it healthy and productive. If there are branches that are not producing any fruit, they will be cut off completely. As we follow Jesus, we also require pruning in order to grow and change. Love is a fruit. Patience, kindness, gentleness, joy, faithfulness, goodness, and self-control are all fruits of the Holy Spirit (Galatians 5:22–23). These characteristics are evident in people who are connected to Jesus, the vine.

What others see is a reflection of what's going on inside of us. As a follower of Jesus, others should see fruit in your life. If you are not seeing fruit in your life, maybe it's time to connect with Jesus. Get connected to the source that will give you abundant life and produce that fruit in you.

"Remain in me, as I also remain in you. No branch can bear fruit by itself; it must remain in the vine. Neither can you bear fruit unless you remain in me" (John 15:4).

If you are in a season of pruning, it is because you are connecting to Jesus. You are growing, you are changing, and Jesus is making you into something more beautiful, something richer and better than what you already are. Jesus is not content with letting you stay the way you are — He wants more for you. He wants the absolute best for your life! 1 Peter 5:7 says, "Cast all your anxiety on Him because He cares for you." Jesus cares for you, and although the process may be painful and uncomfortable, He is not OK with letting you stay where you are when something more beautiful is waiting. Jesus will perfect you because He is concerned for you.

Facebook: Roz Jones **LinkedIn:** Rosalind Jones ladyrosalindjones@gmail.com

July 15
Erica Hicks

Matthew 6:34

"So don't worry about tomorrow, for tomorrow will bring its own worries. Today's trouble is enough for today."

One of the most prominent scriptures of the bible, and why do you think so? I can tell you, because our God is not a God that want you to worry or stress, he wants you to live for today. He has already taken care of tomorrow so its not our job to worry about it. We are to live for today not worry. I love how, if we seek, God will give us all we need to get thru "THIS" day. As for tomorrow, he will give us what we need to get thru THAT day.

Mserica.Hicks@yahoo.com

LinkedIn-https://www.linkedin.com/in/erica-hicks-0106aa174

Facebook-erica.hicks.980

July 16

Terri Sharmaine

Get Up, Get Going

"I press on toward the goal to win the prize for which God has called me heavenward in Christ Jesus." – Philippians 3:14 (NIV)

As my son began to walk at 9 months old. He didn't quit after he fell, he got up and he kept going. You can get up too! When we fall, we focus on our failures. That failure is potentially a blessing in disguise because God has something greater prepared for us. During your prayer time ask God for continued guidance so that you can press on toward the goal and GET UP!

Terri Sharmaine, a Little Rock native, wears many hats. She is a Proud mother, Change Agent, Business Owner, and Servant to name a few. Terri enjoys working with her outreach ministry through social media ministry, hosting empowerment events, hosting and collaborating with health fairs and community outreach seminars. When she is not working her full-time job as an IT Business analyst, Adjunct professor, her new business venture TF Solutions Center, LLC and being a full-time mom. She strives to continue to share positive news and information to help her community through a servant's heart. During her free time, she enjoys reading, writing and spending quality time with her son and family. She strives each day to show her son that all things are possible through Christ, Faith, hard work and determination.

FB: TF Solutions Center, LLC
IG: TeeFloSpeaks
Twitter: TeeFloTweets Website: www.thegoaldiggersblueprint.com

July 17
Lorrie A. Simmons

Psalm 139:14 NIV
"I praise you because I am fearfully and wonderfully made; your works are wonderful; I know that full well."

"I Am Who God Says I Am"

God made us, he shaped us, and formed us in his own image. But somewhere along the way we forget and underestimate our value. Whether it's our first heart break after a bad relationship or even something more sinister like being violated, or taken advantage of, or abused; you are not what happened to you! You are who God says you are. You were sculpted from nothing into something marvelous, glorious, lovely and magnificent in God's eyes. You are beautifully and wonderfully made.

Lorrie A. Simmons a native of Leesburg, began her education at Florida State University with a bachelor's in accounting. She later received a Master's in Accounting and a Master's in Business Administration/Public Administration from University of Phoenix.

A Minister and Accountant for the Christian Worship Center of Central Florida, Kids of Distinction, and serves on the Board for Men of Distinction. Lorrie is the mother of 2 boys. Lorrie is currently the Manager of Accounting & Payroll Systems for the City of Sarasota. Lorrie also has operated her own Accountant business for over 12 years preparing and filing tax returns for individuals and small businesses. Providing training and consultations for non-profit organizations, churches, and those starting their own businesses.

Lorrie began a non-profit organization, Victory Over Violence of FL, Inc in October 2017 due to an overwhelming need to bring awareness of the effects of domestic violence and sexual violence in families within her community. Lorrie has been ministering and mentoring for over 22 years. A survivor and overcomer of both sexual violence and domestic violence. Her vision is to empower people with education and connect victims to resources, so they can walk in victory over violence one day at a time.

Lorrie1174@gmail.com

July 18
Dr. Mary J. Huntley

DON'T FEAR

"Do not fear, Daniel, for from the first day that you set your heart to understand, and to humble yourself before your God, your words were heard" (Dan. 10:12 NKJV)

Does it seem as if God is taking forever to answer your prayers? Rest assured that you are not alone. Be still and know that HE IS GOD. While waiting remind yourself of the many times He has answered your prayers. Use your past experience to boost your confidence. This will help you to encourage yourself in difficult times. He's done it before and HE WILL do it again. Wait I say on the Lord!

Dr. Mary J. Huntley is the Chief Executive/Encouragement Officer of Trinity Global Empowerment Ministries, Inc. She is also a wife, an international best-selling author, prayer warrior, domestic violence awareness advocate, licensed clinical counselor, clinical supervisor, and certified master life coach. She is on a mission to empower others (especially women) to soar above their challenges and reach their God-given potential.

Website: www.drmaryjhuntley.com
Facebook: DrMaryJ Huntley
Twitter: drmaryj_huntley

July 19
Vernita Stevens

1 Corinthians 16:13-14 (NIV) "Be on your guard; stand firm in the faith; be courageous; be strong. Do everything in love."

Good Morning! Today be on the lookout for what is next in your life and stand firm on understanding. Courageous are those that remain faithful, and your strength lies in confidence knowing that "HE" is with you always.

Today "I WILL"
Lead in Love
Smile until my face is sore
Dance until my feet hurt
Today is my day
I AM COURAGEOUS, I AM A CONQUEROR, I AM UNAPOLOGETICALLY ME!!!

Vernita Stevens is a retired United States Marine, Professional Trainer, Motivational Speaker, and Owner of 2p – Paradigm of Possibilities, LLC. She has a passion for helping others embrace that "ANYTHING IS POSSIBLE". She uses an inspirational approach to convey positive results to empower others to live in health and happiness.

City/State: Huntersville, NC

Email: 2p.paradigmofpossibilities@gmail.com

July 20
Yvette English

Exodus 14:14 NLT "The Lord himself will fight for you; just stay calm."

"God whispers ""I Got You""! Have no worries God is in control always; especially when we do not see the light at the end of the tunnel. God wants us to fully surrender all to him; the good, the bad and the ugly. When things are going wrong and you do not see a way out; the word say (Exodus 14:14) "Just stay calm". He wants us to trust Him; without doubt. He will fight for us. What a wonderful thing; all He wants us to do is stay calm and rest assure on our pillowtop faith. I just adore His comfy love!"

Yvette English is a creative writer from New York, NY residing in Philadelphia, PA.

She is sure to captivate an audience with vivid expressions and colorful words. Relatable traits and imaginative descriptions give every character in her story a heartbeat.

Beautiful visions come to her through dreams. Her writing provides strength, inspiration, and motivation to all who welcome the words of Yvette English into their atmosphere.

Website: www.dakotathenovel.com
IG: yvette.english
City/State: Philadelphia, PA
Email: yvetteenglish.ye@gmail.com

July 21
Johnnia Mitchell

Psalm 121:1. "I lift my eyes to the Hills from whence cometh my help"

I say Trust that is a big word. When life is so stressful trying to build a business, run a household, be a wife, being a Beacon light in your grandchildren lives and just life. Sometimes illness comes, how you going to meet rent to keep your doors open. We let the small things in life stresses us out. But we forget that God is right there waiting for us knowing ours help is coming from God. But We forget to take a deep breath and look around and realize to be grateful and knowing your Help Cometh from Him. **TRUST!**

My name is Johnnia Mitchell I am a CEO of **just be beautiful natural hair care& hair loss practitioner I have been in the industry for over 20 years I am passionate about serving.my contact information is**
Johnnia.Mitchell@gmail.com

July 22
Fayola Delica

"I can do all things through Christ who strengthens me."
Philippians 4:13, NKJV of The Holy Bible

In life there are challenges and obstacles that "seem" to prevent us from reaching our goals and dreams. However, I would beg to differ as a child of God. We have to believe that without a shadow of doubt that we are more than conquerors, and the greatest example we have of being able to overcome is Jesus Christ (Romans 8:37). Therefore, we already know that God would not set us up to fail no matter how it looks. But the secret is that we have to be aligned with the will of God for our lives. Once we realize that then we have the ability to succeed at whatever we seek to accomplish.

Fayola Delica is a native from Miami, FL. She is a Minister, Registered Nurse, Educator, International Award-winning Speaker, International Best-selling Author, Serial Entrepreneur, Beauty Queen, Youth Advocate, and a Community Leader. Ms. Delica is in the process of establishing her five-fold ministry. She is a woman after God's own heart. Her passion is about doing her Heavenly Father's business by advancing the Kingdom of God.

Facebook: www.facebook.com/FayolaDelica
Twitter: @fayoladelica Instagram: @fayoladelicallc
LinkedIn: www.linkedin.com/user/Fayola Delica
W: www.fayoladelica.com
E: info@fayoladelica.com P: 954-562-7706

July 23
Temitope Oyewole

A timely intervention saved a couple from shame at their wedding. Situations may arise out of no fault of ours or as a result of what we have failed to do well. In this situation, the couple made provision for wine, but at some point, in the party, the wine finished. This could be an aftermath of improper planning or just a case of uninvited guests showing up. Whichever is the case, there was a timely intervention. Not only was there wine to serve the guests, the best of wine was available to drink! A timely intervention from God is going to happen over that matter! Just make sure God is invited.

John 2: 10- "and said, "Everyone brings the choice wine first and then the cheaper wine after the guests have had too much to drink; but you have saved the best till now."

Temitope Oyewole is a UK based published author and Gospel Movie Producer. She is the founder of Beauty Makers Academy, an institution to raise and empower women to adorn the world with God's beauty. She also runs a brand story studio. She is married and blessed with children.

SOCIAL MEDIA TAGS/ WEBSITES: http://www.beautymakersacademy.com, http://www.temitopeoyewoleblog.com, https://www.instagram.com/temi0ye/ https://www.instagram.com/beauty_makers_academy/

topeibikunle@yahoo.com

HE IS YOUR PROTECTOR (Summary 2 of 2)

"God is our refuge and strength, a very present help in trouble"- Psalm 46:1

Let God lead you step by step through this day so that you can walk along dangerous paths without being afraid while relaxing and enjoying the adventure of your journey together because His Sovereign Presence protects you. Release your worries into God's care while resting in the knowledge that He is taking care of you and all that concerns you so that you can relax in His Presence finding refreshment in the refuge of His everlasting arms.

Rose Hall is a Resourceful, Outgoing, Servant-leading Entrepreneur Motivating and Helping All. She is a faithful wife, loving mother of 4, a Registered Nurse and Health Solutions Expert. She is currently the publisher of the digital newspaper, "Daily Wellness Lifestyle News." She loves God, writing poetry, and encouraging others to GROW to their maximum potential.

Email: askrosehall@gmail.com
Website: www.about.me/rosemhall
Facebook: www.facebook.com/Destinations4u2
Instagram: www.instagram.com/ubhealthe2

July 25
Janelle R. Dawkins

"Rejoice not against me, O mine enemy: when I fall, I shall arise; when I sit in darkness, the Lord shall be a light unto me." Micah 7:8 KJV

You are not exempt from others celebrating your misfortunes and failures. This sort of action can drag us lower than what we already are. Handling this type of negativity appropriately will determine the manner in which you bounce back. God created us to get back up despite our critics and He has created a light within us powerful enough to navigate through any misfortune or failure. Affirm to yourself daily, "I may be down, but don't count me out. I'll be back better than ever." Let God be the light and trust the process. You deserve to win too!

Meet Janelle R. Dawkins, The Resilient Mom Strategist, Life Coach, Author and Speaker who focuses on helping people develop strategies to overcome and face the adversities associated with parenting, work-life balance, relationships and business. This wife, mother and entrepreneur believes you can overcome any obstacle through strategy, faith and determination.

Facebook: @Janelle Sampson Dawkins
Instagram: Janelle Dawkins
Periscope: @JanelleDawkins
Email: janelle@theresilientmomstrategist.com
www.theresilientmomstrategist.com

City: Onancock, VA

July 26
Nichelle B. Crump

John 7:38 (KJV) "He that believeth on me, as the scripture hath said, out of his belly shall flow rivers of living water."

If you give birth to what's inside of you, what's inside of you will save you! You are an incubator of LIFE....life filled with desire, purpose, passion, vision, strength, power, compassion, ideas, knowledge and wisdom (just to name a few). Allowing those attributes to flow creates a ripple effect and brings *JOY INWARDLY*. Water that sits still is stagnate...Water that moves is a catalyst of *LIFE.*

Nichelle B. Crump is a mother of 4 (3 girls/1 son), Business Owner, Personal Trainer, Executive Administrator of a local gym and a Minister of the Gospel. Her commitment and dedication have led her to a successful career; uniquely training the "whole" personal NOT just their physical being. And she does it One Body At A Time.

crumpnichelle06@gmail.com
avesselofhonor14@gmail.com
https://www.facebook.com/nichelle.crump
https://www.instagram.com/vesselsofhonor/

City/State: Burlington, NC

Email: crumpnichelle06@gmail.com

July 27
Majidah "HisGlory" Smith

We all make bad choices that we thought would have good results. Our testimonies of failure can be God's stories of success. God will never waste our pain, our tears and our disappointments. A regret to you may be an opportunity for God to get the Glory out of your life. Don't get stuck in the wilderness. If you invite God into your mess, he will set you free from the bondage and you will walk away victorious instead of a victim.

Romans 8:28 "And we know that all things work together for the good of (Make it personal, insert your name) to them that love God, to them who are called according to his purpose."

Don't be ashamed of who knows your story. Never allow anyone to throw your past, your mistakes back in your face. Repent to God and ask for his forgiveness. The only one who you have to answer to is God. When we make an error and admit to it, it allows God the opportunity to show us who we are and the areas that we need his help in. There is always room in our lives for improvement. So, don't run from God because of shame and guilt. Run to God. He promised to never leave us, and he is waiting with open arms.

Majidah "HisGlory" Smith
Author of God's Gonna Make It Good, A Journey to Forgiveness.
Website: www.mygloriousmajidah.com
Facebook: Author Majidah HisGlory Smith
Instagram and Twitter: HisGlory Majidah
Email: majs827@gmail.com

July 28
LaTashia Prince

Nothing is Impossible the word itself says "I'm Possible" - Audrey Hepburn

Summary: through, adversities comes Strength, with pain builds resilience, with the struggles of life you learn optimism, but with love, courage, confidence & the higher power builds you! It is you and only you that can manifest the destiny of your life, so when you look in the mirror, it is you that must know I am Numero Uno, it is you that must know that I am the winner, it is you that must know any challenges that comes I will defeat it, it is you that must love you, it is you that must know that I do not just exist, but I am and can do the IMPOSSIBLE !

LaTashia Prince is a Devoted Mom who stops at nothing, she was born and raised in Detroit, Michigan and relocated to Atlanta and started her own business. She is the founder of Hearts For Healing LLC in Atlanta, Ga. and plans to release a caregiver book in 2019. LaTashia wants to set an example for everyone around the world that nothing is impossible!! Believe in yourself, "why reach for the stars, when I am the star!"

Website: www.heartsforhealingllc.com
Social media: http://instagram.com/HeartsForHealingLLC
https://www.linkedin.com/in/latashia-prince-74234352
https://m.facebook.com/Hearts-For-Healing-LLC-2032414213659853/
Email: info@heartsforhealingllc.com

Instagram @bundlesbypopulardemand Facebook Bundles by Popular Demand

July 29
Bridget Jackson

Jeremiah 29:11 (NIV) "For I know the plans I have for you", declares the Lord, "Plans to prosper you and not to harm you, plans to give you hope and a future.

I never knew how strong of a woman I was until being strong was the only choice I had. Anyone can give up; it's the easiest thing in the world to do, but to hold it together when everyone would expect you to fall apart is true strength. Sometimes you have to humble yourself, swallow your pride and put your brave face away and break down. Hug someone who loves you just as much as you love them, have a good cry wash out your heart. Perhaps our eyes need to be washed by our tears every once in a while, so that we can see life with a clear view again. Always remember that no matter how hard life gets God has a plan for you!

Bridget Jackson is a Service Coordinator with Arnesta Healthcare of Virginia. Bridget specializes in home health care where she is responsible for complying with all relevant federal, state and local laws in her region. She is a strong believer in the power of positive thinking in the workplace, Bridget regularly executes In-Service training programs and competent supervision to improve employee efficiency and patient care. Bridget liaise with private organizations and patients on behalf of her agency. Bridget is dedicated to helping the community with the proper resources they need to live at home in good health, safety and comfort.

City/State: Meherrin,Virginia Email: bjackson@onediversity.org

July 30

Terri Booker

"The greatest among you will be your servant."-Matthew 23:11

I believe there is a master plan for each of our lives. We each have a unique role in the movie called 'Kingdom Life. I often wonder what part in this movie have I been given to play. This I know for sure, I want to be used by God. Growing up I wanted to be the Star. As I mature, I understand that Jesus is the star and that is as it should be. God uses ordinary people to lead His people. On a number of occasions God changed the characters names to better describe their leadership objective. It seems there is power in a name.

My name means harvester. So today I ask myself, how can I be a harvester for God's Kingdom? How can I play my role with perfection? This scripture reminds me, I must be a servant yes even a servant leader. – TB

Terrie Booker is a wife, mother, entrepreneur, author, realtor, motivational speaker and a renaissance woman in every sense of the word. She is a licensed Realtor and has her MBA. Terrie lent her brilliance as a business leader to Fortune 50 companies before embarking on her own as an entrepreneur. Terrie shares her expertise and empower people to change their financial legacy. Inspired by her love for fashion Terrie has become a Founding Member and B.O.S.S. Brand Ambassador, her motto is," If you have faith the size of a mustard seed you can achieve anything'. Terrie and her husband have two adult children and live in North Carolina.

http://www.beaglamourboss.com/   http://www.premierbeautyshop.com/
Iamterrie@wilsonrealtync.com   Facebook=Terrie   Booker
Instagram=IamTerrieBooker

July 31
Susie Lynnette Sanders

Proverbs 31:24-31 (NIV)

"24 She makes linen garments and sells them, and supplies the merchants with sashes. 25 She is clothed with strength and dignity; she can laugh at the days to come. 26 She speaks with wisdom, and faithful instruction is on her tongue. 27 She watches over the affairs of her household and does not eat the bread of idleness. 28 Her children arise and call her blessed; her husband also, and he praises her: 29 "Many women do noble things, but you surpass them all." 30 Charm is deceptive, and beauty is fleeting; but a woman who fears the LORD is to be praised. 31 Honor her for all that her hands have done, and let her works bring her praise at the city gate."

Strive to be a Proverbs 31 Woman- A Virtuous Woman.

Maintain acts of services to others. Be giving and kind. Maintain your responsibilities. Ask GOD for wisdom and have faith at all times. Use your money and resources of the earth wisely. Have good time management. Special Note: We are not perfect, but we can strive for it at all times.

Susie Lynnette Sanders loves Life! Susie is the owner of Something By Net. A provider of fabulous accessories and gift items. She has worked several years in the pharmaceutical industry and the telecommunications industry. She enjoys working with people. Susie is a woman of God, who loves her family, music, reading, traveling, and making people smile.
Website: www.SomethingByNet.com Facebook: www.facebook.com/SomethingByNet
Instagram: www.instagram.com/somethingbynet
Email: SomethingByNet@gmail.com Facebook: @Susie Lynnette Sanders
www.linkedin.com/in/susiesanders10
SomethingByNet@gmail.com

August 1
Andrea Maine

PSALMS 34:4

"I SOUGHT THE LORD, AND HE ANSWERED ME, AND DELIVERED ME FROM MY FEARS"

Often times we go through things in life that cause extenuating circumstances in our lives and we find ourselves wanting to give up and throw in the towel…. I just wanted to take an opportunity to remind you that God never leaves us nor forsakes us and HE knows all about our troubles. We need to allow God to fight our battles and guide us to our victories. We go through "seasons" and some seasons will be tougher and more demanding than others but you can handle IT… remember "God Gives HIS toughest battles to HIS strongest Soldiers" You can get through "IT", whatever your "IT" is. STAY ENCOURAGED!!!

At the tender age of 32 I was dealt a blow that I thought I could never bounce back from; at 32 I was diagnosed with Stage II Ductal Carcinoma Breast Cancer and I questioned God, "WHY ME!!" and I heard a small voice answer "WHY NOT YOU" I accepted my diagnosis and I leaned on God for strength and comfort and He answered my call. Although I fought two battles with breast cancer, I never lost my faith in HIM, because I truly believe that HE chose me…. because HE knew I could handle it and be a testimony for someone else.

Facebook: Andrea Maine   Email: spellbnd@gmail.com

August 2
Latonya L. Turner

"Believe in yourself, so others believe in you too".

Wake up each morning and thank God for this day. Look in the mirror and tell yourself I love you, smile and give yourself a huge. Say three thing positive things about yourself for example: I am beautiful, I am blessed and highly favored, I am smart, and you are can continue as much as you like. Once you finish walk in your place of business are where you need to go walk with confident, boldness and know that you are ready to serve the people with full confident in what you are giving.

My name is LaTonya L. Turner I am the founder and president of Executive Three Consulting Firm in 1995 and have served companies and Individuals from around the state of Georgia, which I am a native of Atlanta. I am a single mother of three beautiful children and working to leave a legacy for them.

I have served clients ranging from Individuals as well as Small Business owners to making their business a profitable success. With my education background includes a Bachelor of Management (BA), Accounting and Finance (MBA). With their Accounting Principle, Communication, Management, Leadership needs to assist in growth of the organization. My experiences include government as well private sector. In these organization as Account Manager, Budget and Financial Analyst. As Minority Business Enterprise (MBE), we strive to exceed each and every clients' expectations. We help clients succeed today...and educate them to plan.

August 3
Minister Taneshia Curry

Jeremiah 29:11 (NIV)

"For I know the plans I have for you," declares the Lord, "plans to prosper you and not harm you, plans to give you hope and a future."

Philippians 4:13 (KJV) "I can do all things through Christ which strengtheneth me."

Galatians 6:9 (NLT) "So let's not get tired of doing what is good. At just the right time we will reap a harvest of blessing if we don't give up."
"Quitting is NOT an option!"

Even Jesus came close to quitting in the Garden of Gethsemane knowing what He was about to face. But He found strength from within and cried out to God, His Father, "Nevertheless!" As we navigate through life and find ourselves facing situations that seem so overwhelming, we must push pass our flesh and get to the NEVERTHELESS! Cry out to God, Your Father... He will help you. Keep pressing forward because quitting for you is NOT an Option!

Taneshia Curry, a native of Altoona, PA, now a resident in Maryland was licensed as a Minister under the Mt. Calvary Holy Churches of America, Inc. in Washington, DC. Taneshia is an anointed psalmist, worship leader and professional singer. She was recently appointed to serve as the Minister of Worship at The Voice Church, in Laurel, MD. Minister Curry is an Amazon Best-Selling Author through her contribution in "Faith for Fiery Trials". An advocate for single parents, she herself is a proud single-mother of two beautiful daughters.

Facebook: Taneshia Curry Instagram: taneshiacurry www.taneshialcurry.com
LinkedIn: Taneshia Curry Email: taneshia.l.curry@gmail.com

August 4

Kierra Si'Mone

"Yet God has made everything beautiful for its own time. He has planted eternity in the human heart, but even so, people cannot see the whole scope of God's work from beginning to end." (Ecclesiastes 3:11)

Have you ever wondered why the Lord created a concept such as time? I never could fathom this until I began to walk into my purpose. I look back at my journey of disappointments, tears, setbacks and even good times and notice that God truly makes all things beautiful in his time. So, to those of you who are wondering God when will I walk in my purpose? Let me say, just go in your next season. In that season, God will continue HIS schedule. The husband will come, the business will begin to take off, and know that the Lord will complete every work in you from the beginning to end. He has made you that promise.

Instagram; KierraSiMone_
Email:Simonespeaks17@gmail.com
Email: simonespeaks17@gmail.com

Kierra Si'Mone is a Certified Life Coach and visionary of Purpose and PowHer. Kierra is from Jacksonville, Florida and best known for her infectious personality, vibrant smile, and compassionate hugs. Graduate of Bethune Cookman University where she received a Bachelor of Arts in Mass Communication and a member of Alpha Kappa Alpha Sorority Inc. Kierra's philosophy is to turn your can't into can and the impossible into possible.

August 5
Trenee' M Fountain

1 Peter: 2:9 "But ye are a chosen people. You are royal priests, a holy nation, God's very own possession. As a result, you can show others the goodness of God, for He called you out of darkness into his wonderful light."

Throughout life's journey, there are several instances when insecurities, circumstances, and society allow you to question your worth. Despite the inaccurate depictions of this word, God have already pronounced His people as royal, chosen, and even peculiar. Therefore, today is the day you realize you weren't placed on this earth randomly. Today is the day you realize WHO you are and WHOSE you are. You were chosen specifically to fulfill His plan. Now allow Gods light to shine through you.

My name is Trenee' M. Fountain and I am a twenty-two-year-old aspiring entrepreneur from Baton Rouge, Louisiana currently residing in the Dallas-Fort Worth Area. My purpose has driven me to pursue my scholastic ambition, dual majoring in Business Marketing and Communication: Advertising and Public Relations. I am determined to make a difference by challenging the mentalities of society's stereotypes and statistics. I deeply cherish the values of my family, culture, and community which have molded me into the woman I am today. My goal is to show young women to not let their circumstances determine their future. I enjoy writing, which is why I started a blog called "She The Boss Blog". I created this blog to inspire girl bosses through all things fashion, beauty, and lifestyle. God is continuously blessing me, and I want to do the same for others. My prayer is that I pursue my purpose by uplifting other women with the knowledge I'm currently gaining throughout my life's journey.

FACEBOOK:@shethebossblog INSTAGRAM:@shethebossblog & @treneemfountain PINTEREST:@shethebossblog

"We are God's workmanship created in Christ Jesus to do good works, which God prepared in advance for us to do." Ephesians 2:10 NIV

You were created to give God glory! God sees you as a priceless treasure. Your value does not come from your achievements or even from how people feel about you. Your value comes from the fact that you are a child of the Most High God. Make the commitment to love yourself how your heavenly Father loves you. Be happy with who God created you to be. There is only one you! God is continuing to shape and mold you. Always remember that you are fearfully and wonderfully made, beloved of God, complete in God, and uniquely designed for success.

Lakeshia Trumaine Robinson is the ultimate Confidence Coach who known for her amazing resilience. Many chapters of her life stole her confidence. She fought to get her confidence and voice back. Her pain fuels her passion to educate, equip, and empower people to walk in their maximum potential.

Email: excelwithlakeshia@gmail.com
https://www.facebook.com/lakeshiatrumainerobinson
https://www.linkedin.com/in/lakeshia-robinson-638498105
https://www.instagram.com/kingdombeautykee/

August 7
Jessie C. Love

Psalm 139:13-14 "For you created my inmost being; you knit me together in my mother's womb. I praise you because I am fearfully and wonderfully made; your works are wonderful; I know that full well."

"Wonderfully Made"

Dear _____,

Always love yourself and behold your beauty.

You were designed with precision and sculpted phenomenally.

God knew you before you came to be.

Out of millions that could have made it, it was you that God wanted to see.

The dimples in your thighs, the moles on your face, you make life better because your aura shifts every space.

God designed you strategically.

Take a look and cherish who you see!

You're a masterpiece!

Today is a new gift.

Rejoice, shine bright, and thrive.

Fearlessly march forth well to add glory to your story.

jesslovenaturally@gmail.com

August 8
Debra Reed, LICSW

Habakkuk 2:2-3
"And the Lord answered me, and said, Write the vision, and make it plain upon tables, that he may run that readeth it. For the vision is yet for an appointed time, but at the end it shall speak and not lie: though it tarry, wait for it; because it will surely come, it will not tarry."

Your miracle is in the making! I encourage you to embrace the vision that God has for your life. Those close to you may not understand and may not support you completely. Remember, God's plan is for YOUR life. What is understood doesn't need to be explained. I am a firm believer that what God has for me is for me. If he said it, it will come to pass!

Debra Reed is a PlanNet Marketing Representing and an Independent Travel Agent. Providing an effective way for people to create entrepreneurship opportunities in the largest industry in the world, TRAVEL.

Ms. Reed also has over 25 years of diversified clinical social work practice offering psychotherapy, supervision, training and consultation. Her areas of expertise include childhood trauma, grief and loss, and domestic violence. Ms. Reed's educational background includes a Bachelor of Science Degree in Health Education and a Master's Degree in Social Work from Howard University.

www.plannetmarketing.com/dfreed88
www.debrareed.inteletravel.com

August 9
Doral Rolle

Philippians 4:19

"But my God shall supply all your need according to his riches in glory by Christ Jesus!"

Have you ever felt like your back was against the wall, and you were going under, and even though you prayed, it looked like the end? You are not alone, I can tell you from personal experience where my husband and I were having a major financial crisis, we began to seek Jehovah Jireh, our provider with all sincerity, and I can tell you that God made a way out of no way, and He opened doors that no man could have opened, and closed doors that no man could close, I truly believe that God is waiting for us to remind him of his promises He has made to us, He is waiting for you to speak his word.

Freeport Grand Bahama, Bahamas
Facebook: Doral Butler-Rolle
Instagram: Doral Butler-Rolle

August 10
Tammy Wilkins

Ephesians 6:12
"For we wrestle not against flesh and blood, but against principalities, against powers, against the rulers of the darkness of this world, against spiritual wickedness in high places."

As we think about what distracts us from the joy of the Lord, prosperity, and good health we usually attach it to an individual. We associate anger, resentment, frustration, and disappointment to who we see rather than what we don't see. The enemy uses this to his advantage when Jesus is the strongest in our lives. He attacks to steal, kill, destroy and distract us from our purpose by using others. Be encouraged, if we continue to be strong in the Lord and the power of His might, we will resist the enemy and he will flee.

Tammy Wilkins | tammyw@foryouconcierge.com | www.foryouconcierge.com

A devoted wife and mother with a love for God's people. I'm a friend, business partner and entrepreneur building relationships through travel as well as an Associate Manager within the pharmaceutical Industry.

August 11
DeShonda Monique Jennings

Philippians 4:13
"I can do all things through Christ which strengthened me" (KJV)

As you face challenges, don't lose sight on the end result. Remember that as long as God is in your life, you will make it. Sometimes you may feel weak or don't know which way to go. You can do it, keep going. Set your daily goals... If you face a challenge or a situation comes up, you may feel it is too much or too hard to keep going. You may even feel weak. Remember that you can do ALL, not some, but ALL things through Christ. Don't stop, keep pushing yourself.

She is the epitome of what a strong wife, mother, daughter, grandmother and woman of faith is. She grew up in a small rural town of Kenbridge, VA. She serves as an advocate for children and a mentor. She is the owner of Save On Travel which offers people discounts on everyday travel at www.DeeJTravel.org

Website: deshondajennings.com
IG: deshonda_j
FB: DeShonda.jennings
Twitter: DeShondaMonique
City/State: Chesterfield, VA
Email: deshondajennings@outlook.com

August 12
Gwendolyn V. Smith

Habakkuk 3:17-19

The Message Bible and The King James Version

Firstly, Habakkuk, absolutely knew how to Praise our GOD. Moreover, one writer said fig tree and the other said cherry, however, all Habakkuk saw was a tree. We must realize that the "housing" or "container" for our Blessing is already in place. In as much as, no fruit on the vine, remember the vine (housing) is in place! In addition, "Oh Glory" I feel a definite leap in my spirit!!!! Good GOD Almighty....We must have a come what May existence, because our GOD, Has The Stage Set, even when we can't physically see it. Instantly, start shouting, the more desolate a situation seems to be, shout and Praise harder. Thusly, like that deer, Habakkuk speaks about and do cartwheels, and wave your hands in the air and dance like you don't care if someone sees you ..." Oh Glory"

Let me stop writing and dance right NOW! Love you and keep Soaring!

Gwen Smith Ministries, River of Live Inc.
FB Gwendolyn V Davis Smith
Email: gwendolyn4718@att.net

August 13
Karmelita Stevans

"But those who trust in the Lord will find new strength. They will soar high on wings like eagles. They will run and not grow weary. They will walk and not faint." Isaiah 40:30 NLT

God chose to compare His trust and strength to that of an Eagle. The special thing about an Eagle is they don't mix with other birds and fly higher than any other bird. Eagle wings are so strong and wide that instead of seeking shelter from the storm it flies into the storm allowing the storm to lift it higher. When you trust in God there is no other direction to go but UP, taking you above what you are facing in life. Trusting in God elevates you higher than your current situation. You can guarantee that trusting in God gives you strength to face the chaos that seems to be tearing your whole world apart. Trusting in God allows you to see adversity and know there's hope in the end. Do not faint beloved, look at your mountain and command it to move through your faith and trust in God.

Karmelita dedicates her time to educating within Cosmetology schools while imparting into future Beauty Professionals. She continues to educate "beyond the walls" by teaching her clients, mentoring & speaking at seminars.

For more information email hairrehabstudio@gmail.com.

FB: www.facebook.com/hairrehab2014

Instagram: @hairrehab2014

Linkedin: https://www.linkedin.com/in/hair-rehab-studio-98a10884/

August 14
Jacqueline Knowles

Romans 8:28 - "And we know that all things work together for good to those who love the Lord, to those who are called according to His purpose."

To be in the sovereign will of God, means regardless of every situation that happens in our lives, we are confident that if we put our trust in God, it will work for our good and God's Glory.

The plan of God is not to hurt or harm us, but to give us good success. Remember, God is Omniscient and is in control. He is All Knowing. Therefore, He might be saying just wait on My timing.

I believe there is divine purpose for every battle that you may have to fight. We must trust God believing that all things are working together for good to them who love Him.

Jacqueline L. Knowles (Mrs.)
Principal
P. A. C. E.
East Street opposite Deveaux Street
Phone: 356-0943/676-5944

Email: Jackie_Knowles@hotmail.com

"For our light affliction, which is but for a moment, worketh for us a far more exceeding and eternal weight of glory." 2 Corinthians 4:17

I have been fascinated with butterflies for as long as I can remember. It's something majestic about their colorful beauty as they gracefully fly from flower to flower. The graceful beauty displayed however is the result of much inner turmoil and struggle. The morphosis of a butterfly is a crucial process to watch yet it is a very necessary process. The excruciating morphosis of a butterfly creates the beauty, elegance, and grace we all admire while butterfly watching. Isn't it amazing how such a struggle can produce such a victory? So often we pray to forego the struggle, the conflict, the not so good parts of life. But it is through the struggle where we develop the stamina and endurance and patience needed to get to the next level of our purpose. So, the next time you are faced with adversity think of the outcome. Recognize adversity for what it really is and that is an opportunity to grow in your character and further develop into the awesome person Almighty has created you to be.

About Cynthia M. Williams I am the founder of Pink Platoon Empowerment Group. Pink Platoon Empowerment Group is a for profit business with a heart for ministry, outreach, and the office of helps. My main goal is to share empowering information that has helped me overcome a situation or circumstance to other women so they can do the same. I believe what you don't know can and surely will hurt you therefore I've committed myself to a life of personal development and spiritual maturity for advancement in all areas of my life. Currently live in South Georgia with my beautiful daughter, McKenna.

Social media and Contact Info:
Facebook: @PinkPlatoonEmpowers   Instagram: @PinkPlatoonEmpowers
Website: www.PinkPlatoonEmpowers.com Phone Number: 800-811-2618 Email:
Cynthia@PinkPlatoonEmpowers.com

August 16
Chou Hallegra

You Are It!
"I took you from the ends of the earth, from its farthest corners I called you. I said, 'You are my servant'; I have chosen you and have not rejected you."
Isaiah 41:9 NIV

Stop saying, "I don't have what it takes!". There are people who are more talented and who have more experience, but God still called you. YOU ARE IT! God knows what you're made of. He knows your past experiences, present weaknesses, and future mistakes, and He still says, "I've chosen you!"

You're chosen in spite of yourself. Therefore, put the excuses, the fear, the shame, the guilt, and everything else aside. It's time to rise up to your calling. Seize it and embrace it, but most importantly live it out and enjoy every moment of it because YOU ARE IT!

Chou Hallegra is a Board-Certified Christian Counselor and Certified Spiritual Life Coach. She is passionate about helping individuals and families live out the abundant life that is theirs in Christ. Through her writing, speaking, counseling, and coaching, she empowers others to achieve emotional wellness and reach their full potential.
Website: www.graceandhopeconsulting.com
Facebook: https://www.facebook.com/ChouHallegra/
Instagram: https://www.instagram.com/chouhallegra/
Twitter: https://twitter.com/GHConsultingLLC
LinkedIn: https://www.linkedin.com/in/chouhallegra/
Podcast: https://anchor.fm/chouhallegra

August 17
LaTasha Alex

Jeremiah 17: 7
"Blessed is the man that trusted in the Lord, and whose hope the Lord is."

Why do we allow worrying to deter us from reaching our fullest potential? Can you refocus your mind and think about what could be done? I want you to put all your worries away. The Bible tells us not to worry about life or anything else. Take a moment and read, Philippians 4:6-7 KJV, "Be careful for nothing but in everything by prayer and supplication with thanksgiving let your request be known unto God. And the peace of God, which passeth all understandings, shall keep your hearts and your minds through Christ Jesus." Now, Take a deep breath and exhale!!! Enjoy your day

LaTasha was born and raised in Shreveport, LA. She obtained her Associates of Science Degree in Surgical Technology from Southern University at Shreveport and Bachelors of Science Degree in Nursing from Grambling State University. She's a member of Delta Sigma Theta, Inc. She is a woman of God who loves telling others about his works. Her life motto is live your best life because tomorrow is not promised. She's been through many obstacles in life. Her faith in God is what keeps her going, fueled and motivated.

Facebook- Tasha Alex
IG @ohitsjusttasha and @plannernursenmore
http://linkedin.com/in/latasha-alex-b65b2767
Email: latashadalex@yahoo.com, tashada03@gmail.com

August 18
Toni Garvin

Romans 8:1 (NKJV)
"There is therefore now no condemnation to those who are in Christ Jesus, who do not walk according to the flesh, but according to the Spirit."

When you are in Christ, old things have passed away and you become a new creation. You have been washed in the blood of Jesus that covers all of your sins. You receive a pardon and a clean slate. There is no more guilt or shame. You have been freed from the bondage of sin. God loves you so much, when He looks at you doesn't see your past because you have been washed whiter as snow.

Toni is a devoted wife and mother, born and raised in Brooklyn, New York, currently living in Denver, Colorado. She is the CEO of Royally Scent LLC. She enjoys spending time with family. She also enjoys cooking and converting everyday recipes to vegan friendly dishes.

Social Media/Website

Facebook: www.facebook.com/toni.garvin.3

Website: www.royallyscent.com

Email: mstgarvin1@gmail.com

August 19

LaDonna Ann Morgan

"Let it be known, no matter what you face in life, you can overcome, you will overcome and you shall overcome" -Author of book Memories of A Girl Once was by Ann Morgan

When the creator said let there be light, there was light. This shows you the power in the words you speak and thoughts you think. Are you speaking peace, hope, and prosperity into your life or are you speaking words of detriment? Take this time now to think on that which is good and hopeful. What you speak and think on most you create. So, I encourage you to speak words of power and optimism over your life. If life is good be thankful and keep thinking on those good things, if life is not so good start speaking the change you seek into existence now.

Email: lamorganann@gmail.com

Location: Goldsboro, North Carolina

August 20
Theresa Head

Matthew 9:37 "Jesus talks to his disciples The harvest is so great, but the workers are so few. So, pray to the Lord who is in charge of the harvest, ask him to send out more workers for his fields."

We all have a purpose that was given for us to do. Are you do it and sharing with others to help encourage them?

I am the CEO of Head Art Works family business. I am a wife, mother and grandmother. I have a bachelor's degree in business management. I also am a legal secretary, medical assistant and Emergency Medical Technician. We make scented hand craft items.

Website- http://www.headartworks.online
Social Media- Head Art Works- Facebook,
Instagram- Twitter- Pintress- LinkedIn

headartworks@gmail.com

August 21
Rachel E. Bills

Woman of Virtue Arise Scripture:

Proverbs 31:1 " Who can find a virtuous woman? For her price is far above rubies."

You're not accepted by many. A Woman of Virtue has strength that is intimating. You're not easily understood. A Woman of Virtue actions are guided by God and therefore misunderstood. You're judged and criticized. A Woman of Virtue leans on God depends for things she needs instead of friends and family. You're different and don't fit in. A Woman of Virtue was not created to fit in, but to stand out. You may have experienced scrutiny from other (peers, colleagues, even those closest to you). This is because you are a woman after God's own heart. If they talk about you, let them talk. DO NOT underestimate who you are or who's you are. You were created in the image of God, beautifully and wonderfully. You must tell yourself that and believe it regardless of your current situation. God will be there for you because he promises never to leave nor forsake you. Now, go be the Woman of Virtue Go created you to be!

Rachel E. Bills is a native of the Bay Area, born and raised in Pittsburg, California. Rachel has worked in the administrative field for over 20 years and in the counseling field for about ten years, which includes mental health, addictive and Christian counseling. Rachel holds a Bachelor of Science in Business Management and a Master's in Counseling/Marriage & Family Therapy. She is currently a registered Marriage and Family Therapist Intern in the state of California.

Rachel is also the Founder and Director of Women of Virtue Organization, an organization designed to improve the health and wellness of women, children and their families. She believes the organization to be a divinely appointed assignment to serve the community by helping those in need to reach their full potential. She refers to the Power for 4-E's, Educate, Equip, Empower and Encourage as the key to help accomplish the mission of Women of Virtue and refers to herself as the "The Motivator". Rachel has experienced many trials and hardship and is a survivor of depression, low self-esteem and anxiety. But she explains that it is through those very experiences, she is able and determined to help women who are currently facing or who are recovering from similar circumstances.

Rachel is a Transformational Strategist and has launched her per mentoring business where she can help women, who desire one-on-one coaching, to live their best life as God intended.

Bus Phn: (916) 399-3413
Email: womenovorg@gmail.com
Instagram: instagram.com/rachelebillswov
Facebook: facebook.com/wovorg
Facebook: facebook.com/rachelebillswov

August 22
Cheryl Kehl

Psalms 48:5 "God is within her she will not fail."

Living in a world full of negativity makes it hard to believe that we are everything God intended us to be. We look down on ourselves when things are not always perfect the first time. I studied business administration in college and learned that so many successful people failed many times before getting it right. I remember growing up being raised by my grandparents and thinking that nothing was every right for me. I was given away by my mother to my grandparents to raise so I thought from the start I was a failure. I was a secret child of my father's only being known as his child in a small circle of family. This made it very hard for me to believe that life could only be less than perfect. Once I accepted the Lord as my personal savior the failure mentality still remained a strong hold in my life until the age of 53.

Once I really started understanding that God is my real Father and that He is in control of my life my thoughts began to change. I really started believing that I was fearfully and wonderfully made. God is the Master Creator and he has a plan for my life. My plans may not always go as I want them but God's plans are always at work. My life is not my own and God will never be a failure so how could I if I am walking and carrying out His plan for my life. See yourself as God sees you. Lift up your head and understand that God's plan for you is perfect. Once we allow the Holy Spirit to dwell in us and direct our paths in all areas of our lives, we can see that failure is not an option. Woman of God walk in your purpose. Your purpose that God has for you is more than a success it is designed to make God shine through you and cause others to want what is inside of you.

Failure is not an option for those walking in the will of God. So many times, we believe the lies of the enemy. God has fearfully and wonderfully made us in His image. When we look and act like our Heavenly Father there can be no failure present. God cannot failure so you cannot fail while in His presence. I have had May ups and downs in my life but have come to the conclusion that the God is me is always winning.

Cheryl received the Lord as her personal savior at the tender age of 13. Originally from Trenton, NJ she now resides in Jacksonville, FL. She is very active in ministry. Wife of John Kehl and mother of 6 Children with 10 grandchildren. She is an ordained minister and operates four businesses currently. She loves the Lord and His people.

Cheryl can be found on Facebook at www.Facebok.com/Cheryl.kehl.1

Email: cherylkehl@gmail.com

August 23
Pastor Tangela P. Lane

Luke 8:43-48 New King James Version (NKJV)
43 Now a woman, having a flow of blood for twelve years, who had spent all her livelihood on physicians and could not be healed by any, 44 came from behind and touched the border of His garment. And immediately her flow of blood stopped. 45 And Jesus said, "Who touched Me? "When all denied it, Peter [a]and those with him said, "Master, the multitudes throng and press You, [b]and You say, 'Who touched Me?' " 46 But Jesus said, "Somebody touched Me, for I perceived power going out from Me." 47 Now when the woman saw that she was not hidden, she came trembling; and falling down before Him, she declared to Him in the presence of all the people the reason she had touched Him and how she was healed immediately. 48 And He said to her, "Daughter, [c]be of good cheer; your faith has made you well. Go in peace."

Like this woman, we are often only identified by our issue, our problem, our habit, or our addiction. We search for answers from our friends, family, church members, doctors, and even our pastors. Only to find out that their solution, is not the answer we are looking for. We go to every extreme attempting to solve what we consider a problem that no man can solve. BUT that's the key, no man can solve your problem. The true problem solver is God. He knows what we are going through before we even go through it. We have to make up our mind and have a determined spirit that we are pressing forward, reaching out to touch the One that has all power and is all powerful. It is He that gave sight to the blind and made the lame man walk. It is He that can turn your pain into purpose, your hurt into hallelujah, and your worry into worship. Today stretch forth your hand to touch his hem and you will surely touch Him.

First of all, Tangela Phillips-Lane is a woman of God. She is the Pastor of Mt. Zion Missionary Baptist Church in Mt. Ulla, NC. A wife, a mother of 3 daughters, and a grandmother. Pastor Lane accepted the call into ministry in 2010 and delivered her initial sermon on September 30, 2012. She is also a licensed nursing home administrator, licensed assisted living administrator as well as a BSN, RN. She has a heart for the youth and seniors. Pastor Lane is a member and secretary of Women In Progress, owner and CEO of NuVision Travels.

Contact Information: nurse23rcc@gmail.com, pastorlane1765@gmail.com, nuvisiontravels@gmail.com

"For assuredly, I say to you, whoever says to this mountain, 'Be removed and be cast into the sea,' and does not doubt in his heart, but believes that those things he says will be done, he will have whatever he says." Mark 11:23 (NKJV)

You are powerful beyond measure and the words you speak have the ability to lead you victoriously into the Promised Land or tragically derail your future into turmoil and bondage. Boldly declare that all of the promises of God over your life are yes and amen. Nothing is impossible for you! Use your words coupled with consistent and corresponding action to take you from where you are to where He has called and positioned you to be. You have greatness dwelling on the inside of you. Speak to the mountains in your life and command them to be removed.

Sayra Kohen is a home-based business entrepreneur, lifestyle design strategist, and success coach. She specializes in helping ordinary people get extraordinary results using simple step by step systems. Sayra is a revolutionary voice in a failing world system that is equipping men and women to break free from the status qou and live the life of their dreams!

Phone: 623.533.8788 Email: sk@sayrakohen.org
Website: www.SayraKohen.org
Facebook: https://www.facebook.com/SayraHKohen
Instagram: https://www.instagram.com/sayrakohen/
Twitter: https://twitter.com/sayrakohen
Pinterest: https://www.pinterest.com/sayrakohen/
LinkedIn: https://www.linkedin.com/in/sayrakohen/

August 25

Alonya Moore

2 Corinthians 12:9 -"But he said to me, "My grace is sufficient for you, for my power is made perfect in weakness." Therefore, I will boast all the more gladly of my weaknesses, so that the power of Christ may rest upon me."

People! I beg of you to please understand, because we are here with a profound purpose in life. Don't forget! You have a guided light within you even at your weakest point. When you feel that there is no return, no way out of darkness and your mind is congested with confusion. Remember to pull deep, because it's just an obstacle, meant for you to overcome and be strengthened. If you just hold on, there is light right around the corner. So, stay strong! Because God's grace and mercy is sufficient, and he is always on time ready to prepare you for your next level.

August 26

Dr. Marie O. Etienne

How do you discern whether you are walking in God's path?

"Now to each one the manifestation of the Spirit is given for the common good. To one there is given through the Spirit a message of wisdom, to another a message of knowledge by means of the same Spirit, to another faith by the same Spirit, to another gifts of healing by that one Spirit, to another miraculous powers, to another prophecy, to another distinguishing between spirits, to another speaking in different kinds of tongues, and to still another the interpretation of tongues. All these are the work of one and the same Spirit, and he distributes them to each one, just as he determines."
1 Corinthians 12:7-11, NIV

God has given us spiritual gifts for a reason. Those gifts given by the Holy Spirit that are stirring up inside of you should draw you to doing God's will for your life. When we use our gifts in the right perspective, we inspire others to live out their lives with divine purpose. Also, when in tune with the proper use of your God given gifts, you are able to impact the lives of people everywhere. That's why we should not be envious of others, especially as women, because each of us are special vehicles in the kingdom of God.

Dr. Marie O. Etienne, PhD (Hon) in Ministry Education, DNP, APRN, PLNC. Dr. Etienne is a full tenured Professor of Nursing at a local college. She is a mother, wife, a community advocate, and loves to serve God's people. She has a gift of inspiring others to be change makers and social innovators.

LinkedIn: Dr. Marie O. Etienne
W: www.drmarieetienne.com E: info@drmarieetienne.com
P: 305-731-7976 Email: Metienne777@icloud.com

August 27
Brenda Welch

"Let us not become weary in doing good, for at the proper time we will reap a harvest if we do not give up" Galatians 6:9

Do not grown weary in doing good. When your inner self says "this is so unfair"! and you feel your efforts aren't appreciated, and negative thoughts pull you down, think of Galatians 6:9. When you hear the whispers "what is the point"? remember "for a due season we shall reap" and know to be patient. Do not give up, for that is the place and time your situation will turn.... It does not matter how slowly you go as long as you do not stop. Never stop dreaming, Never stop believing. The seeds we sow are powerful, something good is happening even if we suffer initially. We WILL reap a harvest in God's perfect timing, in His "due season" Don't give up!

Brenda, born/raised and currently reside in Cleveland, Ohio. Loving wife, mother, grandmother of six. Brenda is a Realtor, Notary Public and Entrepreneur. Brenda has decided to use her trials and tribulations to encourage women to follow their dreams of home & business ownership by sharing her story of resilience to overcome brokenness. Her family are her number one priority, and her drive for life is greatly inspired by them.

website: choicesivlife.com

Facebook: facebook.com/brenda.bates.52

facebook.com/Choices-IV-Life-1826394707487886/

August 28
Dr. Vernita Roach

Psalm 27:10

"When my father and mother forsake the Lord will take me up."

At the passing of my mom I was six. A presence came upon me that I knew not. At seven, I came to know the Lord. A special anointing was released upon me. He never let go. Much later in the fieriest trial of my life everything given was taken. Enduring persecution, hatred, rejection, sickness and death of a child. The enemy said God has left you. I ran in the secret place not to family. And he saturated me with his Glory. So, when he come, I shall know him for I shall be as he is.

Dr Vernita Roach, motivate others on her radio/tv show "Health Matters & More on the secrets of longevity by use of Natural Health. And through her personal life changing revelation by God people are impacted, and empowered to embrace change and succeed in their everyday life and fulfill their purpose they are destined to do.

pastorvernita@gmail.com

August 29
Brenda Colter

We all experience moments when we just don't feel good enough. Much too often, we allow the thoughts and opinions of others govern the way we assess ourselves. Today I pray that you know that no matter your failings or shortcomings... you are one of a kind! You are beautiful, you are loved and you are blessed with something that God wanted to give to no one besides YOU! That thing is called Purpose. Seek it, live it and love it.

"But the Lord said unto Samuel, Look not on his countenance, or on the height of his stature; because I have refused him: for the Lord seeth not as man seeth; for man looketh on the outward appearance, but the Lord looketh on the heart."
1 Samuel 16:7 KJV

HER Beautiful Mind merges Brenda's role as life coach, mentor and public speaker with the Word of God to present it in a way that makes it clear and practical to others. Her mission is to show the world that no matter where you've come from, no matter how you've been burned, it's always possible to rise up from the ashes and begin anew.

Facebook: @HERBeautifulMind220
IG: @HERBeautifulMind220
Twitter: @HER_BeauMind220
Website: brendacolter.com
Email: info@herbeautifulmind220.com

August 30

Keyuna Faye Webster

"Empowerment for the Powerless"

"Yea though I walk through the valley of the shadow of death, I will fear no evil; for thou art with me; thy rod and thy staff, they comfort me".
–Psalm 23:4

No matter what you are up against, or what you may go through in this life always remember that GOD is with you. You don't have to allow rock bottom to control you or stop you. Don't hold your head down, instead look up to the hills for which come your help, says the Lord.

Imagine a future greater than your past, where you've gone through the worst and still your dreams manifested in spite of. The enemy comes to kill and destroy but take the lessons learned and eventually it will all start to make sense. The suffering will soon end so peace can and will begin. You are much closer to your breakthrough than you may realize. The life you envision is close keep your head held high, push your shoulders back, and keep giving GOD the glory through prayer, praise, and worship. I am Keyuna Faye Webster "Empowerment for the Powerless".

"Empowerment for the Powerless"

Founder/Executive Director/CEO of LoveYuna Outreach, Inc.

Owner, Kay's Kakes and Georgia Anger Academy

Respected businesswoman and community servant Keyuna Faye Webster is on a mission to bring awareness to domestic violence worldwide. By overcoming many horrific experiences, this voice of hope renders empowerment for the powerless. She is God's child, mother, entrepreneur, empowerment speaker, Certified Anger Management Counselor, and Life Skills Management Coach.

Keyuna Faye Webster
"Empowerment for the Powerless"
email: info@keyunafayewebster.org
www.facebook.com/keyunafayewebster
www.instagram.com/keyunafayewebster
LinkedIn: www.linkedin.com/in/keyunafayewebster
Phone: 678.847.4728

LoveYuna Outreach, Inc
"Empowering the Powerless"
Email: info@loveyunaoutreach.org
Web: www.loveyuna.org
FB: @loveyunaoutreachinc
IG: @loveyunaoutreachinc__
Twitter: @loveyunainc

August 31

Sharice Rush

Psalm 34:4-5(KJV) "I sought the Lord, and he heard me and delivered me from all my fears. They looked unto him and were lightened: and their faces were not ashamed."

Today is a new day! Seek the Lord in the good and the bad. He wants to be there to deliver you out of anything that may cause you harm or fear. When you have a conversation with him, he will not only deliver you from any fears but he will continue to lighten your path. Don't be ashamed of your past failures or experiences or even what happened yesterday. God cares all about what you care about and will keep you in peace no matter the situation. Your testimonies of victory will help others to overcome.

Sharice Rush is a Mother, Wife, Author, Entrepreneur, Mentor and Counselor. C.E.O of Sharice Rush Enterprises as well as Signer's Touch of Paparazzi Jewelry. She also serves as a Minister, Youth leader, Prayer Intercessor and Community Outreach Leader for her local church. Among other endeavors she is a Co-Author of Upcoming Book collaboration H.E.R. Extreme Makeover: Reflections of Healing, Equipping and Restoring Life's Messes into Masterpieces. Sharice is a Lover of God and truly has a heart for people.

Email
sharicerush@gmail.com
Social Media
https://www.facebook.com/signerstouchofpaparazzi/
https://www.facebook.com/sharice.rush

September 1
Kiyona Brooks

Matthew 18:21 KJV 21 "Then came Peter to him, and said, Lord, how oft shall my brother sin against me, and I forgive him? till seven times?"

Forgiveness

We have all been wronged and or misused a time or two. It hurts but hurts worse when we are hurt by someone who's close to us. Though we are wired to retaliate, The Most High tells us to forgive our brothers.

I have learned through life lessons that forgiving the offender isn't for them, it is for you. Just as our Father forgives you, you are to forgive your brothers, despite what they've done. Not forgiving only holds you captive. I encourage you to release what they have done, so you can be set free.

Kiyona is a wife, mother and entrepreneur. She is the owner of Voice Voyages Travel, Royal Tax Services and Royal Recruiting Agency. She is known for praising The Most High and her love for family. She lives knowing that you must meet people where they are, not where you believe they ought to be.

FACEBOOK https://www.facebook.com/mashayachqawal
INSTAGRAM https://www.instagram.com/mashayach_qawal/
TWITTER: N/A
LINKEDIN:www.linkedin.com/in/kiyona-alvis-54b35b14

September 2

Nikki Denise

Matthew 19:26 NIV Study Bible (2011). "With GOD all things are Possible".

Jesus looked at him at them and said, with this is impossible, but with GOD all things are possible.

Everything has a time and a season in our lives. However, dont ever give up on yourself, your goals or your dreams because God is always on time. In your planting season you will endure many things but remember that you will never be alone. God will always show up and show out on you each day. When things look impossible to your naked eye understand that it is possible for you today and always. Never mind what others will say or think. In the scripture God reminds you that he looked at them and said with this is impossible but with God all things are possible. Matthews 19:26NIV (2011). Study bible. When faced with adversity that is the primary example of when God is shaping and molding you for greater. Do not ever think that you cannot Win. Because all things Are Possible. "FAITHFULNESS with the strength to believe.

Social media tags: Facebook:Nikkidenise IG: Nikkidenise7

September 3
Chelsea Chase

Rest

"For the Lord God, the One of Israel has said this, "In returning (to me) and rest you shall be saved, In quietness and confident trust is your Strength."
Isaiah 30:15 AMP

I have a tradition of going away by myself every year. My goal is to disconnect from my normal activities and find time to reconnect with God and Myself. This scripture sums it up so clearly for me by reminding me that in returning to God and Rest; we are saved. And that is where we find our strength.

Return my sister HE is waiting!

September 4
Miriam M. Wright

"The biggest adventure you can take is to live the life of your dreams!"
-Oprah Winfrey

Remember when you were A child you had dreams of how you wanted your life to be? Remember the question "what do you wanna be when you grow up?" Are you living that life now? Many people say they try but life happens and they get side tracked.

Dreams cannot become reality without action, take the first step today; everything is possible in this life if you try! Remember the heart of that child and the dream they had. Get started on your adventure trip today, there is no time like the present God bless you on your journey.

Miriam M. Wright
Dream Life Coach/Network Marketing Consultant, Orlando, Florida

www.mmwdreams.com

livingyourdream@mmdreams.com

https://www.facebook.com/wrightwaytoyourdreams/

September 5
Nicole Gaines

2 Kings 4:7 "When she told the man of God what had happened, he said to her, "Now sell the olive oil and pay your debts, and you and your sons can live on what is left over."

I always knew God created me for a greater purpose. I didn't always understand my value. Then the pressures of life forced me recognized that I had the ability to create more wealth for my family. Sometimes Gods allows the pressures of life to squeeze us until we remember that we already possess everything we need to create more.

Do you want more? It's already inside of you. The instructions were written.

1. Use the skills and knowledge you already possess and sell it

2. Pay your debts

3. Live off of what is leftover.

It's your God given responsibility.

Nicole Gaines who is called the "Cashflow Queen." for her business and accounting acumen hails from Detroit, MI. Nicole specializes in helping start-up and small businesses create a solid financial foundation. Nicole is no stranger to entrepreneurship. She is the co-owner of Gaines Construction Services. Her newest entrepreneurial endeavor is Regal Tax Pros, LLC a full-service accounting and tax agency. You can reach Nicole at Nicole.gaines@regaltaxpros.com and 313-952-9099.

September 6
Debbie Tucker

Psalms 100:1-2 "Make a joyful noise unto the Lord, all ye lands. Serve the Lord with gladness: come before His presence with singing."

Arise early every day, giving God praise. Worship Him continually throughout the day. Sing unto Him a new song.

Praising God for what He has done and for what He is going to do shows gratitude and faith that you trust Him.

Your praise can refresh you and has the awesome power to tear down walls. Give God true, genuine praise through singing, zamaring on a musical instrument, lifting up your voice, or in a dance. Praise Him with your life.

He is a mighty God and is worthy of all of the praise!

Debbie Tucker's passion is music, motivating people to walk in their purpose, and sharing God's Word. She has recorded and produced her CD "OH Praise", which can be heard on YouTube her Channel, Debbie Tucker Music Channel. Her mission is to help and serve to make the world a better place.

dtsehguhmusic@gmail.com.

https://www.youtube.com/channel/UCH1LK3WJP8SVkICNX6ik-Xg

September 7
Wyetha Renee Cairns

James 4:7 "Submit yourself therefore to God. Resist the devil and he will flee from you."

Rebuke vs. Submitting. We are encouraged to submit ourselves to God and then we will have the power to RESIST the devil. Even the Archangel Michael in response to Satan's attacks said in Jude 1:9, "...the Lord rebuke you..." So, when attacked by the enemy, submit yourselves to God, obey His Word, put on the full armor of God and stand AGAINST the devil. As Believers of the Lord Jesus Christ, when we submit ourselves to God, we will be equipped and fully empowered to resist the devil. You are more than a conqueror and destined to win EVERY battle, Selah.

Social Media Links: https://www.facebook.com/wyetha.cairns
https://www.linkedin.com/in/wyetha-renee-cairns-993ab9123/
https://www.facebook.com/pearlsofwisdim/ reneecairns@yahoo.com

Wyetha Renee' Cairns resides in Winterville, NC with her husband Jim. Renee' is an Ordained Minister, and is the host of Pearls of Wisdom, a Live Facebook Broadcast. Renee has ministered on countless platforms for over 25 years. She mentors, disciples and serves as a role model for many women desiring to live an on purpose, dedicated Christian life. She is passionate about seeing the Body of Christ living a victorious life in Christ Jesus. Her purpose driven scripture is found in Philippians 3:10 "...That I may know Him, and the power of His resurrection, and the fellowship of His sufferings, being made conformable unto His death..."

Jeremiah 32:27

"Behold, I am the Lord, the God of all flesh: is there anything too hard for me?"

Circumstances will make you think that there's no way out and/or the situation has won. I too have felt this same sentiment and wanted to give up or throw in the towel. Moping around feeling sorry for myself, is what I have done in the past until I found this scripture. This verse has given me so much strength and restores my soul every time I say it. Now I find myself saying the scripture as a question to put things in perspective. I get so much joy when I internalize these words. Rest in knowing that God can handle any situation that we think is impossible. Cast your cares on him for he cares for you. God has your back. Let him do it!

Email:

lynnmeyer616@gmail.com

Just when the caterpillar thought the world was over: it became a butterfly.

Social Media: FB Lynn Meyer & Adrenalynn, IG lynn_is_she

September 9
Sheila E. Morton

Psalm 71:18

"Even when I am old and gray, do not forsake me, my God, till I declare your power to the next generation, your mighty acts to all who are to come."

Purposed Woman: There were times when we cherished the counsel from our elders; the founders and keepers of our heritage. There was a time when we valued their opinion and were esteemed by their spiritual presence in every situation. Through prayer, they guide and protect us. We are their hopes, dreams, possibilities and expectations. For they have been where we yearn to go, seen what we yearn to see. Their truths are more than a moment in time. They are the link that connects us. We honor their names, and we should never forget their wisdom and contribution to our lives.

Sheila Morton is a mother of 4 and grandmother of 14. She is a retired teacher, an online business owner, wife of a retired pastor and active in her woman's ministry at her church. She has her view set on writing more books soon.

Email: smorton28@hotmail.com
Facebook: Sheila Brice-Morton
Facebook: Financial Lifestyle Coach
Website: http://www.iwantitallback.com/

September 10
Latasha WOP Williams

"Choose people who lift you up."   Michelle Obama

Let's be honest, we all have had at least one person in our lives' who was a complete DOWNER. They complained, criticized and argued about the sun and the moon. Regardless of their blessings nothing ever seemed to be right in their lives and they made it a point to sour anyone else's mood. Whoever this person was to you or still is, it's time to start focusing on surrounding yourself with a strong support system.

Find like-minded people who reflect the person you are and who you want to become. Work on dedicating energy to developing and maintaining high-quality healthy relationships. It isn't easy letting go of bad relationships and it doesn't mean you aren't sympathetic. It just means that you now acknowledge that your personal health and growth comes first.

From this moment forward you know your worth and will only allow positive people into your life on PURPOSE.

Latasha "WOP" Williams - Wife, Mother, Daughter, Sister, Friend and The Unapologetically Purposed Woman.

September 11
Charmaine E. Betty-Singleton

2 Kings 4 v 26-28 NASB "IT IS WELL."

When you have lost it all, you can sincerely say "IT IS WELL" knowing that God is the God of the impossible. Last year I was in a car accident, lost my job and did not have a place to call home. I immediately took my cares only to God boldly demanding that He fix it. Many people, not knowing my circumstance, asked me how I was doing, and I merely replied "IT IS WELL". Long story short God fixed it. It is okay to get upset and even angry with God. Why hide it when He knows and sees all? You don't have to tell anyone about the problem, just take it straight to God and plead your case. If you don't know what to say, the Holy Spirit with help you and show you how to trust God, even during your anger. I did not know the how, when or even why, but I knew in my heart that God did not set me on a certain path to fail. I stood on the Word and His promises to me. Trust me, when I say that in brief time, God miraculously turned it around for my good (and God is still working behind the scenes). God is in the miracle working business, what God has done for me He can and will do for you. No matter, what you are going through, you can say "IT IS WELL".

Charmaine E. Betty-Singleton aka CBS, author, advocate, veteran, entrepreneur, attorney, and transformational speaker extraordinaire, is the CEO/Owner of PTK Enterprises LLC, a business focused on supporting other business owners, community activism, and empowering individuals to greatness. Additionally, she is the owner of Victorious Vibes radio station housed on SIBN. Charmaine is an avid lover of God and all people. She attributes her success first to God, and then to her parents and mentors, one of which is the late Dr. Myles Munroe. Charmaine strongly believes that with God ALL things are possible and wishes to "die empty" successfully fulfilling ALL that God has called her to do. Charmaine is a native of Kingston, Jamaica and refers to Queens, New York as home. Charmaine currently lives in Sacramento, California.

You may connect with Charmaine at:
ptkenterprisesllc@gmail.com
https://www.ptkenterprises.com
www.facebook.com/CharmaineBettySingleton

"No one has ever become poor by giving." Anne Frank

What is giving? Giving is freely presenting something to someone without expecting anything in return. Giving can be done monetarily, by performing Random acts of Kindness (Smiling, paying for someone else's meal, Helping the environment by picking up trash), Volunteering (working with non-profit organizations, homeless shelters, or nursing homes) and Donating (giving away clothing that you don't wear, books you don't read, donating blood).

When you think of giving, people look at the size of the gift or the goodness of the cause. But Jesus measures generosity by the condition of the giver's heart. Giving is more than an obligation for followers of Christ; it is an opportunity to lay up treasure that will last for all eternity. Jesus said: 'It is more blessed to give than to receive'. Our attitude in giving matters much more to God than the size of our giving. Giving freely and with a good heart, will never go unrewarded. Don't expect your reward from man; your reward will come from God. Everyone can experience the joy and blessing of generosity; because everyone has something to give. The more you give the more you will receive. Give for the sake of giving and give in secret. God loves a cheerful giver.

Matthew 6:3-4 (NLT) "(3) But when you give to someone in need, don't let your left hand know what your right hand is doing. (4) Give your gifts in private, and your Father, who sees everything, will reward you."

2 Corinthians 9:6-7 (NLT) "(6) Remember this—a farmer who plants only a few seeds will get a small crop. But the one who plants generously will get a generous

crop. (7) You must each decide in your heart how much to give. And don't give reluctantly or in response to pressure. "For God loves a person who gives cheerfully."

Bio: I am Yolanda Sinclair, a Certified Event Planner with over 8 years of experience planning weddings and special events. I am also a travel professional with over 2 years of experience planning and booking travel. I have a Master's Degree in Business Administration with a Concentration in Accounting and have worked as an administrator within several State agencies in North Carolina for over 19 years.

Contact info and Social Media Tags
Yolanda A. Sinclair, MBA CWP, CEP
A Red Carpet Affair, LLC
http://aredcarpetaffairllc.com/
https://www.facebook.com/pg/ARedCarpetAffairllc

http://redcarpetexcursions.traverusglobal.com

September 13
LaTasha Alex

Joshua 1:9 KJV
"Have I not commanded thee? Be strong and of a good courage; be not afraid, neither be thou dismayed: for the Lord thy God is with thee whithersoever thou goest."

Sometimes life takes us through storms that we'll one day understand. Every storm is part our journey. The storms prove our strengths. God knows what you're going through. He promised to bring the good out of the storm. Are you going to shout or question God about the storm raging in your life? I want you to call out to him, uplift his holy name and praise him. After the storm there is always sunshine. Today my sister, I want you to tell your storm that you will win!

LaTasha was born and raised in Shreveport, LA. She obtained her Associates of Science Degree in Surgical Technology from Southern University at Shreveport and Bachelors of Science Degree in Nursing from Grambling State University. She's a member of Delta Sigma Theta, Inc. She is a woman of God who loves telling others about his works. Her life motto is live your best life because tomorrow is not promised. She's been through many obstacles in life. Her faith in God is what keeps her going, fueled and motivated.

Facebook- Tasha Alex
IG @ohitsjusttasha and @plannernursenmore
http://linkedin.com/in/latasha-alex-b65b2767
Email: latashadalex@yahoo.com, tashada03@gmail.com

September 14
M.Latea Newhouse

1 John 1:9 (NKJ)

"If we confess our sins, He is faithful and just to forgive us our sins and to cleanse us from all righteousness."

Have we forgiven ourselves? God has forgiven us and has cleansed us from all unrighteousness. Just Like the cycle of clothes in a washing machine. We also have to go through cleansing cycle. We must go through the necessary steps to properly forgive ourselves. Here are few idea Prayer, Confession, Self-Reflection and Humility can all be the start towards self-forgiveness.

Heavenly Father I pray for every woman struggling towards self-forgiveness. Guide, Lead and Direct us in the steps to receive complete wholeness and self-forgiveness. In Jesus name Amen.

As a woman who has endured yet overcome many obstacles with the Love and Support of God, Prayer, Family and Friends please remember God uses ordinary woman to do extraordinary things. You may reach me @ latea.newhouse@yahoo.com or Facebook under Latea Foreevah Newhouse.

September 15
Donna G. Robinson

James 2:20 NKJV "But do you want to know, O foolish man, that faith without works is dead?"

There is probably some pain that you've endured or some pleasure that you've experienced that leads to your purpose. Some people may feel that the hardest task is discovering it but maybe the most difficult part isn't finding it but executing it. At some point you've got to take a leap of faith and go for it. Stop waiting for your life to become perfect before you start. Just start. Start right where you are with what you have. Remember, faith without works is dead. Stop living a life of death but move and live in your purpose today.

Self-Published Author and Speaker, Donna G. Robinson, spends her time-sharing messages of hope, healing and faith after enduring a traumatic life experience. She has been successful in speaking to others about overcoming trauma, dealing with depression, attending counseling and finding purpose in pain.

Instagram: donnagrobinson
Website: www.donnagrobinson.com
Book: "Courageous and Strong: A Survivor's Story of Hope and Healing"
Email: survivordonnagrobinson@gmail.com

September 16
Edie Price

Upon sitting & reflecting on us as Women, Mothers, Wives, Sisters, Daughters, Aunts, Grandmothers, & Friends. I can only say that we wear many hats throughout our lives. No hat is greater than the other & no pain or heartache is felt any less.

Our strength & determination is Phenomenal. Our strength is not just for ourselves but for our children & families. It allows us to deal with challenges. My question to you ladies is "How do you handle unexpected challenges "?

I gain encouragement & strength from this scripture from:
Philippians 4:13 I CAN DO ALL THINGS THROUGH HIM WHO STRENGTHENS ME

Ms. Edie Price is native of Detroit. She is a loving Mother of one daughter. She is an Entrepreneur in a few Businesses, a Professional in the Automotive Industry. Ms. Price loves the Lord & enjoys helping others. Her goal is to start a Nonprofit organization that helps Single Moms & children.

Connect with me on Social Media:

Facebook - Edie Price
Instagram - Edietravelsprice
LinkedIn - Edie Price

Facebook Business Page - Wholesale Travel and Financial Freedom

Luke 2:52 New King James Version (NKJV)
"And Jesus increased in wisdom and stature, and in favor with God and men."

Every day is a day filled with new opportunities for increase.

What you believe and speak is creating your reality.

Today awake and arise in a spirit of increase, use the most powerful weapon you have your tongue:

Affirm:
I am increasing in favor
I am increasing in knowledge
I am increasing in love
I am increasing in wisdom
I am increasing in stature
I am increasing in wealth
I am in tune with my destiny
I am grateful
I am healthy
I am in direct alignment
I am creating my best life!

Tunda Wannamaker is a mother of two, Speaker Coach and Prophetess. She is passionate about teaching women to face fears, remove blocks, to speak life and step out of their comfort zone. She is the Founder and creator of Nurturing Our Women (now) and Balance Lyfe Coaching.

Email: Tundawan17@gmail.com
Instagram: Www.instagram.com/instabundance
Facebook: https://www.facebook.com/tunda.wannamaker/
LinkedIn: https://www.linkedin.com/in/tunda-wannamaker-98b2bb13/
Twitter: https://twitter.com/TundaWannamaker
Website: https://www.mybalancelyfe.com/

September 18
Pastor Kimberly Hall

"And it came to pass, that, when Elisabeth heard the salutation of Mary, the babe leaped in her womb; and Elisabeth was filled with the Holy Ghost."
Luke 1:41

When the two women pregnant with greatness meet, as soon as Elisabeth hears Mary's voice she is filled with the Holy Spirit and so was her unborn child. The sound of Mary's voice made Elisabeth's baby Leap!

Throughout my life I have had so many great women speak into my destiny and they seem to always have a word or connect with me at the right time!! As women, we need a Mary in our lives who will make our baby leap, ones who will make the vision come alive, or motivate us to become better at what we do! So today, go out and Make another person's baby leap! or pray and ask God to send your Mary to awaken the sleeping Giant on the inside of you!

Facebook- Taskministries

City/State: Wake Forest NC

Email: khall777@live.com

September 19
Kiyona Brooks

Colossians 4:6 KJV

"Let your speech be always with grace, seasoned with salt, that ye may know how ye ought to answer every man."

Check Yourself

My mother would always tell me, "It's not what you say, but how you say it." Once I truly understood the meaning of this, I begin checking myself. I would take deep breaths and think before I opened my mouth. Isn't it amazing how The Most High provides us with instructions to deal with every aspect of life? it changed the way in which I speak to others. Can you imagine walking around always in the I wish somebody would mode? Self-control is vital in our daily walk of life. You cannot get so consumed in emotions and or thoughts that you forget to use your God given power to check yourself.

Make today the first day you check yourself by taking deep breaths, speak slowly and use a softer tone.

Kiyona is a wife, mother and entrepreneur. She is the owner of Voice Voyages Travel, Royal Tax Services and Royal Recruiting Agency. She is known for praising The Most High and her love for family. She lives knowing that you must meet people where they are, not where you believe they ought to be.
FACEBOOK https://www.facebook.com/mashayachqawal
INSTAGRAM *https://www.instagram.com/mashayach_qawal/*
TWITTER: N/A
LINKEDIN:*www.linkedin.com/in/kiyona-alvis-54b35b14*
(ONLY FOR THOSE WHO CHOSE THE OPTION)

September 20
Tamekia Boswell-Taylor

Psalm 46:10 "Be still, and know that I am God: I will be exalted among the heathen. I will be exalted in the earth."

Many times, when we are faced with life's challenges, we want to fix them on our own. We need to come to a place where we are willing to submit ourselves to God and acknowledging that he is in sovereign control. Even in the darkest hour, he never leaves us. Let your fears feed your faith and trust in God Almighty. He is working it out on your behalf. Let Go and Let God Daily reminders: God is Holy, God is Faithful, and God is good all of the time.

Tamekia Boswell-Taylor is the Founder of Sincerely Yours By Tamekia. She believes in giving back in the community and promoting H.O.P. E. "Helping Organizations and People Excel." There is more GOOD to be DONE and Tamekia is the woman to see that it gets done.

- IG: @sincerelyyoursfr

- FB: www.facebook.com/sincerleyyoursfr

- Website: www.sincerelyyoursfr.com

City/State: Fours Oaks, NC

Email: Tamekia@sincerelyyoursfr.com

September 21
Qiana Davis

"I can do all this through him who gives me strength." Philippians 4:13 (NIV)

One of our greatest tests should not keep us in bondage. Through my divorce God showed me how to love myself. There are a lot of women stuck in unhealthy relationships and I encourage you to get out.

As women we tend to lose ourselves when we become a mother or wife. Women we can't have true love until you know how to love yourself. Look in the mirror daily "Look at the beauty God created."

Learn to Love Yourself
Qiana

Qiana Davis, was born September 21, 1981 in Farmville, VA. She was raised in Kenbridge, VA and graduated from Highland Springs High School in 1999. She received her Associates Degree from J. Sargeant Reynolds Community College.

She is the mother of three amazing children: Hoover IV, Asaiah, and Qiair.

Qiana is the owner of Unity Children Learning Center, LLC. and has her own travel company. "Worldwide Travelers 365"

Qiana's energy is a delight and her smile can light up the room. She is the life to any party and truly living her best days. Qiana is determined to fulfill her purpose in life.

Unity Children Learning Center, LLC
804-562-6409
Facebook- Qiana Nicole
Worldwide Travelers 365 www.worldwidetravelers365.com
IG- Worldwide Travelers 365

September 22
Rochelle Redding

Psalm 37:23-24 King James Version (KJV)
"23 The steps of a good man are ordered by the Lord: and he delighteth in his way.24 Though he fall, he shall not be utterly cast down: for the Lord upholdeth him with his hand."

I have learned the hard way that although I am a person of faith, I am not exempt from experiencing difficulties, disappointments and despair. There have been times I have felt damaged and broken, but even in my darkest hours I was reminded that "I am fearfully and wonderfully made". No mistake or shortcoming can ever be too great to stop God's plan for your life. No matter what you have been through, please know that God has a plan and a purpose for your life.

Rochelle Redding is an author, certified life coach, and motivational speaker. She is dedicated to helping women achieve wellness in all aspects of their lives.

Social Media Tags
Facebook – Rochelle Redding Coaching and Consulting
Instagram – Rochelleliveswell
Twitter – RochelleRedding
Website – www.Rochelleliveswell.com
Email – Rochelleliveswell@gmail.com

"The past is a place of reference, not a place of residence; the past is a place of learning, not a place of living." By Roy T. Bennet

I chose this quote because I wanted something that could resonate with anyone and every situation. I wanted to touch deeply the heart of someone in need of a message to uplift, inspire, and comfort them. Sometimes when we're faced with hardships, we tend to blame our past. We tend become so distracted by past situations that we lose focus on what's really important-NOW. By focusing on NOW, we let go of things that no longer serve us. By doing that we discover the most precious gifts life has to offer us NOW.

Precious is a rising entrepreneur and vlogger. She's a former foster child and victim of domestic violence. She enjoys spending time with her five kids, being creative with her hands, and making people smile. Interact her on social media for more details on who she is and collaborations.

Social media tags:

IG@_50shadesofp

https://www.facebook.com/50shadesofp/

https://www.youtube.com/channel/UCdVMjX3wyYA9GiRJSWNdLGA

SnapChat@pbelcher2016

September 24
Kim B. Wells, M.Ed. Pottstown, PA

Jeremiah 29:11 – "For I know the plans I have for you, declares the Lord, plans to prosper you and not harm you, plans to give you hope and a future."

I am the Founder of SISer's In Stilettos. The purpose of this organization is to empower, motivate and encourage women to walk in their "Purpose". This organization encourages a Sisterhood of Women to "Walk in their Destiny" by enjoying life, traveling, and making a difference in our community, wearing Stilettos.

Ladies, I could not have been successfully in life without God's grace, mercy and direction. I have HOPE and FAITH" I can do all things through Christ that strengthens me", and so can you. I am determined to walk it out by empowering, inspiring, uplifting, supporting ALL Women, one pair of Stilettos at a time.

Kim B. Wells is a Women of God who wears high heels, walked up many high mountains and made several detours in the valley wearing my Stilettos. She has been featured in a Christian magazine and hosted Women Conferences globally, encouraging and motivating women to live their best life, wearing their Stilettos.

Social Media
Facebook Kim Wells
Email kimbwells80@yahoo.com

September 25

Genell Aikens

"I can do all things through Christ, which strengtheneth me." Philippians 4:13

Accomplish Goals!

Philippians 4:13 is one of my favorite scriptures. Written by Paul while in prison, this scripture encourages me to believe that any goals I set my mind on can be accomplished. Christ always gives us the necessary strength to overcome the enemy and face our battles. In tough times, He will guide us every step of the way. When parenting, I would often express to my kids that they were just as good as the next person and could achieve their dreams as long as they kept God in their lives. The goals you set are achievable. You have to believe it to receive it and then you shall achieve it!

Genell Aikens was born and raised in Winston-Salem, NC. She's a woman of God, wife, mother, sister, and business owner. She received a BS in Business Administration and a Minor in Religion from Salem College and an MBA in Business Management from Strayer University. She loves studying God's word, traveling, reading, spending quality time with family/friends, and lending a helping hand to those less fortunate.

Facebook:

https://www.facebook.com/Menells-Catering-195798121022061

https://www.facebook.com/MenellsTA

https://www.facebook.com/Menellsessentialoils

https://www.facebook.com/genell.aikens

Instagram:

https://www.intagram.com/nells52

LinkedIn:

https://www.linkedin.com/in/genell-aikens-20208728/

Email address:gaikens@hotmail.com

September 26

Destiny Amanda Johnson

Psalm 136:26 "Give thanks to the God of Heaven, For His lovingkindness (graciousness, mercy, compassion) endures forever"

As an only child, I am always reminded of God's unfailing, unending and constant love through the love my mother has for me. No matter how many times I fail to listen, I disappoint and I make the wrong decisions, she just never seems to love me any less.

Our failures, our missteps and even our inconsistencies do not cause God to change his mind about how much He loves us. Like every parent, He hurts and sometimes He punishes but His Love is and will always remain constant.

Know today, that no matter what you are Loved!!! AMEN.

dajj2591@gmail.com

2 Corinthians 6-18 NIV "And I will be a Father to you, and you will be my sons and daughters, says the Lord Almighty."

I went through life without a Father. I always wondered if my life would have been different for me if he was in my life. I feel that being fatherless affected my life in a great way. I grew up seeing one side of love and it dimmed my vision to recognize real love from a man. I suffered from low self-esteem, rejection and feeling I wasn't pretty enough. I had no positive male in my life to love me and pour into my life and give me direction for my life. Later in life I had to woman up and learn to love and forgive and to love who God created me to be and I had a Heavenly Father that loved me unconditionally. God is my loving Father like no other. In him I was made complete. It's a blessed assurance that our Father God will never leave us nor forsake us.

FB: Beauty4ashes

Email: rountree45@me.com

Teesbeauty4ashes.wixsite.com

September 28
Raquel Hernandez

"I DON'T THINK OF MYSELF AS A POOR DEPRIVED GHETTO GIRL WHO MADE GOOD. I THINK OF MYSELF AS SOMEBODY WHO, FROM AN EARLY AGE, KNEW I WAS RESPONSIBLE FOR MYSELF, AND I HAD TO MAKE GOOD."
~~ OPRAH WINFREY~~

SELF AFFIRMATIONS AND A PROMISE TO YOURSELF!!

- -I APPRECIATE EVERYTHING THAT I HAVE, THE THINGS THAT I DON'T HAVE WILL
- COME SOMEDAY. I AM CAPABLE. I CAN DO THIS, AND I AM EQUIPPED. I AM
- POWERFUL. I CAN DO ANYTHING, BUT NOT EVERYTHING. WHAT I AM DOING IS
- ENOUGH. I AM STRONG. I HAVE SURVIVED SO MANY THINGS TO GET TO WHERE
- I AM. I HAVE RESPONSIBILITY FOR MYSELF, NOT FOR ANYONE ELSE. MY VOICE
- MATTERS. MY OPINION COUNTS. I BELONG HERE AS MUCH AS EVERYONE ELSE.
- I AM JUST WHO I WAS MEANT TO BE AT THIS POINT OF MY LIFE-NO MORE, NO
- LESS. I AM WHOLE, FLAWS AND ALL. I TRUST MYSELF. I FORGIVE EVERYONE

- THAT HAS EVER HURT ME. I AM FREE. I WILL ONLY SURROUND MYSELF WITH
- PEOPLE WHO BRING OUT THE BEST IN ME. I WILL NOT COMPARE MYSELF/MY LIFE
- WITH STRANGERS ON SOCIAL MEDIA. YES, I AM ALLOWED TO SAY "NO" TO OTHERS
- AND "YES" TO MYSELF. I CHOOSE TO BE POSITIVE. I RELEASE MY NEGATIVE
- THOUGHTS, TO CREATE SPACE FOR POSITIVE THINKING AND OPTIMISM. I HAVE THE
- POWER TO CREATE THE LIFE THAT I DESIRE. I CAN. I WILL. I REFUSE TO GIVE UP
- BECAUSE I HAVEN'T TRIED ALL POSSIBLE WAYS YET. I AM PROUD OF MYSELF. I
- BELIEVE IN MYSELF. I AM EXCITED ABOUT THE PERSON I AM BECOMING. I ACCEPT
- MYSELF. THE GREATEST GIFT I CAN GIVE MYSELF IS UNCONDITIONAL LOVE. I AM
- UNIQUE. I AM DIFFERENT IN MY OWN BEAUTIFUL WAY. TODAY, I LET GO OF ALL THAT
- NO LONGER SERVES ME. GOD DIDN'T CREATE US TO HIDE WHO WE REALLY ARE. WHEN
- YOU'RE LIVING IN GODS PURPOSE AND BEIGN YOUR AUTHENTIC SELF, YOU CAN
- FINALLY UNLOCK INNER JOY AND CONTENTMENT. EVERYDAY BE GRATEFUL. HELP
- OTHERS. FORGIVE. LOVE. ALLOW SELF-CARE. MOST IMPORTANTLY PRAY.

RAQUEL HERNANDEZ IS A WIFE AND A MOTHER OF THREE AMAZING KIDS. SHE WAS BORN IN PUERTO RICO. SHE COMES FROM A BIG FAMILY. SHE IS THE YOUNGEST OF 10 SIBLINGS. HER MOTHER BROUGHT HER TO LIVE IN NEW YORK AT THE AGE OF SIX MONTHS OLD. SHE GREW UP POOR AND HAD MANY HARDSHIPS THROUGHOUT HER LIFE. SHE LIVED IN A DOMESTIC AND VIOLENT HOME. SHE STRUGGLED FINDING HERSELF AND TRUSTING ANYONE. THIS DIDN'T STOP HER FROM GRADUATING HIGH SCHOOL OR ATTENDING COLLEGE. SHE MOTIVATED HERSELF AND ALWAYS MOVED FORWARD IN LIFE. REGARDLESS OF THE STRUGGLES, SHE KNEW IN HER HEART THAT LIFE HAD MORE MEANING. SHE THEN FOUND JEHOVAH, GOD. SHE NOW RESIDES IN RALEIGH, NORTH CAROLINA WITH HER SPOUSE AND CHILDREN. SHE IS A CERTIFIED HEALTH COACH. AS A COACH SHE IS A GUIDE AND MENTOR WHO EMPOWERS YOU AND PROVIDES ONGOING SUPPORT SO YOU CAN MAKE SUSTAINABLE CHANGES THAT IMPROVE YOUR HEALTH AND HAPPINESS. SHE LOOKS AT HOW ALL AREAS OF YOUR LIFE ARE CONNECTED. SHE'S DONE LOTS OF SELF DEVELOPMENT, AND CAN GUIDE YOU TOO. MOST IMPORTANTLY, SHE IS A WOMAN OF GOD, LOVES FAMILY AND IS AUTHENTIC AND SINCERE IN ALL ASPECTS OF HER LIFE.

FACEBOOK: http://facebook.com/rockys1life

INSTAGRAM: 1972star and @balancingdailylife

TWITTER: 1972starRaquel

LINKEDIN: linkedin.com/in/raquel-hernandez-a04a3a70

WEBSITE: http://www.balancingdailylife.com/

EMAIL: raquel.hernandez93@yahoo.com

Brigitte Denise Andrews

Beloved Daddy's Girl/Luke 15: 11-32

Beloved, The presence of God is your place of peace. Don't allow the distractions of money, fame or even the popularity of this world lure you away from what or who you love most. When the superficial formalities fade and they will, you may find yourself in the proverbial "pig pen". Just before you succumb to your surroundings, remember Daddy's voice, His abundant supply and His loving touch. It's in that moment when… "you come to yourself"! Running home to Daddy's open arms, He smiles and whispers, "I've been waiting all along, in My presence is where you belong".

Brigitte Denise Andrews
Mother of 3 grown sons
Child and Domestic Abuse Survivor and now an Advocate
Praise & Worship Leader-New Life Interfaith Ministries
Email: bdandrews5@gmail.com

September 30
Wyetha Renee Cairns

Hebrews 4:9-11 "There remaineth therefore a rest to the people of God. For he that is entered into his rest, he also hath ceased from his own works, as God did from his. Let us labor therefore to enter into that rest lest any man fall after the same example of unbelief."

It takes laboring to enter into God's rest, but once there, don't allow anything or anyone to move you from that place. It is awesome to look around and say, "Yep, I see all that is going on, but I am NOT moved by it". In this world we will have trouble, but we are admonished to be of good cheer for Jesus has already overcome every trouble we will ever face. He has given us His peace where we can rest from the burdens and cares of this world. So, sit down my friend and rest, Selah.

Social Media Links: https://www.facebook.com/wyetha.cairns
https://www.linkedin.com/in/wyetha-renee-cairns-993ab9123/
https://www.facebook.com/pearlsofwisdim/ reneecairns@yahoo.com

Wyetha Renee' Cairns resides in Winterville, NC with her husband Jim. Renee' is an Ordained Minister, and is the host of Pearls of Wisdom, a Live Facebook Broadcast. Renee has ministered on countless platforms for over 25 years. She mentors, disciples and serves as a role model for many women desiring to live an on purpose, dedicated Christian life. She is passionate about seeing the Body of Christ living a victorious life in Christ Jesus. Her purpose driven scripture is found in Philippians 3:10 "...That I may know Him, and the power of His resurrection, and the fellowship of His sufferings, being made conformable unto His death..."

October 1

Kiyona Brooks

"Rest and self-care are so important. When you take time to replenish your spirit, it allows you to serve from the overflow. You cannot serve from an empty vessel." – Eleanor Brown

Self -Care

I had an Ah-ha moment when I was reflecting on taking care of my family and friends. I realized that I take care of everyone else better than I take care of myself and give far too many people full access to me. Many of us are suffocating while helping others breath. Be good to yourself first. Stop allowing everyone to gain access of your time and set boundaries. It is not selfish to take some me time. Pencil in some much-needed time for yourself today and everyday moving forward. The more you digress, you will be better equipped to care for everyone else.

Kiyona is a wife, mother and entrepreneur. She is the owner of Voice Voyages Travel, Royal Tax Services and Royal Recruiting Agency. She is known for praising The Most High and her love for family. She lives knowing that you must meet people where they are, not where you believe they ought to be.

FACEBOOK https://www.facebook.com/mashayachqawal

INSTAGRAM *https://www.instagram.com/mashayach_qawal/*

TWITTER: N/A

LINKEDIN:*www.linkedin.com/in/kiyona-alvis-54b35b14*

October 2
Sandra Hardy

1 Chronicles 29:11-12
"11 Thine, O Lord, is the greatness, and the power, and the glory, and the victory, and majesty; for all that is in the heaven and in the earth is thine; thine is the kingdom, O Lord, and thou art exalted as head above all. 12 Both riches and honor come of thee, and reinvest over all; and in thine hand is power and might; and in thine hand it is to make great, and give strength unto all."

There are times when we go through so many challenges in life. Our first response is to try and handle everything without assistance. If we fail or if we succeed the results is credited to ourselves. 1 Chronicles 29:11-12 is a constant reminder to not only give our test and trials to God but that the results will be due to is power and majesty. I get so much comfort knowing God is in control my life!!! Just understanding that nothing you can ever encounter is outside God's control is the peace of God.

Sandra Hardy is the founder of Bootz to Heelz, a retired veteran, a federal employee, and entrepreneur of two multilevel marketing companies. Master's in Human Resources, son Marcus.
Social Media Tags:
www.facebook.com/BZ2HZ
City/State: Raleigh/NC
Email: sandra.hardy44@gmail.com

October 3
Karshena McCain Adkins

Psalm 3:3 New International Version (NIV)
"But you, Lord, are a shield around me, my glory, the One who lifts my head high."

No matter what happens today, or what will happen or has happened, LIFT YOUR HEAD. I remember my mom constantly telling me to not to drop my head. EVER.

You are fearfully and wonderfully made. You are special. God has you in the palm of his hand.

Hold your head HIGH. Be bold. Be confident. BE YOU!

Email Karshenamccainadkins@gmail.com

October 4
Lashawn Farmer

Isaiah 55:11
"So shall my word be that goeth forth out of my mouth: it shall not return into me void, but it shall accomplish that which I please, and it shall prosper in the thing whereto I sent it."

We are often affected by the things people say to us or about us. Words hurt and verbal abuse is just as prevalent as physical abuse. It's time to make a shift in the atmosphere and use our tongues to bring about hope and inspiration. We should make it a mission to pour positivity into everyone we meet. Words of aspiration and divine guidance can reach the heart and soul of a person and give them a desire to make it through the day and plant positive roots into their purpose.

October 5
Lisa-Gaye Richards

Isaiah 40:29 NIV
"He gives strength to the weary and increases the power of the weak"

God will give you strength when you feel overwhelmed by the circumstances of life. Be encouraged that no matter how stressed and pressured you may feel as soon as you cry out to God, He will answer you! He will give you strength when you are weary and increase your power when you are weak. No matter what difficulty you may be experiencing, God is greater than any challenge and He will give you strength to stand strong in your storm. Trust **Him!**

Lisa-Gaye Richards is a Jamaican native who holds a Master's Degree in Child and Adolescent Psychology. She strongly believes that her purpose in life is to be of service to others… She enjoys volunteering and giving back to her community. As a Brand Awareness Ambassador, Lisa-Gaye is passionate about spreading the "Now We No" Mission to young girls and women and a healthy lifestyle. She is a wife and a mother who loves the Lord with all her heart.

EMAIL: leeceg@live.com

SOCIAL MEDIA TAGS: Website: www.easethesuffering.com
FB:
https://www.facebook.com/NowWeNowithLisaGaye/

Instagram:
https://www.instagram.com/r.lisagaye/

October 6
Teresa Robinson

Romans 14: 22 KJV "Hast thou faith? Have it to thyself before God? Happy is he that condemneth not himself in that thing which he alloweth."

Sometimes, God places us in positions in life to make us stronger or to be a testimony unto someone else. As human nature, when something is unfamiliar to us, at times we begin to fear and have doubt. But, I'm here to tell you, fear and doubt is not of God. Do you not trust God enough and believe that what He say he'll do, that its already done? He said that if you have faith the size of a mustard seed, you can say to the mountain move and it shall be done. You must remember when taking any position or whatever the situation may be, you are in control of what you allow in you. Don't doubt nor condemn yourself. Stand firm and you shall do great things.

City: Greenville, SC Facebook: @Teresa Robinson @Sweet & Frosted
@ S.I.S.T.A.S FYC Instagram: ladiit_rachelle Sweetnfrosted
Email: t.rachellerobinson@gmail.com

Teresa R. Robinson is a very outgoing, strong-willed, and loving mother of two. Teresa is also an inspiring author, entrepreneur and owner and founder of Sweet & Frosted Custom Confectioners and Savory Foods LLC and founder of S.I.S.T.A.S. FYC a nonprofit organization encouraging females of all ages to smile and take hold of life. Teresa is a firm believer in Fabienne Fredrickson's quote, "The things you are passionate about are not random. They are you're calling." So, she spends her time encouraging family and others to find something that they love to do and make a difference.

October 7
Latasha "WOP" Williams

Psalm 27:1

"The Lord is my light and my salvation; whom shall I fear? the Lord is the strength of my life; of whom shall I be afraid?"

This is my Favorite Scripture in Its Entirety but this part speaks to my soul daily. Dear Sister Reading This Today, Know that God is there in the darkest of places to illuminate his light of Love; therefore, you don't have to fear anything. He is there to be your Strength when you're weak therefore don't be afraid of what looks challenging or what is unknown. When we put our Faith in God and mix our Works according to our Gifts....We Become Unstoppable. Today My Sister Be Not Afraid God Is With You On Purpose.

Latasha "WOP" Williams - Wife, Mother, Daughter, Sister, Friend and The Unapologetically Purposed Woman.

October 8
Teneisha Robinson

"The cave you fear to enter holds the treasure you seek". Joseph Campbell

Imagine standing on the shore alone, peering through the entrance, and being able to see a flicker of light. You need that light but are afraid to enter. You need the light as a guide, for nourishment. You are not physically bound by anyone or anything, yet, your feet are cemented firmly in place.

What's in your cave? A business? A new relationship; letting go of an old one? Believing in and loving yourself unapologetically? Your feet will follow when you make up your mind that you are ready for bold and courageous action. *Enter. That. Cave.* There's freedom there.

Linkedin.com/in/teneisharobinson Facebook: @msmagnoliacoach
Twitter: @magnoliacoach

Teneisha Robinson is the founder of Magnolia Coaching, LLC; an integrative coaching provider that works with clientele looking to improve interpersonal and professional communication and conflict resolution skills. A native Mississippian, Ms. Robinson, earned her undergraduate degree at Delta State University. She went on to earn her MACR from Bethel University. Currently, Ms. Robinson serves as a coach mentor for LITE Memphis, an entrepreneurial innovation program for high school students. Ms. Robinson also sits on the board of a local fatherhood organization and is co-creator of a small business professional development program. Her education, training, and natural ability for communication contribute to clients being able to create and maintain healthy, vibrant relationships within their families and professions. In her spare time, she loves to read, binge-watch Criminal Minds, travel, and drag her Mom to estate sales.

October 9
Latasha "WOP" Williams

"'Though the mountains be shaken and the hills be removed, yet my unfailing love for you will not be shaken nor my covenant of peace be removed,' says the LORD, who has compassion on you." Isaiah 54:10 (NIV)

I wonder what would happen in our lives if we really lived in the absolute assurance of God's love. I mean, as Christians we know He loves us. We sing the songs, we quote the verses, we wear the T-shirts and we sport the bumper stickers. Yes, God loves us.

I'm not talking about knowing He loves us.

I'm talking about living as if we really believe it. I'm talking about walking confidently in the certainty of God's love even when our feelings beg us not to. I'm talking about training our hearts and our minds to process everything the way God wants us to.

Latasha "WOP" Williams - Wife, Mother, Daughter, Sister, Friend and The Unapologetically Purposed Woman.

October 10
Demetria Burren

Philippians 4:6

Is there something in your life that has you worried? Worry derives from fearing what we cannot control. I used to worry about my daughter when she'd walk home from school, because I couldn't control who had access to her along the way. Philippians 4:6 tells us that God's antidote to worrying is prayer. Prayer places our trust in the one person that can be everywhere at all times and has all power. And He loves us! So, the next time you are tempted to worry, see it as God calling you to trust Him with your life at a new level.

EMAIL: demiburren@gmail.com

Demetria Burren is an IT Support Analyst for a Healthcare IT company and also CEO of Brown Sugar Beauty Supply. She is married to Isaac Burren and has 3 children: Jonathan, Amira and Jackson. Also, she serves Social Media Manager for the Dallas Chapter of Black CEO organization.

SOCIAL MEDIA TAGS: FB and Twitter @demiburren
WEBSITES: www.brownsugarbeautysupply.com

October 11
Candace Wilkerson

You are designed and destined for greatness. Don't be discouraged when others don't believe in your dreams or support your goals. Remember to keep looking up! Look to heels for which cometh your help, and put your trust in God. When you feel like you are sinking, like quick sand, just remember on Christ the solid rock, you will forever stand. David said about him:

"'I saw the Lord always before me.
Because he is at my right hand,
I will not be shaken."
Humble Servant, Candace L. Lynch-Wilkerson, Ed. S

October 12
Theresa Head

"Great minds discuss ideas; average minds discuss events; small minds discuss people. — This is a moving statement, not to conform to being like everyone else."- Eleanor Roosevelt

I am the CEO of Head Art Works family business. I am a wife, mother and grandmother. I have a bachelor's degree in business management. I also am a legal secretary, medical assistant and Emergency Medical Technician. We make scented hand craft items.

Website- http://www.headartworks.online
Social Media- Head Art Works- Facebook,
Instagram- Twitter- Pintress- LinkedIn

headartworks@gmail.com

October 13

Raquel Hernandez

"I, JEHOVAH GOD, AM GRASPING YOUR RIGHT HAND, THE ONE SAYING TO YOU, DO NOT BE AFRAID. I WILL HELP YOU."
ISAIAH 41:13

MY SECRET IS SIMPLE. I PRAY.

YOU ARE NOT READING THIS BY ACCIDENT. EVERYTHING IS GOING TO BE ALRIGHT. THIS IS YOUR CONFIRMATION. JEHOVAH GOD, IS MAKING A WAY FOR YOU RIGHT NOW. "THE PAIN YOU'VE BEEN FEELING, CAN'T COMPARE TO THE JOY THAT'S COMING." YOU ARE NOT ALONE. YOUR PAST DOESN'T DETERMINE YOUR FUTURE. YOU OWE YOURSELF THE LOVE THAT YOU SO FREELY GIVE TO OTHERS. FIRST EMBRACE YOUR PAINS BECAUSE "WHERE THERE IS NO STRUGGLE, THERE IS NO STRENGTH." THIS MEANS YOU HAVE LIVED LIFE. START PRAYING, FORGIVING AND LETTING GO OF EVERYTHING THAT'S HELD YOU BACK. WE ARE NOT WHAT WE'VE BEEN THROUGH.

FORGIVING IS THE BEGINNING OF HAVING A PEACEFUL LIFE. BECOME THE PERSON YOU ARE MEANT TO BE. I APPLAUD YOU IN ADVANCE, BECAUSE I KNOW AFTER READING THIS, YOU HAVE BECOME!! "TRUST IN JEHOVAH WITH ALL YOUR HEART, AND DO NOT RELY ON YOUR OWN UNDERSTANDING. IN ALL YOUR WAYS TAKE NOTICE OF HIM, AND HE WILL MAKE YOUR PATHS STRAIGHT." (PROVERBS 3:5,6)

RAQUEL HERNANDEZ IS A WIFE AND A MOTHER OF THREE AMAZING KIDS. SHE WAS BORN IN PUERTO RICO. SHE COMES FROM A BIG FAMILY. SHE IS THE YOUNGEST OF 10 SIBLINGS. HER MOTHER BROUGHT HER TO LIVE IN NEW YORK AT THE AGE OF SIX MONTHS OLD. SHE GREW UP POOR AND HAD MANY HARDSHIPS THROUGHOUT HER LIFE. SHE LIVED IN A DOMESTIC AND VIOLENT HOME. SHE STRUGGLED FINDING HERSELF AND TRUSTING ANYONE. THIS DIDN'T STOP HER FROM GRADUATING HIGH SCHOOL OR ATTENDING COLLEGE. SHE MOTIVATED HERSELF AND ALWAYS MOVED FORWARD IN LIFE.

REGARDLESS OF THE STRUGGLES, SHE KNEW IN HER HEART THAT LIFE HAD MORE MEANING. SHE THEN FOUND JEHOVAH, GOD. SHE NOW RESIDES IN RALEIGH, NORTH CAROLINA WITH HER SPOUSE AND CHILDREN. SHE IS A CERTIFIED HEALTH COACH. AS A COACH SHE IS A GUIDE AND MENTOR WHO EMPOWERS YOU AND PROVIDES ONGOING SUPPORT SO YOU CAN MAKE SUSTAINABLE CHANGES THAT IMPROVE YOUR HEALTH AND HAPPINESS. SHE LOOKS AT HOW ALL AREAS OF YOUR LIFE ARE CONNECTED. SHE'S DONE LOTS OF SELF DEVELOPMENT, AND CAN GUIDE YOU TOO. MOST IMPORTANTLY, SHE IS A WOMAN OF GOD, LOVES FAMILY AND IS AUTHENTIC AND SINCERE IN ALL ASPECTS OF HER LIFE.

FACEBOOK: http://facebook.com/rockys1life
INSTAGRAM: 1972star and @balancingdailylife
TWITTER: 1972starRaquel
LINKEDIN: linkedin.com/in/raquel-hernandez-a04a3a70
WEBSITE: www.balancingdailylife.com
EMAIL: raquel.hernandez93@yahoo.com

October 14

Tamala Coleman

Hebrews 11:16- "But without faith it is impossible to please him: for he that cometh to God must believe that he is, and that he is a rewarder of them that diligently seek him."

Faith is the substance or the guarantee that those things which you are waiting for will come to pass. Faith is the evidence when we cannot see the Manifestation. Faith begins when you drown your doubts, cast off fear and anchor in the truth.

God is a rewarder of those who diligently seek him. If you don't have grace or deliverance, seek Him again.

https://www.facebook.com/tamala.coleman.1
https://twitter.com/tamala_coleman
https://www.instagram.com/iam_tamalacoleman/
https://www.iheart.com/podcast/966-spiritually-speakin-29260154/

Email: tcpraise14@gmail.com

October 15
Mary Beasley

1 Corinthians 10:13 "No temptation has overtaken you such as is common to man; but God is faithful, who will not allow you to be tempted beyond what you are able, but with the temptation will also make the way of escape, that you may be able to bear it."

A Way of Escape!

When life's situations seem impossible and circumstances overwhelm you to the point you feel there's no way out. Remember this, God is faithful and He has an escape designed just for you! The temptations are nothing new. Someone else is going through just like you. Now this is the best part! With every temptation, God provides a way of escape! Yes! Be encouraged, no matter the test, trial or temptation, hold on! God knows how much you can bear and if you can no longer bear it, He has a way of escape!

Mary Beasley is a Licensed Clinical Pastoral Counselor, Published Author and CEO of LewMar Innovations, we offer Christian counselor's licensing and degree programs. To provide quality training for pastors and mature Christians who feel God's call to counsel and make available credential that the community (Christian and non-Christian) will recognize.

lminow.com
maryb.lewmar@gmail.com

October 16
Rochelle Redding

John 10:10 King James Version (KJV)
"The thief cometh not, but for to steal, and to kill, and to destroy: I am come that they might have life, and that they might have it more abundantly."

There are many times in our lives when we feel as though "All Hell is breaking loose" all around us. You may be going through a divorce, struggling with addiction, experiencing domestic violence, or suffering from depression. But God will use our challenges and difficulties to teach, grow, and even protect us from situations in our lives. Bishop T.D. Jakes often says "There is a blessing in your pressing". We must continue to press on and not grow weary as God will reward our faithfulness.

Rochelle Redding is an author, certified life coach, and motivational speaker. She is dedicated to helping women achieve wellness in all aspects of their lives.

Social Media Tags
Facebook – Rochelle Redding Coaching and Consulting
Instagram – Rochelleliveswell
Twitter – RochelleRedding
Website – www.Rochelleliveswell.com
Email – Rochelleliveswell@gmail.com

October 17
Briearra Toeran

Philippians 4:13
"I can do all things through Christ who strengthens me!"

-At times we all interrogate God about his spirit
and resolution in our lives
whether it's by Design or not
we all have been guilty of it. Perhaps today's pressure is a bit more fearing than
others
so today begin your personal affirmations
I am an advocate for my TRUTH LIFE!
I am an advocate for knowing the death of the strength that MY GOD has given
me!

At times we all interrogate God about his spirit and resolution in our lives whether it's by design or not. We all have been guilty of it. Perhaps today's pressure is a bit more fearing than any other day so today begin your personal affirmations. I am an advocate for my TRUTH LIFE! I am an advocate for knowing the death of the strength that MY GOD has given me! At the age of 21 I had my first child. Kyree is the love of my life. About 6 weeks after birth I received a letter from the Sickle Cell Foundation to schedule an appointment. I was beyond afraid. Although the outcome was that he only carries this trait, had it been any other way I would still give My Savior All The Praise Ye The Lord's!

Today remember WE all can Do All Things Through Christ That Strengthens US!

Email: brunette_smith@yahoo.com

October 18

Krystle Bradley

Psalm 23:4 NLT

"Even when I walk through the darkest valley, I will not be afraid, for you are close beside me. Your rod and your staff protect and comfort me."

God's promises are guaranteed. They WILL happen. While waiting on the promise we have to go through a process. The process is where your faith (trust) is put to the test. No matter how rough, there is purpose in this season. You need to become weighted. It is the time where you pray, fast, read, study, grow, change, develop and reflect and become spiritually mature. Remember the teacher is always quiet during the test. He has entrusted you with silence for a greater reason. Don't allow what you see to forget what God said. I was picked on purpose!

Krystle Bradley is the founder of Brave University, a nonprofit organization that aims to end the bullying epidemic. She is an author, mentor, public speaker, educator, graduate of North Carolina A&T and member of Delta Sigma Theta Sorority, Incorporated. She believes in seeing the good in everyone she meets.

Instagram: KMilli84 and BraveUniversity3
Facebook: KMillionaire Bradley and Brave University
Twitter: b_krystle and @BraveUniv3
E-mail address: bravebradley3@gmail.com

October 19
Cheena R. Headen

Philippians 4:8-9 "Finally, brothers, whatever is true, whatever is honorable, whatever is just, whatever is pure, whatever is lovely, whatever is commendable, if there is any excellence, if there is anything worthy of praise, think about these things."

Your living is determined not so much by what life brings to you, but by the attitude you bring to life! 100% of your ATTITUDE contributes to you surviving a trial in life. It helps with keeping a healthy outlook on life. Here is a mathematical formula to the word: A-T-T-I-T-U-D-E would be 1+20+20+9+20+21+4+5 which equals 100%. Each of these letters are numbered by their position in the alphabet. Practice daily what Philippians 4:8-9 says when faced with adversity and watch how the peace of God guards your heart and mind.

https://www.motivationalmemo.com/100-mathematical-reasons-for-developing-a-great-attitude/

Certified Emotional Healing Life Coach and founder of Breakout Mindset Mentoring and Coaching, focusing on helping women strategically develop the mindset that will change the dynamics of their life Spiritually, Mentally, Emotionally, and Physically. Cheena is the 2018 recipient of the ACHI WSWA Magazine Awards Charlotte/Triad Chapter Woman of the Year Award and the 2018 recipient of the Trials to Triumph Award. She has been seen on many platforms sharing her huge vision and passion to impact the lives of women, young ladies and girls for Christ. Encouraging them all to have faith in the power they possess within to take back their life and OWN IT! Cheena is also the founder of Triple Empowerment Network,1000WomenInMotion, and PINK4CHEE Inc. She is the Author of Spiritual Steps to Surviving a Triple-Negative Diagnosis, Until Further Notice Celebrate Everything the Journal and Compiler of the Anthology Unleashed Travails: From Pain to Purpose.

Cheena is a friend to many, a mother of two and a caring sister to four brothers and one sister. She enjoys availing herself to opportunities to know and serve others as a Certified Mentor for the American Cancer Society, program called Reach to Recovery in Greensboro, NC. She is a Moses Cone Systems Volunteer at the Wesley Long Cancer Center. An active member of Lambda Tau Upsilon Christian Sorority and also an active member of NCNW, Inc.

Cheena's motto: "I may not captivate my whole audience, but if only one person, then I've done what I was purposed to do". So, Until Further Notice CELEBRATE Everything!

Email:
cheena@cheespeak.com

Social Media Tags:
www.facebook.com/cheenarheaden
www.instagram.com/cheenarheaden
www.linkedin.com/in/cheenarheaden
www.twitter.com/cheespeaks

Websites:
www.breakoutmindset.com
www.unleashedtravailsbook.com
www.cheespeaks.com

October 20
Sheree "Sunshine" Cox

2 Timothy 1:7 New International Version (NIV)
"For the Spirit God gave us does not make us timid, but gives us power, love and self-discipline."

There are days when we may feel non- adequate, timid or even confused. Just know, those are lies attempting to shadow the greatness and power that lies within you. Arise! You hold the Spirit of God, the power that holds your destiny to fulfill your purpose. You were uniquely created to love and have self-discipline over your life. God has given you the plan, power and purpose. Now use it! Live life with Greatness.

October 21
Naomi Roe (Schaffer)

It is possible!

"What do you mean, 'If I can'?" Jesus asked. "Anything is possible if a person believes."" Mark 9:23 NLT

As I walked through the doors of my senior classroom, I knew this would be my last chance to prove to myself and my Teacher that I could complete an assignment. I was graduating a year behind my fellow classmates and the pressure was on. You see I didn't have a track record of finishing strong, in fact just about all of my past work was either incomplete or missing however, on this day something was different. I don't know if it was the pressure of time catching up to me or the fact that my classmates had moved on without me.

As the final hour approaches my teacher walks over to me and quietly kneels down to whisper in my ear "you only have 30 minutes left; you're not going to make it." Something inside of me almost broke into pieces as she settled there with a serious look in her eyes. Yet I knew that I've come to far to give up now! I began to find comfort in a tiny voice inside my head that said "keep going!" The thirty minutes had passed and it'd finished the test. I knew I could do it. You see all things are possible to them that believe. I pray that you take from this story the courage to go on even when the clock is winding down because anything is possible if you believe"

Naomiroe30@yahoo.com

Facebook Naomi Roe

October 22
Rebecca Landers

"God is in the midst of her; she shall not be moved: God shall help her, and that right early." Psalm 46:5 KJV

God Wants You To Victorious!

Dear sister, this scripture is dear to me, because it has helped me to overcome my fears. you may ask how so? well, I know God is all powerful and He has equipped me and you with that same power. There is one key, we have to believe in Him and have faith. Belief and faith help me to know that God will not allow me to fail. This scripture has also given me the ump in my triumph's. just as God has helped me to triumph through life's trials, He can and HE WILL HELP YOU AS WELL."

Rebecca Landers was born and raised in Bluefield, West Virginia and currently resides in Hueytown, Alabama. She has an Associate Degree in Liberal Arts and also one in Health Care Reimbursement. She is a Woman of God who believes that your struggle whether mental, physical, or financial is never meant to tear you down, but to help you find your true God given purpose. She believes that God has given each one of us a gift that we are supposed to inspire at least one other person with. One of her favorite Scriptures is, Luke 12:48

https;//www.facebook.com/rebla.vette.landers1

Birmingham, AL

Email: r3klanders@yahoo.com

October 23
Natasha Saunders

II Corinthians 4:8-9 "We are pressed on every side, yet not strained; perplexed, yet not unto despair; pursued, yet not forsaken; smitten down, yet not destroyed."

God will apply pressure on certain areas of our lives to press out the best product possible. The question is, "Are you scared of a little pressure?" Or do you face your obstacles believing that God is about to make something beautiful out of your struggle?

Often, we are not reaching our true potential because we are running from the very thing that can change us for the better, bringing to surface the beauty within -- the potential that God is pleading for us to birth. After all, that unborn potential can ultimately change the world and it begins with you.

Natasha Saunders is Co-Founder of TRIFECTA, an enterprise and social movement empowering youth, individuals and communities through economic and community development. TRIFECTA's mission is to "Guard it, Nurture it and Reveal it," strengthening community collectivism while creating cultural shifts and eliminating disparities. Saunders' passion is to help others actualize their potential.

https://www.trifectainc.org/

https://business.facebook.com/TRIFECTAinc/

October 24

Vernita Stevens

Where I was yesterday, will not prevent me from fulfilling my purpose today.

Even on the rough days remember it is ok to be a seed. Today embrace the darkness for you know that in this space is where your transformation will begin.

**I am a seed being planted, covered in the soil of Grace and Mercy.
Hydrated by the rain of Faith and nurtured with the Glory of His Love.
Breaking through barriers that were meant to hold me back.
I will sprout the new chapters of my life.
With this transformation I WILL fulfill my purpose.
Today the New Me is STRONGER, WISER, and READY to tackle the world!**

Vernita Stevens is a retired United States Marine, Professional Trainer, Motivational Speaker, and Owner of 2p – Paradigm of Possibilities, LLC. She has a passion for helping others embrace that "ANYTHING IS POSSIBLE". She uses an inspirational approach to convey positive results to empower others to live in health and happiness.

City/State: Huntersville, NC

Email: 2p.paradigmofpossibilities@gmail.com

October 25
Melinda Wynn

Many times, we allow people's thoughts and opinions to dictate our decisions about our dreams. Do not give people total power of the choices you make in your life. You and only you have the power to make your dreams happen. I say the recipe of God+ self-belief +self-determination+ self motivation = your dreams. The only way someone can stop you from dreaming or fulfilling it, is if you give them the power too. So, keep and hold on to your power. Speak life and truth into all of your dreams.

email: veryblessedone@hotmail.com

"No one has the power to shatter your dreams unless you give it to them."
Maeve Greyson

October 26
Terri J. Fowler

"Have You not made a hedge around him, around his household, and around all that he has on every side? You have blessed the work of his hands, and his possessions have increased in the land." ~Job 1:10

All people, like you and I; met adversity, had mountains to climb, have problems to deal with. Things are going to come up.

Maybe you are not getting beat up physically, but you are going through trials where you are battling the enemy who wants nothing more than to keep you in those low places.

God knows every strand of hair on your head. Don't you think he knows when you need him the most? You were not built to break. All you have to do is call on him!

Call on him when you're happy! Call on him when you're sad! Call on him when you are about to faint from your circumstances! He's waiting on you; waiting on you to just call on him. Call on him!

He has a hedge of protection around you! Whatever you're going through; you were not built to break. Just call on him and he will see you through!

Email: terrifowler26@gmail.com
Instagram: @Tjfow26
Twitter: @TJFowler26
Facebook: www.facebook.com/nbtbreak

October 27

LaKel Farley

James 2:20 NKJV "But do you want to know, O foolish man, that faith without works is dead?"

There is probably some pain that you've endured or some pleasure that you've experienced that leads to your purpose. Some people may feel that the hardest task is discovering it but maybe the most difficult part isn't finding it but executing it. At some point you've got to take a leap of faith and go for it. Stop waiting for your life to become perfect before you start. Just start. Start right where you are with what you have. Remember, faith without works is dead. Stop living a life of death but move and live in your purpose today.

Self-Published Author and Speaker, Donna G. Robinson, spends her time, sharing messages of hope, healing and faith after enduring a traumatic life experience. She has been successful in speaking to others about overcoming trauma, dealing with depression, attending counseling and finding purpose in pain.

Instagram: donnagrobinson

Website: www.donnagrobinson.com

Book: "Courageous and Strong: A Survivor's Story of Hope and Healing"

Email: survivordonnagrobinson@gmail.com

FOCUS ON GOD

"Delight yourself in the LORD, and he will give you the desires of your heart." - Psalm 37:4

Rest in God's Presence while He fills your inner strength. Relax in His word by asking His Spirit to make it come alive to you. Know that your living relationship with Him helps you to approach each new day with confidence so that you are ready for anything that comes your way. Look to Him and allow Him to be your positive focus today and then you will experience the joy of knowing that only He could fully satisfy it. Remember to delight yourself in Him letting Him become the desire of your heart.

Rose Hall is a Resourceful, Outgoing, Servant-leading Entrepreneur Motivating and Helping All. She is a faithful wife, loving mother of 4, a Registered Nurse and Health Solutions Expert. She is currently the publisher of the digital newspaper, "Daily Wellness Lifestyle News." She loves God, writing poetry, and encouraging others to GROW to their maximum potential.

Email: askrosehall@gmail.com
Website: www.about.me/rosemhall
Facebook: www.facebook.com/Destinations4u2
Instagram: www.instagram.com/ubhealthe2

October 29
Dr. Christine Handy

Above Only Living
Deuteronomy 23:13 tells us – "And the LORD shall make thee the head, and not the tail; and thou shalt be above only, and thou shalt not be beneath"

Let's stop right there! Take a moment and think about your life. What are examples of your Above Only Living? Are you the lender or the borrower, are you the employee or the employer, are you fed or do you feed? Reflect on how you are living and set your goal to live "Above Only". Pay off your debts, plan your dream vacations, fly first class, live where you want, drive what you want, control your time, bless your family, bless your community, live the life that the Lord intended for you! You have God's permission to live Above Only.

Dr. Christine Handy is an educator, entrepreneur, life coach, and author. A respected high school principal and leader, she is also a Senior Manager and Relationship Marketing expert with Send Out Cards and a leader with a health and wellness company. Additionally, she is a collaborating author in the Amazon Best Seller – Dear Fear Volume II and It Takes Money Honey. You can connect with Dr. Handy on Facebook under Christine Handy or by email christine@aboveonly.ws.

October 30
Ijana Nathaniel

"It always seems impossible until it is done." – Nelson Mandela

I know what it feels like to set a goal to complete something and it seems as if there is no end in sight. It is in that very moment that you tell yourself to keep it pushing, and to never give up. You may not see the end, but it is near. A good friend would tell me, do not break down before your breakthrough. When you feel like you are at the end of your rope, remember the quote above, "it always seems impossible until it is done".

Ijana Nathaniel is the mother of two amazing children- Nia and her son, Jeremiah. Ijana holds a Master's Degree in Organizational Leadership from Nyack College.

In 2010, Ijana became the Founder and President of Dare 2 Dream Leaders Inc., a 501c3 nonprofit youth organization based in Brooklyn, NY, serving Middle School and High School students. The organization provides mentoring and educational programs to help youth gain financial, career and entrepreneurial skills.

https://www.facebook.com/ijana.nathaniel
https://www.instagram.com/ijananathaniel/
https://www.dare2dreamleaders.org
about.me/ijana.nathaniel

October 31

Debbie Ann Andrews

"And we know that all things work together for the good to them that love God, to them who are called according to his purpose." Romans 8:28

Those who love God, are in fact, called by God when they encounter our risen Lord and are baptized by His spirit. This is when their divine purpose for their lives is unlocked. Our birthing seeds were planted with fertile soil and essential nutrients so that our dreams will manifest. Therefore, Beloved, stay focused and don't allow immorality of the world's systems to deter you from reaching your "divine destiny." Always dream big, cultivate faith and pray so the Lord can commune more intimately with you. He will give you immeasurable faith to do what He has called you to do. You are a mighty instrument in the hands of God!

Debbie is a breast cancer survivor, advocate and contributing bestselling author for "Faith for Fiery Trials." Debbie is a speaker on the topic of "Living with and Beyond the Breast Cancer Diagnosis." She openly and transparently shares her journey in an effort to encourage and inspire others as they walk through what can be a very "dark night of the soul." She infuses her talks with how she incorporated positive affirmations and indomitable faith to survive breast cancer. Debbie is a woman living on purpose, in purpose and committed bringing breast cancer awareness to women, one woman at a time. Debbie is a member of Greater Mount Calvary Holy Church in Washington D.C., under Bishop Alfred A. Owens and Co-Pastor Susie C. Owens. She serves in several ministries and a graduate of Bible Calvary Institute with a certificate in "Biblical Studies."

prayer1@rcn.com

Facebook, Debbie Ann Andrews

IG, Debbie A Andrews Twitter, Debbie Ann Andrew

www.DebbieAnnAndrews.com

November 1
Jahmia Jackson

"Show me the right path, O Lord; point out the road for me to follow."
(Psalms 25:4)

All paths and journeys in life lead back to experiences that involve a point of learning. Your choices affect what outcome will be experienced. Turn to God for spiritual direction and trust the process. What you are currently experiencing may be for the benefit of you sharing your testimony with someone else. The experience is not to destroy you but, the test that you share through your testimony shows your reverence and honor to God that his grace and mercy is sufficient. Your purpose is preparing room for you to live a life of gratefulness! Push through and bless him today through prayer!

November 2
Asia Edwards

Proverbs 3:5-6

"Trust in the Lord with all your heart and lean not on your own understanding; in all your ways submit to him, and he will make your paths straight."

Your plans are not always the plans that God has ordained for your life. Lean to God, even during times when you don't quite understand! Your day of redemption is on the horizon. Perception is the majority of how you view your life! Wake up with bliss because you woke up and be happy because you can. Understand that life is a journey that we all embark upon but consistent renewal of your strength is how you will survive and to see yourself as the survivor. Believe in yourself and trust that God will make your paths straight.

November 3
Sabrina Jones

2 Kings 6:17-20 King James Version (KJV)

"And Elisha prayed, and said, LORD, I pray thee, open his eyes, that he may see. And the LORD opened the eyes of the young man; and he saw: and, behold, the mountain was full of horses and chariots of fire round about Elisha."

Sometimes just because we have the corners all finished to a puzzle, we think that we can make out the entire picture. Today, look to the END. It may start off shaky, and even now it may not look like it is coming together, but know that Jesus is waiving the box with the finished picture. Open your eyes and look beyond yourself to see that HE has equipped you with everything you need to complete the task. What HE needs of you will take HIM to complete it. No matter how it all began, know that in the END, you have a victory celebration awaiting your arrival.

Sabrina Jones is the founder and director of "The Transformation Experience "which is a deliverance and equipping program for women. She has also recently launched "The Berean Equipping Center" which is a weekly online intense bible study, she holds a Bachelor of Science from N.C. A&T State University in Greensboro, NC. Her gifting within the fivefold are Teacher and Evangelist. Sabrina has a passion for seeing those in bondage find freedom to live as Jesus lived, serve as He served and do as He commanded us to do. She has been married to Terence Jones for thirty years and they have three awesome children. Sabrina Jones is a trail blazer and has a genuine love for the people of God.

Website: www.Transformation4you.com

Email: Sabrinajones88@yahoo.com

Transformation email: Transformationkingdom88@gmail.com
Twitter: @Transformers

November 4

Toni Garvin

Luke 17:5 (NKJV) "And the apostles said to the Lord, "Increase our faith."

Without faith it's impossible to please God. He desires to bless us. If we walk in doubt and unbelief, how can God bless us? Faith is the catalyst that opens the door to God's promises. It doesn't matter what it looks like because by faith IT'S ALREADY DONE! By faith you must believe, knowing that God's word is true. You must have faith knowing you are more than a conqueror and you are victorious. You are a Royal Priesthood. You are an heir to the throne. This is your inheritance. Walk in it!!!

Toni is a devoted wife and mother, born and raised in Brooklyn, New York, currently living in Denver, Colorado. She is the CEO of Royally Scent LLC. She enjoys spending time with family. She also enjoys cooking and converting everyday recipes to vegan friendly dishes.

Facebook: www.facebook.com/toni.garvin.3

Website: www.royallyscent.com

Email: mstgarvin1@gmail.com

November 5

Dr. Mary J. Huntley

DON'T FEAR

"Do not fear, Daniel, for from the first day that you set your heart to understand, and to humble yourself before your God, your words were heard." (Dan. 10:12 NKJV)

Does it seem as if God is taking forever to answer your prayers? Rest assured that you are not alone. Be still and know that HE IS GOD. While waiting remind yourself of the many times He has answered your prayers. Use your past experience to boost your confidence. This will help you to encourage yourself in difficult times. He's done it before and HE WILL do it again. Wait I say on the Lord!

Dr. Mary J. Huntley is the Chief Executive/Encouragement Officer of Trinity Global Empowerment Ministries, Inc. She is also a wife, an international best-selling author, prayer warrior, domestic violence awareness advocate, licensed clinical counselor, clinical supervisor, and certified master life coach. She is on a mission to empower others (especially women) to soar above their challenges and reach their God-given potential.

Website: www.drmaryjhuntley.com
Facebook: DrMaryJ Huntley
Twitter: drmaryj_huntley

November 6

Lorrie A. Simmons

Psalm 139:14 NIV

"I praise you because I am fearfully and wonderfully made; your works are wonderful; I know that full well."

"I Am Who God Says I Am"

God made us, he shaped us, and formed us in his own image. But somewhere along the way we forget and underestimate our value. Whether it's our first heart break after a bad relationship or even something more sinister like being violated, or taken advantage of, or abused; you are not what happened to you! You are who God says you are. You were sculpted from nothing into something marvelous, glorious, lovely and magnificent in God's eyes. You are beautifully and wonderfully made.

Email: Lorrie1174@gmail.com

Lorrie A. Simmons a native of Leesburg, began her education at Florida State University with a bachelor's in accounting. She later received a Master's in Accounting and a Master's in Business Administration/Public Administration from University of Phoenix.

A Minister and Accountant for the Christian Worship Center of Central Florida, Kids of Distinction, and serves on the Board for Men of Distinction. Lorrie is the mother of 2 boys. Lorrie is currently the Manager of Accounting & Payroll Systems for the City of Sarasota. Lorrie also has operated her own Accountant business for over 12 years preparing and filing tax returns for individuals and small businesses. Providing training and consultations for non-profit organizations, churches, and those starting their own businesses.

Lorrie began a non-profit organization, Victory Over Violence of FL, Inc in October 2017 due to an overwhelming need to bring awareness of the effects of domestic violence and sexual violence in families within her community. Lorrie has been ministering and mentoring for over 22 years. A survivor and overcomer of both sexual violence and domestic violence. Her vision is to empower people with education and connect victims to resources, so they can walk in victory over violence one day at a time.

November 7
Yolonda Marshall

Hebrews 6:10-12

"For God is not unjust. He will not forget how hard you have worked for him and how you have shown your love to him by caring for other believers,[b] as you still do. ¹¹ Our great desire is that you will keep on loving others as long as life lasts, in order to make certain that what you hope for will come true. ¹² Then you will not become spiritually dull and indifferent. Instead, you will follow the example of those who are going to inherit God's promises because of their faith and endurance."

Health issues, Job loss, divorce, overworked and undervalued? As women we do it all and still keep going. Remember Sister, we are the daughters of the King! God sees everything you have poured out and will never let what you have done for Him to go unrewarded.

Facebook: Yolonda Marshall
Email: phenomenalfreedom@gmail.com

November 8
Crystal Glasper Wright

"Every great dream begins with a dreamer. Always remember, you have within you the strength, the patience, and the passion to reach for the stars to change the world." -Harriet Tubman

I believe as young girls we all start with a dream of what we can be. There is no dream that is not reachable with hard work and dedication. In order to achieve our dreams, we must have patience and know it will happen if we trust the process. We have all been little girls with dreams and will grow into women with a passion. I always tell myself to reach for the highest star. If I can't change the world knowing I had the ability to help one person makes me feel accomplished at the end of the day.

Crystal Wright has overcome many obstacles. She was considered a statistic at an early age having her first child at 14. She has gone on to complete 2 college degrees and obtain a successful career even though the odds were against her.

Facebook: Crystal Christyle
Instagram: newnewchristyle

City/State: Raleigh, NC

Email: glasper81@gmail.com

November 9
Gwendolyn Demby

Discovering the Benefits of Joy

Joy is a position that we must possess at all times. My brethren, count it all joy when you fall into divers' temptations James 1:2. This is why it's important to remain in a state of joyfulness.

"There will always be strength present, even through trials. Thou will show me the path of life & being in His presence brings us fullness of Joy"
Psalm 16:11.

"No matter what we go through make the Joy of the Lord your first priority. The Joy of the Lord is my strength" Nehemiah 8:10

Gwendolyn is first a woman that loves and fears the Lord, married 33 years and has one biological son, two stepdaughters, one adopted daughter who is her biological niece. She was also a guardian to her youngest nephew, who is now an adult. She has returned to school, aspiring to become a licensed professional counselor.

"She's learned that whatever state she's in therewith to be content."
Philippians 4:11

November 10
Karshena McCain Adkins

Psalm 3:3 New International Version (NIV)
"But you, Lord, are a shield around me, my glory, the One who lifts my head high."

No matter what happens today, or what will happen or has happened, LIFT YOUR HEAD. I remember my mom constantly telling me to not to drop my head. EVER.

You are fearfully and wonderfully made. You are special. God has you in the palm of his hand.

Hold your head HIGH. Be bold. Be confident. BE YOU!

Email Karshenamccainadkins@gmail.com

November 11
Meltona Bryant

Exodus 20-12 "Honour thy father and thy mother: that thy days may be long upon the land which the LORD thy God giveth thee."

So if you have a mother and a father that's alive the Bible says you should honor your parents that means if you at any time in your life had a disagreement with your mother, grandmother cursed your father, grandfather disrespected them and did anything's that you should have not done , go back and apologize and beg for their forgiveness you have yashua and then you have your parents they love you , be an asset and not a deficit you should give them flowers while they are alive, do whatever you can do for them now and make their lives more comfortable while you can and yashua will bless your days if you don't he will shorten your days

Born June 8th 1961 to Vivian and Eddie in lakeside hospital long island NY, grew up in Wyandanch 11798 a Hamlet in the town of Babylon. Everyone knew each other you had a curfew to be in at a certain time you could sleep with the doors unlockedl,1 of 10 children 8 girls 2 boy, mother still living father has passed, graduate high school 1979, ,my first job was at Estee Lauder working on the assembly line it was like slave labor , I gave birth to my daughter Vivian (love you) in 1981,(have 3 grandchildren jahlil, Chiniah , Victoria love you) son in law Jason)got married in 1983 ,the ,moved to Washington state, lived in Tacoma, Olympia and Lacey, from there went to Virginia, live there a couple of years, then went to Germany was there 1987-1991, returned to the USA   present Acme Bus   I love all my family and friends helping people, I thank everyone who has come into my life , to help make me the Queen I am and thank you mommy, for all you have done for me love you and thank you yashua for my days Mrs. Williams for letting me be a part of your vision. Never quit on your dream.

https://www.linkedin.com/in/meltona-bryant-19175235 Text me at 631-693-4352
Twitter Meltona Bryant@meltonabryant www.helpmyhealth.prosystem101.com
meltona.savedmoremoney.com Luvmy.petcbd101.com
Meltona.freecable4Life.com www.erewards.shop/L584510 meltonas1002@gmail.com

November 12
Tocha Moore

Ecclesiastes 3:1-8 "To everything there is a season, and a time to every purpose under the heaven: 2 A time to be born, and a time to die; a time to plant, and a time to pluck up that which is planted;3 A time to kill, and a time to heal; a time to break down, and a time to build up;4 A time to weep, and a time to laugh; a time to mourn, and a time to dance;5 A time to cast away stones, and a time to gather stones together; a time to embrace, and a time to refrain from embracing; 6 A time to get, and a time to lose; a time to keep, and a time to cast away; 7 A time to rend, and a time to sew; a time to keep silence, and a time to speak;8 A time to love, and a time to hate; a time of war, and a time of peace." (KJV)

There is a time for everything! No matter where life takes us or what happens there is a reason for it all. When we find ourselves in the rough places in life, we can take refuge in the fact that it will not be forever, the hard times will end. Purpose is the reason something is done or created, everything has a purpose remembering that will help you deal with anything! There is always a lesson to be learned as long as you are willing to be the student. It all Serves a Purpose. You have a Purpose!

Email: yourtochamoore@gmail.com

November 13
Keyuna Faye Webster
"Empowerment for the Powerless"

"She silently stepped out of the race she never wanted to be in, found her lane and proceeded to win". –Unknown

There comes a time where you have to stop trying to make things right with certain people in your life, especially when they don't want to own their part in what went wrong. Listen! Forgive yourself for not knowing better at that time. Forgive yourself for allowing them to take away your power. Forgive yourself for the behaviors that may have pulled you of out character. Forgive yourself for being who you they needed you to be instead of everything you needed to be for yourself. Forgive yourself for the survival patterns and traits you adapted to while enduring the trauma of a toxic situation. There is a strong message in the way a person treats you, all you to do pay attention. Take your power back, forgive them, adjust your crown, and go WIN! You are a DIAMOND, not a rock!!

"Empowerment for the Powerless"

Founder/Executive Director/CEO of LoveYuna Outreach, Inc.
Owner, Kay's Kakes and Georgia Anger Academy
Respected businesswoman and community servant Keyuna Faye Webster is on a mission to bring awareness to domestic violence worldwide. By overcoming many horrific experiences, this voice of hope renders empowerment for the powerless. She is God's child, mother, entrepreneur, empowerment speaker, Certified Anger Management Counselor, and Life Skills Management Coach.

Keyuna Faye Webster
"Empowerment for the Powerless"
email: info@keyunafayewebster.org
www.facebook.com/keyunafayewebster

www.instagram.com/keyunafayewebster
LinkedIn: www.linkedin.com/in/keyunafayewebster
Phone: 678.847.4728

LoveYuna Outreach, Inc
"Empowering the Powerless"
Email: info@loveyunaoutreach.org
Web: www.loveyuna.org
FB: @loveyunaoutreachinc
IG: @loveyunaoutreachinc__
Twitter: @loveyunainc

November 14
Lakisha Harris, MA, LPC

Healing is Power!

For years we have heard that "Money is Power" and then "Knowledge is Power" but yet we have seen those with both money and knowledge succumb to depression, low self-esteem, poor decision making, and even suicide. Your true living happy power comes from healing! Healing emotionally, mentally, and physically. We are not able to pick our upbringings, or why things affect us negatively but we can gain healing from them both. This often means exploring difficult times and taking a deep understanding on what brought you to this point. Exploring and correcting negative thoughts.

It is possible to be heal and it is possible to be truly and consistently Happy! You must however seek out your healing process! Find a therapist or a group and do the work to Heal! You Got This!

Lakisha Harris, MA, LPC
Is a mental health therapist specializing in trauma, a parent coach and author of "Every Woman's Little Black Book - Heal. Date. Thrive!
www.HarrisCandC.com
www.healingispower.net
Facebook: @HarrisCandC and @HealDateThrive
Instagram: @HarrisCandC
YouTube: @HealingIsPower
Twitter: HarrisCandC

November 15
Leticia Hicks

Season of Adversity
"Often times God demonstrates His faithfulness in adversity by providing for us what we need to survive. He does not change our painful circumstances. He sustains us through them." ~ **Charles Stanley**

We will encounter adversity in different seasons of our lives. I pray, you are coping with the current challenges in your life. God will help you overcome the struggles, pain and negative thoughts. Shed tears of sorrow and joy, knowing God is there to comfort you. Your testimony will be greater than the adversity that you encounter. You are on the path to the manifestation of God's promises. Trust him on the journey. Release and allow God to do a greater work in and through you. Remember, God is in love with you.

Letitia Hicks is an women empowerment strategist, entrepreneur minster and author. I help women transform their lives with a renewed sense of power, passion and purpose.
Letitiahicks.com

Email: letitiahic63@hotmail.com

November 16
Nikki L. Goodloe

"But understand this, that in the last days there will come times of difficulty. For people will be lovers of self, lovers of money, proud, arrogant, abusive, disobedient to their parents, ungrateful, unholy, heartless, unappeasable, slanderous, without self-control, brutal, not loving God, treacherous, reckless, swollen with conceit, lovers of pleasure rather than lovers of God, having the appearance of godliness, but denying its power. Avoid such people." 2nd Timothy 3:1-17

In the words of Iyana Vanzant "It's not selfish to put yourself first, it's self-ful." It's your life. You have permission to remove yourself from any relationship, situationship, job, etc. that no longer serves you in a positive, meaningful, uplifting manner. You don't owe any explanations to anyone who has not walked a day in the life of YOU! You have one life to live and owe it to yourself to make it your best! It's time to break out those brand-new heels, lace up those sneakers and give yourself permission to walk straight into your God purposed destiny!

https://www.facebook.com/nikki.goodloe2018
https://www.facebook.com/nikkilgoodloe/
www.instagram.com/nlgoodloe

Email: nikkilgoodloe@gmail.com

Resilience

The truth is everyone needs resilience this is what allows us to overcome adversities in our everyday lives. However, it's what we do when we incur life's major setbacks that is the true test of our resiliency such as losing a job, a failed relationship, financial loss as well as a health-related issues. Activating and increasing our resiliency muscles allows us to address obstacles that may come our way.

Making strides to increase your resiliency will require effort on your part and it will require your own transparency with yourself about how you view yourself and others around you. Knowing what works for you and being aware of your feelings, emotions and thoughts can help strengthen relationships and build a positive future. When learning about yourself and those closest to you, it is important to recognize your strengths and those of others, as well as coping strategies that have been helpful in the past.

Resiliency is under your own control. Resiliency transforms trials into triumphs, victims into survivors, failure into success, and hardships into challenges.

Psalm 145:14 "The Lord upholdeth all that fall, and raiseth up all those that be bowed down."

For over 18 years Althea Bates has worked in social services and workforce development. Growing up in a strong Jamaican family that always encouraged her to dream and work hard Althea has found her way to becoming more than she had initially set her eyes onto. She has found herself functioning as an Entrepreneur, a Professor/Lecturer, a Nonprofit Leader, Directors for various organizations and most recently an author and a Champion for women empowerment issues. Within her educational pursuits she has received a Bachelor's of Science in Psychology from Temple University, Masters of Science from Springfield College in Human Services with a concentration in Organizational Management and Leadership and is currently a Doctoral Candidate at Capella University.

Ms. Webber-Bates currently operates as the CEO and Founder of A. Bates Consulting which provides a range of training -related consulting services to nonprofits/municipalities relative to topics and areas in youth development, case management, workforce development and human services practices. In August of 2016, Althea launched and founded TAlthea Webber-Bates continued her work as an author & co-author putting put book projects including: Favor in Failure (2018); Life Balance for the Women on the Rise (2017) and Soaring into Greatness (2017) as well as Brokenness, Baggage and Blessings (2018). In finding her voice and owning her journey she also found in herself the gift of presenting high energy messages that takes the audience through her own personal journey and the purpose she found as she built her Resiliency. Throughout her years as a motivational speaker and author Althea relates to teens, adults and corporations alike inspiring and motivating them to begin the process of healing through empowerment.

Althea Webber-Bates continued her work as an author & co-author putting put book projects including: Favor in Failure (2018); Life Balance for the Women on the Rise (2017) and Soaring into Greatness (2017) as well as Brokenness, Baggage and Blessings (2018). In finding her voice and owning her journey she also found in herself the gift of presenting high energy messages that takes the audience through her own personal journey and the purpose she found as she built her Resiliency. Throughout her years as a motivational speaker and author Althea relates to teens, adults and corporations alike inspiring and motivating them to begin the process of healing through empowerment.

Social media handles:

Facebook Business Page:
Project Resiliency Movement
A Bates Consulting Group

Personal Facebook: Althea Webber Bates
Instagram: Projectresiliencymovement
Twitter: @projresmovement
Website: Abatesconsultinggroup.org
Email: Projectresiliencymovement@gmail.com
Abatesconsulting@gmail.com

November 18
Viva Lewis-Harris

Psalm 3:3 "But you, Lord, are a shield around me, my glory, the One who lifts my head high."

Our father is our protector IN SPITE of what we experience. Once we look at what He has protected us from, HIS glory manifests; as we realize that our trials and tribulations are not in vain. The beautiful thing is, He lifts our heads high coming out. NO GUILT, NO SHAME, NO REMNANTS of what we went through. Remember, we are NOT what we did or experienced in our lives, we are who GOD says we are.

Email: only1viva@gmail.com

November 19

Minister Robyn Curry

Luke 9:23-24

"Then He said to *them* all, "If anyone desires to come after Me, let him deny himself, and take up his cross daily, and follow Me. For whosoever will save his life shall lose it: but whosoever will lose his life for my sake, the same shall save it."

As we follow Christ, many crosses will be laid upon our path. These crosses are not meant to be stepped over or handed off to another, rather, we are instructed to take them up. These are the crosses we bare. My cross may not look like your cross, and your cross may not look like mine, but chances are they are both heavy, and they are both painful. For following Jesus does not mean we escape suffering, but instead we should prepare to face it. For the sake of Christ, when we lay down our agendas, our wills, and our lives, it is there that we save them. May God's grace be sufficient each and every day as you pick up your cross.

Min. Robyn M. Curry's spiritual upbringing began in the Otterbein United Methodist Church, in Altoona Pennsylvania, where she was a member for 19 years. Robyn's call to teach the Word of God, has led her, in service, to various ministries such as; Youth Leadership, Women's Ministry, Missions and Outreach, and Director of Sunday School Education while residing in Palm Coast, Florida. Robyn joined Worship World Church, after moving to Maryland in 2010, where she currently serves under the leadership of Pastor W. Andrew Best, Jr. Robyn has been married to Justin R. Curry for Thirteen years and is the mother of four children and two grandchildren. The Curry's felt the Lord was calling them back home and returned to Altoona, Pennsylvania, where they currently reside.

November 20
Rhonda "Ro" Solomon

"Be fearless in the pursuit of what sets your soul on fire." ~ Unknown

At times the challenges of "Adulting" spiral our lives into a world of doubt, despair and depression. There may be times we feel undervalued, or that our life serves no purpose. Listen, God does not make mistakes! You were divinely and uniquely created for your sole purpose. So, rise from the darkness of despair and the ashes of self-doubt. Emerge renewed through faith!

Cultivate a Phoenix mindset in the pursuit to live in your purpose. Never doubt your journey, always let your passions ignite your focus allowing you to proceed fearlessly through life.

Rhonda Solomon, affectionately known as "Ro" (and most recently nicknamed "The Phoenix), is a Media Personality, Life Coach, Speaker and Author. She was born in the United States but spent her formative school years in St. Ann, Jamaica with her Aunt and Uncle. She later returned to the USA to complete her education. As a media personality Ro is able to ignite her community on current events and issues. Ro hosts 'The RoSolo Show" on www.106LiveRadio.com every Tuesday. She works as a host with Caribbean Life TV Network. She is also a cast member of "Women on the Rise Atlanta", which airs on Comcast in the Fall of 2018.

As a Certified Life Coach, she has mastered the art of helping individuals uncover their true identity by cultivating a love affair with their passions and turning their passions into their life's purpose. Driven by her passion to provide the support to at risk teens that was not provided to her, Ro created "The Phoenix Foundation". The Phoenix Foundation provides a nurturing program, which allows teens to know they are not broken. The focus of the organization is to provide the support young teens often do not receive because society is too busy judging. Ro's organization encourages young women to cultivate a phoenix mindset by rising above their current challenges, brushing off the dust, and becoming a Phoenix. Ro's driven by her purpose to mentor, uplift and walk others through their distractions into their transformation. Her various platforms provide outlets for women to come together and discuss life's challenges in a safe, secure and judgment free environment.

Social Media Tags:
Facebook: Rhonda Fleming-Solomon
Instagram: @rosolo71 and @therosoloshow
Website:
www.rosolo.net
Email Address:
therosoloshow@gmail.com

November 21
Celestine Davis

1 Peter 2:15 (ESV) "For this is the will of God, that by doing good you should put to silence the ignorance of foolish people."

Finding yourself overexposed or misunderstood? Misunderstandings and lies can move at the speed of light through social media outlets. Don't get caught up in how you think you appear to others. Remember to activate your virtuous womanhood. Silence the foolish with your sober-minded righteousness. Seek to present His love and not to win an argument for your sake. In Christ we have freedom. That freedom shouldn't be used for our own desires, but to live as Christ would want us to live. The wisdom of Christ in us will silence the foolish. You only need to believe and live it.

Celestine is a writer, visual artist, emerging filmmaker, speaker, and community arts promoter. She is the Director of the annual Down East Flick Fest held in Greenville, NC and the creator of the visual journaling workshop, "ReCreations: Rewriting Your Life Script ™" and facilitates writing-to-heal workshops.

Social Media tags and Website links

https://www.linkedin.com/in/celestine-davis-75147422/
https://www.instagram.com/faithdame/
http://celestinedavis.com/
https://www.facebook.com/4thecreator/
downeastflickfest.org

November 22
Kimberly Carter

"You may encounter many defeats, but you must not be defeated. In fact, it may be necessary to encounter the defeats, so you can know who you are, what you can rise from, how you can still come out of it." -Maya Angelou

In every aspect of my life I have encountered defeats. In school, at work, within my own business ventures and relationships. But guess what, I'm still here and every defeat has taught me something along the way. I'm still a work in progress, WE ALL ARE, but that doesn't stop me from continuing to try to be the best me I can be. So, ladies if you want to start that business, change careers, get out of that relationship that's no good for you to concentrate on yourself, have that baby, get married... whatever it is that you want to do, don't let fear hold you back. Make your plans and take that leap! We are all meant to shine so SHINE ON LADIES!

Kimberly Carter was born in Bronx, New York and raised in the Washington, DC (DMV) area. She is a published Poet, the owner of I Like it RAW, an all-natural bath and body company, and the Founder of Because We Care Network, an organization dedicated to helping the community. She is currently continuing her education at Southern New Hampshire University with a Business Management focus of study.

www.ilikeitrawbodybutters.com
rawbodybutters@aol.com
www.facebook.com/ilikeitraw
Instagram- ilikeiraw_llc

November 23
Brenda Sawyer

2 Corinthians 9:7 KJV "Every man according as he purposeth in his heart, so let him give; not grudgingly, or of necessity: for God loveth a cheerful giver."

God Wants You To Be A Giver: Do you ever feel like you are the one who always gives, but never receives anything in return? Well, nothing could be further from the truth, because every time you awake God gives you a brand-new day of His grace and mercy. How can you top that for giving and receiving? God wants you to know that He is your "Source" who allows you to give back by looking at the intention of your heart. You don't ever have to give to get then worry about whether you made the right decision. Sometimes I think God will test your motive for giving by looking at the sincerity of your heart, not the quality or the amount. Remember, trust God and know that you are His precious beloved child who He is trying to get something to, so that He can multiply back to you some one hundred-fold. Just keep believing and trusting that God will always supply all of your needs according to His riches in glory by Christ Jesus. (Philippians 4:19)

Brenda Sawyer was born and raised in New York City and currently resides in Philadelphia. She is a Woman of God who has a strong spiritual foundation that acknowledges God is the Head of her life and without Him she can do nothing. Brenda Sawyer is a retired elementary school teacher who has always had a passion for teaching and imparting knowledge. Ms. Sawyer's love for education, afforded her the opportunity to receive a second Master's degree in Elementary Education. She is also a published author and the Founder and CEO of GIRLS WALKING WITH INTEGRITY EMPOWERING FOR DESTINY (GWWI) a Christian mentoring program for young ladies between the ages of eight and eighteen. Brenda Sawyer periodically holds workshops to empower the young ladies to become all that God has called them to be to reach their destiny for posterity. Ms. Sawyer strongly encourages everyone to set goals, find their purpose and follow their passions. One of her favorite Scriptures is, "Where there is no vision, the people perish: but he that keepeth the law, happy is he." Proverbs 29:18

WEBSITE: www.brendasawyer.com FACEBOOK: www.facebook.com/brendasawyer.58 INSTAGRAM : www.instagram.com/brendasawyerencourages LINKEDIN: www.linkedin.com/in/brenda-sawyer-5a264530

Philadelphia, PA

Trust the process

The process of life can get crazy at times, heck it is crazy cause you don't know whether to turn left or right, go up or down, or to say yes or no, but trust it. Stay focused. Be committed. It will bring you to a better place in yourself, one of humbleness and appreciation. It takes failures and "do overs" to get it right. All the shoulda's, woulda's, and coulda's, don't prepare us for the future. Nothing really does, but life itself happening. When you yield yourself in the one who made heaven and earth will all your being, things will turn around in your favor. Trust the process. He will give you, patience, strength and endurance to go through and come out as pure gold.

Proverbs 3:5-7(NKJV)

"Trust in the Lord with all your heart, and lean not on your own understanding; In all your ways acknowledge Him, and He shall direct your paths. Do not be wise in your own eyes; Fear the Lord and depart from evil."

Natasha K. Ransom is a woman of God, wife, sister, cousin and friend. Whatever God will have me to be. I love to worship and travel. My husband is my heart and my children bless my soul. I aspire to be someone who leaves a mark. This is only the beginning.

My Facebook is natashablessingsransom

My Instagram is blessings2012

My LinkedIn info is https://www.linkedin.com/in/natasha-ransom-41573b73

November 25

Terrie Booker

"The greatest among you will be your servant."-Matthew 23:11

I believe there is a master plan for each of our lives. We each have a unique role in the movie called 'Kingdom Life. I often wonder what part in this movie have I been given to play. This I know for sure, I want to be used by God.

Growing up I wanted to be the Star. As I mature, I understand that Jesus is the star and that is as it should be. God uses ordinary people to lead His people. On a number of occasions God changed the characters names to better describe their leadership objective. It seems there is power in a name.

My name means harvester. So today I ask myself, how can I be a harvester for God's Kingdom? How can I play my role with perfection? This scripture reminds me, I must be a servant yes even a servant leader. – TB

Terrie Booker is a wife, mother, entrepreneur, author, realtor, motivational speaker and a renaissance woman in every sense of the word. She is a licensed Realtor and has her MBA. Terrie lent her brilliance as a business leader to Fortune 50 companies before embarking on her own as an entrepreneur. Terrie shares her expertise and empower people to change their financial legacy. Inspired by her love for fashion Terrie has become a Founding Member and B.O.S.S. Brand Ambassador, Her motto is," If you have faith the size of a mustard seed you can achieve anything'. Terrie and her husband have two adult children and live in North Carolina.

http://www.beaglamourboss.com/ http://www.premierbeautyshop.com/

Iamterrie@wilsonrealtync.com
Facebook=Terrie Booker
Instagram=IamTerrieBooker

November 26
Carmelesha Matthewson

Give God the Same Time You Give Your Cell Phone.

Put that cell phone down and spend some time with me. I heard God so clearly that morning. I asked for forgiveness immediately. I knew he was right. I was spending more time on my social media than with him. It's so easy to do five minutes turns into thirty. Then you have wasted more than an hour watching useless videos and reading a negative post. We are so quick to watch and listen to things that add no value to our lives. But then we will call it just entertainment when it is only one more thing to distract you. Count how many times you pick up your phone in a day. Then count how much time you spend with God. That cell phone can't answer prayers, heal your body, give you peace, or give you divine protection. Spending time with God will provide you with that. Plus, it's FREE!

City/State: Knightdale N.C.

Email: info@carmelesha.com

November 27
Gaylin Munford

Ecclesiastes 3:1-8 King James Version (KJV)
"To everything there is a season, and a time to every purpose under the heaven"

"My biological clock is ticking !!!!", rings often through my head. I think of my life and my anticipated timeline. College, Career, Marriage, Children and Happily Ever After. Unfortunately, this timeline is still incomplete. "My biological clock is ticking !!!!", This phrase often rings through my head. I think of my life and my anticipated timeline. College, Career, Marriage, Children and Happily Ever After. Unfortunately, this timeline is still incomplete.

It's easy to become discouraged by what seems like our turtle timeline. Remember that God has ordained the seasons for our lives. When doubt and discouragement creep in we must walk by faith believing that our season is ordained in his perfect timing.

Dear Lord, Teach me how to patiently wait for my season, without doubt, and to trust that you are my time keeper.

Gaylin Munford is a business woman and educator. She owns Jennifer Rose Co., a concierge service that offers event, travel planning and decor services. She is a graduate of Loyola Marymount University and Cal State Dominguez Hills University where she earned degrees in Communication and Education.

https://www.facebook.com/jenniferroseeventandtravelboutique/
https://www.instagram.com/jenniferroseeventdesign/?hl=en
Jenniferroseco@yahoo.com **Phone 323 497-3135**

November 28
Sayra H. Kohen

"You will also declare a thing, and it will be established for you; so light will shine on your ways." Job 22:28 (NKJV)

As a child of the Most High King, you have the power and authority to strategically design your future through the power of decrees. Declaring the Word of God over every situation and circumstance will cause His promises to be made manifest and usher you into your divine destiny. Miracles become commonplace when you tap into the power of the written Word of God and begin decreeing it daily over your life. Declare of His goodness. Declare of His mercy, love, and faithfulness. Declare His will be done and experience victory over your enemies and tremendous success!

Phone: 623.533.8788 Email: sk@sayrakohen.org
Website: www.SayraKohen.org
Facebook: https://www.facebook.com/SayraHKohen
Instagram: https://www.instagram.com/sayrakohen/
Twitter: https://twitter.com/sayrakohen
Pinterest: https://www.pinterest.com/sayrakohen/
LinkedIn: https://www.linkedin.com/in/sayrakohen/

Sayra Kohen is a home-based business entrepreneur, lifestyle design strategist, and success coach. She specializes in helping ordinary people get extraordinary results using simple step by step systems. Sayra is a revolutionary voice in a failing world system that is equipping men and women to break free from the status quo and live the life of their dreams!

November 29
Latasha "WOP" Williams

I know this can be hard. But what if we really lived in the absolute assurance of God's love? Oh, sweet sister, in whatever you are facing today, I pray Isaiah 54:10a over you, "Though the mountains be shaken and the hills be removed, yet [God's] unfailing love for you will not be shaken."

Dear Lord, You are good. And You are good at being God. Therefore, I trust Your plan and believe that You're allowing this to happen for a reason. It may be hard, but I'd rather be close to You through a thousand difficult moments than apart from You in a thousand good ones. In Jesus' Name, Amen.

Latasha "WOP" Williams - Wife, Mother, Daughter, Sister, Friend and The Unapologetically Purposed Woman

November 30
Sharon M. Hyman

"Nothing happens until something moves." - Albert Einstein

Often times we put off doing the things that are necessary to accomplish our goals, waiting, hoping and praying that somehow things will miraculously fall into place, without much effort, on our part. The truth is, without action, nothing will happen. So, in order for our goals to materialize, we MUST take action.

Today, I'm encouraging you to quit waiting and take the first step, regardless of how insignificant it may seem. Commit to doing, at least one thing every day, that will bring you closer to your goals. THEN! and only then, everything you've been hoping and praying for, will start to fall into place.

Sharon M. Hyman is a Canadian Entrepreneur, Founder & CEO of HYMAN Realty Inc, real estate career advisor, trainer and coach. Beyond real estate you can find her doing what she loves best—-mentoring young entrepreneurs. She is an interior design enthusiast who enjoys travelling, entertaining and spending quality time with family.

Website: sharonhyman.ca
Instagram: sharon_real_estate
Twitter: sharon_hyman
Email: sharon@hymanrealty.com

Genesis 1:1KJV
"In the beginning, God created the heaven and the earth. "

This first powerful line of the Holy Bible opens the door to faith. There are no variations, or pre story. It just is. No saying we think, or maybe. The reader steps out on faith by choosing to continue the journey or close the book. I remember when I first read those words for the first time as an adult. I didn't question Why? Or How? I didn't scoff and say impossible. I chose to believe, I chose to continue the journey towards faith. Dedicated to Steffond, Adrian, Jordan, Tiara and Dejah. Love and Favor, Mom

Lisa is Southern at heart. Raised in Rutherfordton North Carolina She grew up playing 4 squares and beating the street lights home. Graduating from R-S central, she pursued a career as a Registered Nurse. Lisa enjoys reading and silent auctions in her spare time. She resides in Asheville NC with her Husband Mark and teenage daughter Dejah

lisagray5058@gmail.com
http:www.facebook.com/lisagray
Instagram oilynursern
YouTube Lisa Gray MyGodlife

December 2
Alice M. Jarmin

Colossians 3:13 (NLT)

"Make allowance for each other's faults, and forgive anyone who offends you. Remember, the Lord forgave you, so you must forgive others."

We've all been hurt by someone; be it in word or deed. Relationships end horribly, children act disrespectfully, or coworkers do not respect boundaries. Our nature tells us to hold a grudge or get one up on the other person; but the Word commands us to forgive. Genuine forgiveness is difficult to achieve. Qualities like kindness, patience and love help to make it easier to pardon the offenses. Deciding to forgive, truly forgive, frees you from anger and allows the healing process to begin. Relinquishing your hold on anger will release unimaginable blessings in your life. Try it and see!

Social Media Tags: https://www.facebook.com/amreid.williams

City/State: Creedmoor, North Carolina

Email: amreid-williams@hotmail.com

December 3
Charlette Fairchild

Isaiah 41:10

"Fear not, for I am with you; be not dismayed, for I am your God; I will strengthen you, I will help you, I will uphold you with my righteous right hand."

God's word is a beautiful thing!! Sometimes life gets hard. There are probably days you feel as if you can't go on or want to just lay in bed and sleep life away! TODAY IS A NEW DAY!! Be encouraged! You have a God that loves you so much that he will provide the strength you don't have! No matter what you do or where you go, he is with you! To think at this very moment he is uplifting you, encouraging you and bringing you peace! Get up and rejoice in God's blessings!! YOU are loved, valued and cherished!

December 4

Shannon L. Turner

Psalm 23:1 "The Lord is my Shepherd, I lack nothing."

This faith journey can be a bit of a roller coaster at times, with its ups and downs, twists and turns. Lord when my mind races or heart grows anxious please calm with your peace that surpasses all understanding. Lord please help me to always see that You are with me and providing for me especially in the times I am in survival mode, in my own strength, trying to handle what life seems to have thrown at me. You are my Savior, my Friend, the Lover of my soul, my Constant. Shannon L. Turner

Email: embracinglife@shannonlturner.com

December 5
Keisha Boatwright

So, I like what I see when I'm looking at me
When I'm walking past the mirror
No stress through the night, at a time in my life
Ain't worried about if you feel it
Got my head on straight, I got my mind right
I ain't gonna let you kill it
You see I wouldn't change my life, my life's just" – Mary J. Blige

Know that loving yourself first is not an option it's a must. Know that it matters what you tell yourself your heart is listening. Give yourself permission to embrace your flaws because are enough. There are some things you can't do by yourself, stop and ask for help when necessary. Live life to the fullest by taking some chances. All that to say it's perfectly fine to love yourself unconditionally and to be unapologetic. People will have their opinions but you don't have to feed into. Silence speaks volume but know the power of hearing your voice. Most importantly breathe.

Keisha Boatwright also known as "Kesh" is a native of Newark, New Jersey. She attended Rutgers University in New Brunswick, New Jersey as an engineering major prior to entering the military. Kesh is a fourteen-year Navy Veteran. Keisha is a certified Yoga instructor. She completed 200hr YTT in 2017 at Yoga Mindset in High Point, NC. Keisha is also an author writing her first short story.; "The Meet and Greet" in 2015 which was published in Short Fiction Break literary magazine and co-author of Unleashed Travails - from Pain to Purpose. Keisha is a mother of three and GiGi to one grandchild currently in NC; splits her spare time between writing, teaching yoga or crafting.

Facebook: soulistickesh kreativitybykesh *Instagram:* soulistickes reativitybykesh
Twitter: MzKeshNJ www.soulistickesh.com www.mzkesh.wordpress.com

December 6
Charlisa Herriott

"Where is Your Faith?"

NOW FAITH is the substance of things HOPED for, the evidence of things NOT YET seen according to Hebrews 11:1. Can you place your TRUST in believing in something that you cannot see? Can you have FAITH in something that is intangible, unforeseeable but yet believable? IF you said, "yes", then your level of FAITH is strong. Bu if you struggle with what you believe to come true or manifest within your life, then I ask you this, "Where is your FAITH?"

Charlisa Herriott is an Author, Minister, Speaker, 2x Cancer Survivor and Survivor Coach. She empowers women who experience the frails of life to rise from their ashes to Live on Purpose, Live with Passion and Live Life Full!

Website: www.CharlisaHerriottASurvivorsVoice.com
Instagram.com/CharlisaHerriott
Facebook.com/CharlisaHerriott
Linkedin.com/inCharlisaHerriott
Twitter.com/CharlisaHerriot

December 7

Eve S. Hendricks

"I Exist for This"

In a world where many are trying to find their purpose, there are days in which you are unsure of your existence. Why are you here? What are you supposed to be doing? If everything wrong is happening for me, why do I exist? Well, let me enlighten you, you exist for all of that. Everything that you have endured and will endure is a part of your existence. When we often ask God, why me? His answer is, why not you? Proverbs 3:5-6 NIV reminds us to trust in the Lord with all your heart and lean not on your own understanding; in all your ways submit to him, and He will make your paths straight. Get out of your own way and trust God's way. When life starts to happen and you do not feel strong enough to handle it, remind yourself, YOU EXIST FOR THIS.

Eve S. Hendricks is a youthful and loving mom who credits those attributes to her three beautiful daughters, Akala, Ayana and Alivia. She enjoys thrifting, spending time with her children and inspiring other women to live their best life despite setbacks. She loves God and that is her super power.

Facebook: Eve Hendricks
IG: on the_eve_lifestyle_
City/State: Graham, NC Email: ontheevestyle@gmail.com

December 8
Audrika Danielle

Financial Freedom

DO NOT ever be ashamed of where you've been. Keep on & win. They mock & lie about your story but will never understand your glory. I am ever so thankful for words of wisdom, a knowledge of love & minds of infinite positive energy flowing with momentum along with having developed the ability to positively affect hearts & mindsets for generational prosperity one family at a time...and then some.

Born Audrika Walton in North Carolina and raised in Michigan. The eldest of three children she developed many skills & discovered many gifts along life's journey. Audrika Danielle is a mother of eight children 7 girls & 1 boy. At a young age Audrika Danielle learned how to braid hair and was interested in crafts. Her first finished project was a latch-hooked rug and from there she learned many others such as crochet, weaving, repurposing furniture pieces, clothing and more. Audrika Danielle enjoyed having her creations in local downtown Decatur, Georgia boutiques. She specializes in unique handmade creations.

Audrika Danielle attended Bauder College & learned Fashion Design in the early 2000's and went on to become a nurse in 2012. Audrika Danielle then moved to

Florida where she discovered that she had a passion for helping people to destress as well as a natural knack at listening & problem solving which gave way to both a career as a Full Specialist in 2014 which consists of Manicure/Pedicures, Facials, Foot Detox, and even learning how to do henna tattoos as well as Facial Threading. Audrika Danielle along with opening up a mini spa in Florida enjoyed becoming a Transformational Life Coach and putting together workshops along with mini pampering sessions. Audrika Danielle looks forward to what is next...

Feel free to contact Audrika Danielle @

321-339-8984

artisticsouljah@gmail.com

artisticsouljah.com

facebook.com/artisticsouljah

facebook.com/audrikadanielle

December 9
Janet French-Cannedy

Scripture: Ruth 3:11 – "Now, my daughter, do not, fear. I will do for you whatever you ask, for all my people in the city know that you are a woman of excellence."

As I travel this amazing journey called life, I find fulfillment in encouraging others along the way. Having survived six major back surgeries, I have come to realize that becoming a woman of excellence, may involve many obstacles (including pain), but it should not prevent us from inspiring others to live their full potential. Even through our pain we must remember that we can do all things through Christ who strengthens us, in our pursuit towards excellence.

December 10

Avice Burchett

Joshua 1:9. "Have I not commanded you? Be strong and courageous. Do not be afraid; do not be discouraged, for the Lord your God will be with you wherever you go."

Often times in life, we are faced with giants that seem impossible to defeat. During these moments we must remember God's promises in His Word that we already have victory in Jesus. It is during these darkest hours that we must put our trust and Faith in Him. These storms and challenges have purpose. God allows certain situations to arise so that our faith in Him will grow.

Email: burchettavice@yahoo.com

December 11
Sheree "Sunshine" Cox

Romans 8:6
"For to be carnally minded is death; but to be spiritually minded is life and peace."

In our lives we encounter trials and tribulations that frustrate the mind to believe that all has failed. It's in that moment that you stumble upon a carnal bondage. When we realize that we are of a spiritual mind and soul, we are set free. Every battle starts in the mind; however, we all are uniquely designed to win anything that comes against us! We must determine how we channel our mind spiritually or physically? The spiritual mindset allows abundant power over our calling and the carnal mindset plays on the playground of your mind causing distortion and distraction.

Today, we choose the gifts that God has given us to have self-control, joy and peace.

Jeremiah 29:11 (NIV) "For I know the plans I have for you", declares the Lord, Plans to prosper you and not to harm you, plans to give you hope and a future."

I never knew how strong of a woman I was until being strong was the only choice I had. Anyone can give up; it's the easiest thing in the world to do, but to hold it together when everyone would expect you to fall apart is true strength. Sometimes you have to humble yourself, swallow your pride and put your brave face away and break down. Hug someone who loves you just as much as you love them, have a good cry wash out your heart. Perhaps our eyes need to be washed by our tears every once in a while, so that we can see life with a clear view again. Always remember that no matter how hard life gets God has a plan for you!

Bridget Jackson is a Service Coordinator with Arnesta Healthcare of Virginia. Bridget specializes in home health care where she is responsible for complying with all relevant federal, state and local laws in her region. She is a strong believer in the power of positive thinking in the workplace, Bridget regularly executes In-Service training programs and competent supervision to improve employee efficiency and patient care. Bridget liaise with private organizations and patients on behalf of her agency. Bridget is dedicated to helping the community with the proper resources they need to live at home in good health, safety and comfort.

City/State: Meherrin,Virginia
Email: bjackson@onediversity.org

December 13
Sylvia Pauling

Genesis 50:20 New Living Translation
"You intended to harm me, but God intended it all for good. He brought me to this position so I could save the lives of many people."

God can take that thing that the enemy intended to use to destroy you and turn it around in your favor. God's healing can manifest in all circumstances. You may be experiencing a lost and the grief of that lost has consumed you but hold on because there is nothing too hard for God. He will carry you through. Your faith in God can and will sustain you. The devil wants you to believe he's won the fight but, on this day declare that you are a winner. Take a deep breath, sit in good posture, hold your head up, trust and believe that the devil did not win. Move forward today allowing God to use YOU to be a Blessing to someone else. As you bless someone else you will be blessed. BLESSINGS AND MORE BLESSINGS!!

Sylvia Pauling is a native South Carolinian. She earned her Master of Arts degree in Guidance and Counseling from Trinity College. She earned her Bachelor of Science degree in Psychology from South Carolina State University. Ms. Pauling is a licensed professional counselor who is an activist and advocate in the movement to end domestic violence. Ms. Pauling is the Founder of The Pauling Institute Inc. in Washington, D.C., a mental health agency where she uses a holistic approach through psychotherapy and other counseling skills to help others improve their mental health. Her areas of expertise are domestic violence, posttraumatic stress disorder (PTSD), grief and family therapy.

Ms. Pauling is a Certified Danger Assessor and a DC Victim Assistance Academy Graduate. She is certified in NTU Psychology. She is a current candidate for a PhD in Public Policy at Walden University. She was the first Domestic Violence Specialist for the District of Columbia Child Welfare Agency, where she remained for 15 years. She is currently a Program Manager for the U.S. Department of Justice/Office On Violence Against Women.

Ms. Pauling is passionate about helping others take care of their mental health. She uses a collaborative client-therapist approach, which emphasizes the individual's strengths and insights and is based upon a balance of body, mind and soul. She holds victims and survivors of domestic violence close to her heart and has dedicated her life to helping them break free from the vicious cycle of domestic violence and helping communities respond to domestic violence in a healthy manner.

Social Media Tags
FB (Sylvia Pauling)
IG (paulings1968)
Twitter (THEPAULINGINSTITUTE @ S_Pauling)
Website (www.thepaulinginstituteinc.com)

December 14
Mary Harris

Matthew 5:14-15 NIV "You are the light of the world. A town built on a hill cannot be hidden. Neither do people light a lamp and put it under a bowl. Instead they put it on its stand, and it gives light to everyone in the house."

Live Out Loud - this seems like a simple phrase, but we tend to not live full out, center stage, front and center especially women. We support others' dreams but aren't as passionate in pursuit of our own. Your vision matters! You diminishing yourself to make others feel important does a disservice to you & God! He creates us to be peculiar & bold not to shrink & crumble. So be the bodacious bold and beautiful Y-O-U who can change lives, spread hope & shape nations! Decide to live each day intentionally on purpose. Living Your Life Unapologetically Out Loud!

Mary Harris is a domestic violence and sexual abuse advocate through her foundation; Dvine Beauti, a minister, speaker, contributing author to the bestselling book Faith for Fiery Trial, social media personality, host of From Trial to Triumph Facebook Live Show, and her greatest accomplishment of being proud mother and grandmother.

www.dvinebeauti.com;   www.facebook.com/realdvinebeauti;
www.instagram.com/realdvinebeauti;   www.twitter.com/realdvinebeauti;
https://www.linkedin.com/in/realdvinebeauti/

positivae@yahoo.com

December 15

Gina R. Brown

Matthew 9:20-23
"If he touches it, it has to change."

Be encouraged, knowing God is a Healer, a Deliverer, a Way Maker. Take the initiative like the woman with the issue of blood. Position yourself for a touch. He is a game changer. You may be hurting, exhausted and bleeding from the thorn in your side, but don't give up. Your faith will draw you before him. It will give you strength to endure, to step forward and reach for his touch. Move like you believe his word. If he touches it, it has to change.

Gina R. Brown is the Founder and Executive Director of Exploits International Ministries. She is a Licensed Minister who has been serving in ministry for over twenty-five years. Professionally she is a proven Project Manager, Administrator, Motivational Speaker and Mobilizer who strongly believes the word of God and is on a personal mission to fulfill the call on her life. She passionately serves in the area of missions and outreach and uses that passion to fuel her and others as she works to enlighten, train, mobilize and pray. As a Missionary, she has traveled to multiple countries for overseas mission work. As a Mentor, she shares her education and life experiences to motivate and empower women, youth and young adults to live their best life. As a cancer overcomer and warrior, she uses that experience to bring awareness, support and encouragement to those who are affected by that disease. #takingcancerdown

Email: gina.brown1000@gmail.com

December 16
Donna M. Douglas

Psalms 57:1-7
"Be merciful unto me, O God, be merciful unto me: for my soul trusteth in thee: yea, in the shadow of thy wings will I make my refuge, until these calamities be over past. 2 I will cry unto God most high; unto God that performeth all things for me. 3 He shall send from heaven, and save me from the reproach of him that would swallow me up. Selah. God shall send forth his mercy and his truth. 4 My soul is among lions: and I lie even among them that are set on fire, even the sons of men, whose teeth are spears and arrows, and their tongue a sharp sword. 5 Be thou exalted, O God, above the heavens; let thy glory be above all the earth. 6 They have prepared a net for my steps; my soul is bowed down: they have digged a pit before me, into the midst whereof they are fallen themselves. Selah. 7 My heart is fixed, O God, my heart is fixed: I will sing and give praise."

Scripture reveals David wasn't hiding alone. This anointed but not-yet-appointed king led group of 400 discouraged, distressed, debt ridden and discontented men. Not exactly the people you want with you during one of the darkest seasons of your life. Children of God need to be so confident in who God is and what His words say, that when dark days come, we fix our eyes on the truth of God's goodness. Praise may not shift our circumstances, but it will definitely begin to change our hearts. Has God ever used a dart season in your life to birth something new in you?

Donna Douglas has a true talent for communicating and a deep passion for people. As a certified trainer, speaker and coach, Donna aspires to encourage and motivate others to take action towards the realization of their vision, their dreams and goals. She is an eloquent speaker who delivers persuasive, inspiring and moving words that emerge from her character and echoes the motives of her heart.

EMAIL: dmarie1612@gmail.com

Social Media:

Linkedin - www.linkedin.com/in/donna-douglas-5845283

Facebook – https://www.facebook.com/dmdouglas1

December 17
Pam Dorsey

Psalms 139:13-14 (NKJV)

"For You formed my inward parts; You covered me in my mother's womb. I will praise You, for I am fearfully and wonderfully made; Marvelous are Your works, and that my soul knows very well."

Today your declaration and affirmation are that you are becoming better daily. Be proud of the woman that you see in the mirror because you have fought to become her. You are Fearfully and Wonderfully made, knitted perfectly in your mother's womb. God handcrafted you into who He wanted you to be and who He needs you to be in this earth! No One can do you like you! You are an Original created by the Originator of all mankind. Embrace All of You! Trust God! Trust You! Trust Your Process! You are Needed and Necessary!

Pamela E. Dorsey was born and raised in Greenville, SC and now resides in Columbia, SC. She is a wife, mother, author, entrepreneur, and speaker. Pam is purposed to help women not only discover their God given purpose, but walk it out! At the core of Pam's brand are these three words,

Purpose Passion and Life
Facebook.com/IAmPamDorsey **Instagram.com/IAmPamDorsey**

Twitter.com/IAmPamDorsey LinkedIn: https://www.linkedin.com/in/pamela-dorsey-80a3a344

December 18

D'Tondja M. Foster

Forgiveness for The Little Girl Inside

Forgive me for not protecting you when I could.
Forgive me little girl for believing you could have done any better than you did
with what you were given.
Forgive me for stealing your childhood away and making you grow so fast.
Forgive all the times I told you, you weren't enough because of your size, your
color, disability.
Forgive me for starving you on so many levels I almost took your life.
Forgive me for beating you mentally, suffocating you physically that I took away
your will to just Be.

December 19
Candice Davis

2 Corinthians 12:9-10
"My grace is sufficient for you, for my power is made perfect in weakness.'
Therefore, I will boast all the more gladly of my weaknesses, so that the
power of Christ may rest upon me. For the sake of Christ, then, I am content
with weaknesses, insults, hardships, persecutions, and calamities. For when I
am weak, then I am strong".

You may have endured hardships in life whether financial, with love, or health
and are maybe thinking you will not see better days. God tells us that his grace is
sufficient to not only see us through but to use these adversities to build us up.
Seek God in everything and rest in Him knowing that He is continuously working
it out for your good. The idea and visions of what you think is better are given to
you by God. They are attainable if you keep the faith. You may get knocked down,
you will grow weary, but it is important that in those moments you allow God to
be your rock. He is solid and His love for you is everlasting.

Candice Davis is a mother of four children living in Philadelphia. A teenage mother
and high school dropout, she is currently enrolled in college. Candice enjoys
encouraging others to use their hardships as fuel to excel in life. The cofounder
of Royal Rebels on the Rise Candice is seeking to help others build on and grow
through life's curveballs.

Instagram Tag: Royalrebels215
Facebook: Royal Rebels Inc.
Website: www.royalrebelsontherise.com

December 20
Trina Horton

(Isaiah 43:18-19) "Do not remember the former things, nor consider the things of old. Behold, I will do a new thing, now it shall spring forth; shall you not know it? I will even make a road in the wilderness and rivers in the desert."

Something New

I was about to turn the big 50. Looking back over my life I started thinking about the mistakes, past hurts, disappointments, and pains that I had suffered. I felt like a failure. In this moment I realized that God does not want me looking in the rear-view mirror of life, instead it's time for me to focus on my future. Keep moving forward. This is the only way you will ever accomplish all that God has called you to. Where ever you find yourself today, remember that God wants to do a new thing in your life!

Trina is a native of Atlanta, Georgia where she resides with her beautiful daughter. She is the co-founder of Power of the Pair, a speaking and consulting boutique that educates women on how friendships and collaborations can create thriving lifestyles through accountability, emotional support, and boosting confidence. Trina received a Bachelor of Arts degree from Spelman College, and is presently a Teacher's Candidate for a Master's Degree in Special Education. She enjoys mentoring and volunteering with various organizations.

Social Media: Website- www.powerofthepair.com; Facebook – www.facebook.com/Trina.Horton.39 ; Instagram- @powerofthepair; Twitter - @powerofthepair **Email**: trinahorton0501@gmail.com

December 21

Lisa Harris-Jones

Job 42:12A

'So, the Lord Blessed the latter end of Job more than his beginning"

Life IS Good???

I study the Word, tithe, pray faithfully, treat others right, stay in my lane and I diligently try to do what's right! Yet, I'm continuously going through and sometimes I want to throw in the towel!

Sometimes we feel that we've done all that we can and begin to question God when life gets too tough. God being God, has to step in and remind us of exactly who He is! God knows our heart; our intentions and we have to continue to trust Him and know that He is behind the scenes working on our behalf.

How your story ends is more amazing than you KNOW right now.
Hold on! Trust God, it ain't over!!

Email: telicia13@gmail.com

FB: Lisa Harris-Jones
IG @teliciaj
Website: www.Hisimage.us

December 22
Cassandra F. Ward

Proverbs 18:21
"Death and life are in the power of the tongue, and those who love it will eat its fruit"

Speak life my daughter, the Power of Life and Death are in the Power of the tongue. Do you truly comprehend what that really mean? Words Kill, Words give LIFE, they're either poison or fruit. Which will you choose? You can't talk negative and expect positive results. You can't speak defeat and expect victory. You can't speak lack and expect abundance. Words are like seeds, what you plant, you give life too. My challenge to you is that you speak things as if they were.

Begin your day with this set of affirmations:
I will hear the voice of the Holy Spirit
I will Lead and not Follow
I will create and not destroy
I am the head, not the tail
I am above, not beneath
I am the lender, not the borrower
I am loved by God,
I am chosen by God
I am protected by God

No weapon formed against me shall prosper, and every tongue
That rises against me in judgement shall be condemned. I'm healthy, I'm humble, I'm happy, I'm wealthy. I (state your name) will never be broke another day in my life, and I will live the fullness of life and all God has for me.

Cassandra F. Ward, was born and raised in Rich Square, North Carolina. Cassandra currently resides in Greensboro NC and is the mother on one adult son, Shaquis' Jaquon. Cassandra is a graduate of East Carolina, with a Master's Degree in Middle Grades Math and Language Arts. She is employed as an educator with Guilford County Schools. One of her greatest accomplishments is becoming a Co-author of an Amazon Best Seller in 2017. Cassandra strongly believes in the Power of your words. It is her prayer, that you will use your words to change your life.

"**Every day won't be the same, You will have good days, bad days, trying days, overwhelming days, tired days, invigorated days and days you feel you cannot go on. No matter what day you are having today decide to still show up. Show up and Keep going! @commandingline**

Finding the strength to endure is sometimes the hardest thing and most times you feel defeated. We don't see what GOD has for us and don't understand some of the trails and valleys he puts us through to strengthen us. We fall victim to our circumstances and at the brink of a breakthrough we give up never seeing our destiny. One thing you must remember GOD has a perfect plan and everything we go through has a purpose. So, those days that you feel like giving up, remember all things work for the good of the Lord. Show up and perform in excellence; see all that GOD has for you.

Website
www.uptowndivaaccessories.biz
Email
uptowndivatx@outlook.com

uptown_divaaccessories - Instagram
Uptown Diva Accessories - Facebook

December 24
Theresa Head

Michelle Obama

"Do not bring people in your life who weigh you down. And trust your instincts ... good relationships feel good. They feel right. They don't hurt. They're not painful. That's not just with somebody you want to marry, but it's with the friends that you choose. It's with the people you surround yourselves with. — Words spoken so true; I am sure we all had people around us that did not have our best interest at heart. Positivity bring positive results in our lives."

I am the CEO of Head Art Works family business. I am a wife, mother and grandmother. I have a bachelor's degree in business management. I also am a legal secretary, medical assistant and Emergency Medical Technician. We make scented hand craft items.

Website- http://www.headartworks.online
Social Media- Head Art Works- Facebook,
Instagram- Twitter- Pintress- LinkedIn

headartworks@gmail.com

December 25
Donna Cushenberry

There are times in life when you will be faced with the question " What do I do when I don't know what to do?" It is in these times that you must remember that God has carried you in the past and that He is orchestrating a plan that will position you for the next season in your life. This is not a guarantee that the journey will be free from challenges and trials but it is important to quickly recall the faithfulness of God. Our Sovereign Lord is still your Provider, Protector, Way Maker and our closest Friend.

Isaiah 46:9 "Remember the things I have done in the past. For I alone am God! I am God, and there is none like me."

Donna R. Cushenberry is called "The Encourager". She loves God and inspires others to press and persevere in the face of adversity to live out the greatness within themselves. Donna is an entrepreneur and leader who is committed to building the Kingdom.
Social Media:
FaceBook- Donna Cushenberry
Instagram - Donna_Cushenberry

December 26
Donna Cushenberry

Romans 8:37 NKJV
"37 Yet in all these things we are more than conquerors through Him who loved us."

You are seated in Heavenly Places! You are not your past and every failed relationship, poor decision, reckless act and even the hurt you caused others is behind you. Therefore, consider every challenge and struggle you faced to be God's strategy that lifted you above what was already under your feet. Sometimes we struggle with moving forward in our lives because we do not see ourselves as deserving of the promises of God. Today, I challenge you to see yourself as an amazing woman. You are a Winner, an Achiever and you are an Overcomer.

Donna R. Cushenberry is called "The Encourager". She loves God and inspires others to press and persevere in the face of adversity to live out the greatness within themselves. Donna is an entrepreneur and leader who is committed to building the Kingdom.

Social Media:
FaceBook- Donna Cushenberry
Instagram - Donna_Cushenberry

December 27
Ashante Smallwood

"You may encounter many defeats, but you must not be defeated. In fact, it may be necessary to encounter the defeats, so you can know who you are, what you can rise from, how you can still come out of it."
~ Maya Angelou

You are a woman of many strengths, jewels and gifts. Throughout life you will go through trials and tribulations. You may feel the weight of the world on your shoulders and it just will not let up. Just remember life is not happening to you, but for you. Do not lose focus. You were made for this. Your story is shaping you for your divine purpose. Your divine purpose is to help you fulfil the assignment God has called you to complete. Please hold on a little bit longer. The reward for patience and obedience is great favor and blessings.

Ashante Smallwood is the Founder/Owner of Princess Asia's Collection, LLC and Co-Founder of Avva's Production. I perform as an Entrepreneur, designer, mentor, author and administrative director. My mission is to empower female youth, by promoting self-love, self-care, character building and confidence.

Social media links:
FB: Princess Asia's Collection, LLC
Instagram: princess_asiascollection
Website: www.princessasiacollection.com
Email: Ashante@princessasiacollection.com

December 28
Nikki W. Miller

Jeremiah 29:11 NIV
"God Has A Perfect Plan For Your Life."

The prophet Jeremiah reminds us, "For I know the plans for you, declares the Lord, plans to prosper you and not to harm you, plans to give you hope and a future." As believers of Jesus Christ we must remember that oftentimes the plans of God for our lives may not always feel good as we are promised to experience trials and tribulations in this life. Yes, these times are a part of God's plan for our lives. Why? We must remember that the best growth comes through persevering through these tests, not escaping them, but understanding that in the midst, God will give us hope and joy!

Nikki W. Miller is a passionate Educator, Entrepreneur, Christian Life Coach, and Author. She is the wife of Anthony Louis Miller of 27 years and the mother of two beautiful adult daughters Gabrielle and Moriah Miller. Nikki is the doggie mom of a gorgeous Shih Tzu Macey Ann Miller. Nikki serves in many ministries at her church in Greenville, NC Sycamore Hill Missionary Baptist Church and is an active member of Delta Sigma Theta Sorority, Inc.

December 29
Chantaine Rhoe-Bulluck

Hebrews 12:28-29 (NIV)
"Therefore, since we are receiving a kingdom that cannot be shaken, let us be thankful, and so worship God acceptably with reverence and awe, for our God is a consuming fire."

I start every morning singing along loudly with "For Every Mountain" by Kurt Carr because I need the reminder. It's easy to praise Him when everything is going right. It's real hard to remember to praise him when my world is shaking! It's so good to know we have a God that gives us "a brand-new mercy along with each new day". Praise him now for what He is about to do! Trust Him to conquer and consume the enemies without - and within - that are greater than you. Start your day with praise and watch Him work!

Chantaine is a powerful speaker with an incredible message. As a result of the travel strategies she teaches in her Experience Rejuvenation™ seminars and private coaching, people have epic experiences and amazing memories for years to come.

Connect with Chantaine at www.LettzChat.com
https://www.facebook.com/ChantaineBulluck
https://www.linkedin.com/in/chantainerhoebulluck
Email: crb@rejuvenateyourlife.biz

December 30

Gwendolyn Arnette

Isaiah 65:24 New King James Version (NKJV)
²⁴ "It shall come to pass
That before they call, I will answer;
And while they are still speaking, I will hear."

Our Father always listens for Faith which comes out of our mouths. As we understand who HE is as GOD, then and only then we'll know that every time we call on Him in Faith, *even before we open our mouths*, He's already heard us. OUT OF THE ABUNDANCE OF THE HEART THE MOUTH SPEAKS...so if you find yourself in desolate place, where darkness is all around you, begin to speak out of your mouth "Oh God My God I know you are able" Understand that God has already worked out a plan for your deliverance because of your FAITH!

Gwendolyn Arnette is an entrepreneur and owner of GiGi's Creations an Innovative Branding Solution, focused on Branding Photography while also providing other brand solutions. She is a mother of three and a grandmother of three. Her motto passed down from her grandmother is "TRUST IN THE LORD AND TREAT EVERYBODY RIGHT" the key to longevity.

Contact details are missing:
www.instagram.com/gigis_creativeshots

https://www.facebook.com/gigis.creativeshots

https://gdmacollins.myportfolio.com

December 31

Fayola Delica

"Your Hidden Treasure is in the mess"

"You are as strong as your challenges." By Fayola Delica

At different points in my life, I had faced some very challenging times. I used to think that I was being punished by God. However, over time God had showed me that He was just building my faith and trust in Him. In hindsight, I have a deeper relationship with God and know my inner strength to be much stronger than ever before. Therefore, I encourage you to stand on the promises of Romans 8:28, "And we know that in all things God works for the good of those who love him, who have been called according to his purpose." (NIV, Holy Bible)

Fayola Delica is a native from Miami, FL. She is a Minister, Registered Nurse, Educator, International Award-winning Speaker, International Best-selling Author, Serial Entrepreneur, Beauty Queen, Youth Advocate, and a Community Leader. Ms. Delica is in the process of establishing her five-fold ministry. She is a woman after God's own heart. Her passion is about doing her Heavenly Father's business by advancing the Kingdom of God.

Facebook: www.facebook.com/FayolaDelica

Twitter: @fayoladelica Instagram: @fayoladelicallc

LinkedIn: https://www.linkedin.com/in/FayolaDelica

W: www.fayoladelica.com

E: info@fayoladelica.com

P: 954-562-7706

January

1	Shannon L. Turner	16	Minister Sonya Arrington, LMSW
2	Celestine Davis	17	Gina R. Brown
3	Charlette Fairchild	18	DeShonda Monique Jennings
4	Marnie Pouget	19	Pastor Kimberly Hall
5	Marnie Pouget	20	Audrika Danielle
6	Mary Davis	21	Michelle Bae Prewitt
7	Theresa Head	22	Kyla M. Neil
8	Dien Neubauer	23	Avice Burchett
9	Sharon M. Hyman	24	Brenda Freeman
10	LaTasha "WOP" Williams	25	Chantaine Rhoe-Bulluck
11	Candace Wilkerson	26	Gwendolyn V. Smith
12	Charmaine E. Betty-Singleton	27	Sheila Morton
13	Pamela Davis-Ghavami	28	Linda Latrice Ranson
14	Shacre Bennett	29	Tocha Moore
15	Andrea Maine	30	Tijera Moseley
		31	Ashante Smallwood

February

1	Nateshe Williams	15	Leticia Hicks
2	Tamala Coleman	16	Sayra Kohen
3	Tschanna Taylor	17	Margareth "Maggy" Reed
4	Charlisa Herriott	18	Consuelo McAllister Covin
5	Crystal Bodie Smith	19	Karmelita Stevens
6	Brenda Colter	20	Donna White, M.Ed
7	D'Tondja M. Foster	21	Basheba Maiden
8	Erica Hicks	22	Mary Beasley
9	Linda Feliciano	23	Naomi Roe (Shaffer)
10	Toni Garvin	24	Tunda Wannaker
11	Wyetha Renee' Cairns	25	Nikki Denise
12	LaTasha "WOP" Williams	26	LaTasha "WOP" Williams
13	Camesha S. Williams	27	Lisa C. Gray
14	Vernita Stevens	28	Ava R. Gordon

March

1	Gwendolyn Arnette		17	Stephanie Shelling
2	Key Bentley		18	Yolanda Sinclair
3	Teresa Robinson		19	Tia Kennebrew
4	Sharice Rush		20	Gwendolyn Demby
5	Tameka Bowens		21	Mary Harris
6	Dr. Christine Handy		22	Jacqueline Knowles
7	Maria L. Perryman		23	Doral Rolle
8	Margareth "Maggy" Reed		24	Danielle Mo'nae Worth
9	Rhonda Wilson		25	Sabrina Jones
10	Cathy Harris		26	Chelsea Chase
11	Janae Black		27	Argentina Harris
12	Cecellia Rountree		28	Miriam M Wright
13	Cheena R. Headen		29	Ruby La-Nice Garner
14	Jahmia Jackson		30	LaTasha Alex
15	Pastor Osita S. Osagbue		31	Lena Payton-Webb
16	Jennifer J. Bryant			

April

1	Rasheeda George		16	Cassandra F. Ward
2	Lakisha harris		17	Kimberlee Bilbrew
3	LaToya O. Guion (Olivia G.)		18	Janet French-Cannedy
4	LaTasha Jones, MSW, ASW		19	Candice Simpson
5	LaKel Farley		20	LaToya O. Guion
6	Brenda Brasher		21	Nakiya Jackson
7	Natasha Saunders		22	Gaylin Munford
8	Sheila E. Morton		23	Erica L. Brasher, M.Ed
9	Brunette Kirtdoll Smith		24	Debra Reed, LICSW
10	Sharmaine M. Moore		25	Deanna Murphy
11	Edie Price		26	Dien Neubauer
12	Sharlene Peters		27	Allison Braham
13	Chou Hallegra		28	Kim B. Wells, M.Ed.
14	Celestine Davis		29	Teara Q. Booker
15	Shawnee Palmer, LCSW, LAC		30	Jessie C. Love

May

1	Danielle Mo'nae Worth	17	Rhonda "Ro" Solomon
2	Dr. Christine Handy	18	Krystle Bradley
3	Teneisha Robinson	19	Terri Sharmaine
4	Brittnee Toeran	20	LaToya O.Guion
5	Renee Dantzler	21	M.Latea Newhouse
6	Geanell E. Robinson	22	Angelica Lassiter
7	Linda A. Feliciano	23	Destiny Amanda Johnson
8	Alice M. Jarman	24	Carmelesha Matthewson
9	Debbie Ann Andrews	25	Demetria Burren
10	Keni Fleming	26	LaTasha Alex
11	Dr. LaToya Wiggins	27	Akasha Kinlock
12	Pastor Margareth "Maggy" Reed	28	Kelly S. White
13	Jessie C. Love	29	Atiya Fowler-Myers
14	Sandra Hardy	30	Nicole Gaines
15	Valerie Woodard	31	Shanae Starnes
16	Melinda Wynn		

June

1	Lisa-Gaye Richards	16	Pastor Margareth "Maggy" Reed
2	Theresa Hand	17	Jean A. Garner
3	Nalema Ross	18	Karshena McCain Adkins
4	Candice J. Arnold	19	Lisa Harris-Jones
5	Nakisha Blackwell	20	Nakisha Blackwell
6	Minister Robyn Curry	21	Kimberly Carter
7	Nikki W. Miller	22	Hope Krystal Hood
8	Brieanna Toeran	23	Tempie Walton-Berry
9	Katrina French	24	Queensheeba Kennedy
10	Freida Henderson	25	Lisa Blauvelt
11	Carole Sallid-Times	26	Nichelle B. Crump
12	Rochelle Redding	27	Cheyenne X. Williams
13	LaTasha Jones, MSW, ASW	28	Candice Davis
14	Fredrika Sellers	29	Stacey Florio
15	Michelle Bae Prewitt	30	Hattie Hammond

July

1	Charlisa Herriott		17	Lorrie A. Simmons
2	Viva Lewis-Harris		18	Dr. Mary J. Huntley
3	Eve S. Hendricks		19	Vernita Stevens
4	Rasheeda George		20	Yvette English
5	Alma Holley		21	Johnnia Mitchell
6	Erica Hicks		22	Fayola Delica
7	Nikki Goodloe		23	Temitope Oyewole
8	Natasha K. Ransom		24	Rose Hall
9	Pam Dorsey		25	Janelle R. Dawkins
10	LaShaunda R. Browne		26	Nichelle B. Crump
11	Mary Davis		27	Majidah "HisGlory" Smith
12	Mary ScullyD		28	LaTashia Prince
13	Keisha Boatwright		29	Bridget Jackson
14	Rosalind Jones		30	Terri Booker
15	Erica Hicks		31	Susie Lynnette Sanders
16	Terri Sharmaine			

August

1	Andrea Maine		17	LaTasha Alex
2	Latonya L. Turner		18	Toni Garvin
3	Minister Taneshia Curry		19	LaDonna Ann Morgan
4	Kierra Si'Mone		20	Theresa Head
5	Trenee' M Fountain		21	Rachel E. Bills
6	Lakeshia Trumaine Robinson		22	Cheryl Kehl
7	Jessie C. Love		23	Pastor Tangela P. Lane
8	Debra Reed, LICSW		24	Sayra H. Kohen
9	Doral Rolle		25	Alonya Moore
10	Tammy Wilkins		26	Dr. Marie O. Etienne
11	DeShonda Monique Jennings		27	Brenda Welch
12	Gwendolyn V. Smith		28	Dr. Vernita Roach
13	Karmelita Stevens		29	Brenda Colter
14	Jacqueline Knowles		30	Keyuna Faye Webster
15	Cynthia M. Williams		31	Sharice Rush
16	Chou Hallegra			

September

1	Kiyona Brooks	16	Edie Price
2	Nikki Denise	17	Tunda Wannamaker
3	Chelsea Chase	18	Pastor Kimberly Hall
4	Miriam M. Wright	19	Kiyona Brooks
5	Nicole Gaines	20	Tamekia Boswell-Taylor
6	Debbie Tucker	21	Qiana Davis
7	Wyetha Renee Cairns	22	Rochelle Redding
8	Lynn Meyer	23	Precious Jarrells
9	Sheila E. Morton	24	Kim B. Wells, M.Ed.
10	LaTasha "WOP" Williams	25	Genell Aikens
11	Charmaine E. Betty-Singleton	26	Destiny Amanda Johnson
12	Yolanda Sinclair	27	Cecellia Rountree
13	LaTasha Alex	28	Raquel Hernandez
14	M.Latea Newhouse	29	Brigitte Denise Andrews
15	Donna G. Robinson	30	Wyetha Renee Cairns

October

1	Kiyona Brooks	17	Briearra Toeran
2	Sandra Hardy	18	Krystle Bradley
3	Karshena McCain Adkins	19	Cheena R. Headen
4	Lashawn Farmer	20	Sheree "Sunshine" Cox
5	Lisa-Gaye Richards	21	Naomi Roe (Schaffer)
6	Teresa Robinson	22	Rebecca Landers
7	LaTasha Williams	23	Natasha Saunders
8	Teneisha Robinson	24	Vernita Stevens
9	LaTasha "WOP" Williams	25	Melinda Wynn
10	Demetria Burren	26	Terri J. Fowler
11	Candace Wilkerson	27	LaKel Farley
12	Theresa Head	28	Rose Hall
13	Raquel Hernandez	29	Dr. Christine Handy
14	Tamala Coleman	30	Ijana Nathaniel
15	Mary Beasley	31	Debbie Ann Andrews
16	Rochelle Redding		

November

1	Jahmia Jackson	16	Nikki L. Goodloe
2	Asia Andrews	17	Althea Webber Bates
3	Sabrina Jones	18	Viva Lewis-Harris
4	Toni Garvin	19	Minister Robyn Curry
5	Dr. Mary J. Huntley	20	Rhonda "Ro" Solomon
6	Lorrie A. Simmons	21	Celestine Davis
7	Yolonda Marshall	22	Kimberly Carter
8	Crystal Glasper Wright	23	Brenda Sawyer
9	Gwendolyn Demby	24	Natasha K. Ransom
10	Karshena McCain Adkins	25	Terri Booker
11	Meltona Bryant	26	Carmelesha Matthewson
12	Tocha Moore	27	Gaylin Munford
13	Keyuna Faye Webster	28	Sayra H. Kohen
14	Lakisha Harris	29	LaTasha "WOP" Williams
15	Leticia Hicks	30	Sharon M. Hyman

December

1	Lisa C Gray	17	Pam Dorsey
2	Alice M. Jarmin	18	D'Tondja M. Foster
3	Charlette Fairchild	19	Candice Davis
4	Shannon L. Turner	20	Trina Horton
5	Keisha Boatwright	21	Lisa Harris-Jones
6	Charlisa Herriott	22	Cassandra F. Ward
7	Eve S. Hendricks	23	Linda Latrice Ransons
8	Audrika Danielle	24	Theresa Head
9	Janet French-Cannedy	25	Donna Cushenberry
10	Avice Burchette	26	Donna Cushenberry
11	Sheree "Sunshine" Cox	27	Ashante Smallwood
12	Bridget Jackson	28	Nikki W. Miller
13	Sylvia Pauling	29	Chantaine Rhoe-Bulluck
14	Mary Harris	30	Gwendolyn Arnette
15	Gina R. Brown	31	Fayola Delica
16	Donna M. Douglas		

46291949R00225

Made in the USA
Middletown, DE
26 May 2019